PRENTICE-HALL INTERNATIONAL, INC., *London*
PRENTICE-HALL OF AUSTRALIA, PTY., LTD., *Sydney*
PRENTICE-HALL OF CANADA, LTD., *Toronto*
PRENTICE-HALL OF FRANCE, S.A.R.L., *Paris*
PRENTICE-HALL OF INDIA (PRIVATE) LTD., *New Delhi*
PRENTICE-HALL OF JAPAN, INC., *Tokyo*
PRENTICE-HALL DE MEXICO, S.A., *Mexico City*

PRENTICE-HALL JOURNALISM SERIES
Kenneth E. Olson, *Editor*

© 1964 by Prentice-Hall, Inc.
Englewood Cliffs, N. J.

LIBRARY OF CONGRESS CATALOG CARD NO.: 64-12092

PRINTED IN THE UNITED STATES OF AMERICA [C-19890]

Depth Reporting

An Approach to Journalism

by
Neale Copple
The University of Nebraska

Assisted by
Mrs. Emily E. Trickey

Backed by
The Newspaper Fund, Inc.
of *The Wall Street Journal*

Prentice-Hall, Inc.   Englewood Cliffs, New Jersey

To my wife, Olive,
who soothed when I seethed, was patient when I pouted,
and, somehow, smiled

Foreword

You are about to read a book on the art and science of making news understandable.

Depth reporting, as Neale Copple labels it, is talked of more than practiced. Perhaps that is so because more often than not it is a practice easier said than done.

As you will learn, both by reading and by practice, depth reporting is a combination of many factors. It is something that cannot be applied to every news event, nor should that be attempted. It is something that cannot be achieved by every reporter, although some of its elements can help any reporter. It is something that requires the understanding of editors and publishers as well as reporters, because it is a costly practice, both in time and money. It is an almost certain way to deepen and strengthen a newspaper's relationship with its readers.

Among newspaper folk, depth reporting has become a popular phrase, but one widely misused and misunderstood.

Although facts are a prime ingredient, a mere piling of detail on detail does not alone give a news report depth. Also required is a sifting of the important from the unimportant and then the lucid organization of the important facts to give a reader a clear understanding of the whole.

Words are vital, too. A fact-packed, well-organized story can fall apart if the writing is obscure instead of precise, if the words are confusing instead of simple.

Depth reporting, properly done, provides its own interpretation to a reader. It does not require an opinion of the reporter. And every well-reported, well-written story can better serve its reader by carrying the quality of authoritativeness. But no reporter can convey this quality until he has dug deeply for all the facts, has sorted,

v

analyzed, and finally organized a news package which he knows is accurate and complete.

All this means hard work, infinite curiosity, great patience, a willingness to tackle any assignment, and an unending quest for knowledge.

It's seldom an easy job. But seldom is it unrewarding, for the reporter and especially for the reader.

ROBERT BOTTORFF
Managing Editor
The Wall Street Journal

Preface

In recent months, I have joined that minority which reads prefaces. For years I had skipped them habitually—even maliciously. Then I made the belated discovery that often the most delightfully frank writing to be found in a book was in its preface.

Here, the author writes directly to the reader. Here, he indulges in happy verbal therapy after months, even years, with a manuscript.

Here, too, he explains to the readers why his book may vary from the norm. This is not an apology but an opportunity that gives the preface a real reason for being. In the case of this book, I have varied from the norm in one particular respect, and the readers deserve to know why.

Here and there you will find that the first person "I" and the second person "you" have crept into this manuscript where the third person would be normal. This creeping-in was not by accident. It had two purposes:

First, both the "I" and the "you" are in this book because it is a textbook. In a way, a textbook supplements and is part of the instructor's lectures to his class. That instructor teaches in the first person and speaks to his students in the second. Those two persons are in this book because there is some logic in writing for the classroom just as one would teach for it.

Second, an occasional "I" pops into this manuscript for a very old and very good journalistic reason. You will find that countless good newsmen have been quoted. In accepted journalistic practice, the opinions of these men are attributed to them. But my opinions are here, too, and, so that the reader will recognize them as such, the word "I" often becomes honest journalistic attribution.

Beyond these, there are only two general points I would like to make about this book:

First, simply to say that anything I have done or said in this book was done out of love for the profession.

Second, you should read this book in an order that fits your needs, not necessarily as the sections are organized.

This book was written primarily for two audiences, the advanced journalism student and the young professional already working on a newspaper. Beyond these, I hope there is information for every thoughtful mind in the business. However, this book was organized as a depth reporting textbook and as a professional handbook.

Section I introduces you to depth reporting and makes an abbreviated case for it as the future of American journalism.

Section II deals immediately with the practical problems of this kind of reporting—the planning, research, organization, and writing.

Section III is a liberal arts bibliography for journalists.

Section IV takes up the editing problems that depth reporting creates. It also fulfills promises made in Section I to document the case for depth reporting.

I won't deny that the middle of the book is a strange place for a bibliography. But, I believe when you read it—yes, I said "read it" —you will agree that it is not misplaced. It is also not the usual extra reading list that too often goes unused. It is designed as a working, readable part of this book. It looks critically at the journalist's chances of getting the liberal arts education we all insist he needs. It serves as a practical vehicle to help the student realize how he must use the other academic disciplines as his tools. It serves as a practical guide to the reference material professionals need. Finally, it is a vehicle for comments on writing and the newspapers' use and understanding of the academic areas from which most of man's activities stem.

You will find that the introductions and annotations within the bibliography are opinionated, intended for reading, and always slanted toward the journalist. You will also find a special index devised to make the bibliography a guide to source material for news stories.

Among other comments, you will find several in the bibliography suggesting that many books need not be read in the order in which they are written. That also is true of this one. I have found in using much of this material in experimental depth reporting classes that the more quickly the students get to writing the more quickly they understand the harsh demands of this approach to journalism. So, the major section of this book, Section II on writing, follows the brief introductory Section I. An instructor may then find that it is convenient to introduce the students to the bibliography, and, finally, when they are already writing, send them on to examine editing problems and the documentation for depth in Section IV.

Others may be interested in getting the documentation and looking at the editing picture almost at once. They will find they can make an easy transition from Section I to Section IV. Some may even want to turn first to the bibliography, Section III. I hope they will be surprised, pleasantly surprised.

One final note before proceeding to the pleasant task of thanking those who helped me. You will find in this book a concentration on local—domestic—news. There are three reasons:

First, the wire services have long recognized the need for depth to make foreign news understandable. Second, the students and young professionals for whom this is written will be testing their wings at the local level. Finally, it is in their own backyards that newspapers which practice depth can beat the socks off the competition.

With Thanks to—

When I start to say thank you to all the people who helped me with this book, I neither know where to start nor where to stop. But, I must try. Despite my effort to make no effort to omit my own opinion, I hope that many of those who helped me will also consider it their book.

I already have acknowledged on the title page the part Mrs. Emily E. Trickey played from the start to the last proof mark. Indeed, her own writing and research contributions to the bibliographic section alone were so great that gratitude and honesty compelled me to write "we" instead of "I" where first person pronouns were necessary in that section.

Next, I must thank The Newspaper Fund, Inc., of *The Wall Street Journal* and its executives. The Fund made the depth reporting project at the University of Nebraska and this book financially possible. The executives provided equally or more important moral backing. Particularly, I must express my thanks to Don Carter, now managing editor of *The National Observer,* who as executive director of the Fund added his enthusiasm to mine when I needed the boost. I must also thank his successor to the post of executive director, Paul Swensson.

Thanks also go to The Reader's Digest Foundation, whose grants for student expenses gave substance to our experiment in quality writing.

Dr. William E. Hall, director of the University of Nebraska

School of Journalism, helped in many ways. Not the least of these was as a critic, an adviser, and a builder-upper and a calmer-downer. Furthermore, he left me alone.

My graduate school dean and friend, Kenneth E. Olson, Dean Emeritus of the Medill School of Journalism, served me and my publishers as a wise and patient professional editor.

Throughout this book there are examples taken from the work of professional journalists. They are identified with the excerpts from their stories. However, a number of the country's best editors and reporters also contributed their thoughts and their philosophies. They must be named here as a special note of thanks. This is also true of circulation managers who helped us examine student readership. And, finally, there are my colleagues who advised patiently while we sought the books for the liberal arts bibliography for journalists.

Before proceeding, however, I must call your attention to a man whose name does not appear in this book other than here. He is my former boss, Arville Schaleben, managing editor of *The Milwaukee Journal*. Early in the research for this book his reply to one of my letters provoked me. "Provoked" is an understatement. In what was almost a rage, I redoubled my efforts to "clearly and profanely, if necessary," define for Arv Schaleben what I meant by depth reporting. It was months later, when my definitions had improved greatly, that I realized that I had been had at a game I myself had played many times with young reporters and students. This paragraph is a sheepish thanks to one of journalism's great editors—and teachers.

Now for the thanks to many others:

Robert Bottorff, executive editor, *The Wall Street Journal;* Lowell Brandle, *The St. Petersburg Times;* Erwin W. Canham, editor, *The Christian Science Monitor;* Turner Catledge, managing editor, *The New York Times;* Ed Cony, *The Wall Street Journal;* R. L. Crowley, former managing editor, *The St. Louis Post-Dispatch;* Frank Eyerly, managing editor, *The Des Moines Register* and *The Des Moines Tribune;* Louis B. Fleming, *The Los Angeles Times;* Ben W. Gilbert, city editor, *The Washington Post;* the late James Greenwood, *The Corpus Christi Caller-Times;* T. C. Harris, executive editor, *The St. Petersburg Times;* Don Holm, *The Portland Oregonian;* Anthony Lewis, *The New York Times;* Morton Mintz, *The Washington Post;* Phil Meyer, *The Miami Herald;* Edward M. Miller, assistant managing editor, *The Portland Ore-*

gonian; George Mills, *The Des Moines Register;* Saul Pett, *The Associated Press;* Gilbert M. Savery, *The Lincoln Journal;* Joe W. Seacrest, co-publisher, *The Lincoln Journal;* George M. Straszer, assistant to the editor, *The Los Angeles Times;* William H. Stringer, *The Christian Science Monitor;* Rod Van Every and Robert Wells, *The Milwaukee Journal.*

The following circulation managers also helped:

W. G. Black, *The Norman* (Oklahoma) *Transcript;* Roy Dauble, *The Omaha World-Herald;* Walter I. Evans, *The St. Louis Globe-Democrat;* Helge Holm, *The Daily Oklahoman* and *The Oklahoma City Times;* C. K. Jefferson, *The Des Moines Register* and *The Des Moines Tribune;* Ralph Kothenbeutel, *The Ames* (Iowa) *Daily Tribune-Times;* C. A. Monroe, Jr., *Boulder* (Colorado) *Camera;* Bill Neph, *Stillwater* (Oklahoma) *News-Press;* James R. O'Donnell, *The Kansas City Star-Times;* Myron Peterson, *The Denver Post;* L. F. Pike, *Columbia* (Missouri) *Tribune;* Jack Quigley, *The St. Louis Post-Dispatch;* Mark Seacrest, *The Lincoln Journal* and *The Lincoln Star;* Dolph C. Simmons, Jr., associate publisher, *The Lawrence* (Kansas) *Daily Journal-World;* and H. G. Woodrome, *The Rocky Mountain News.*

Now, my University of Nebraska colleagues:

Dr. William D. Aeschbacher (state historian), history; Dr. Dudley Bailey, English; Dr. Miguel A. Basoco, mathematics; Rexford S. Beckham, science librarian (anthropology); Dr. John Christopher, mathematics; Dr. Don O. Clifton, educational psychology (statistics); Wayne R. Collings, agricultural librarian; Dr. Robert E. Dewey, philosophy; Dr. Donald W. Dysinger, psychology; Dr. Wendell L. Gauger, botany; Dr. Glenn W. Gray, history; Richard H. Hansen, L.L.B., law librarian; Dr. Leslie Hewes, geography; Dr. Preston Holder, anthropology; Dr. Henry F. Holtzclaw, chemistry; Dr. Robert Hough, English; Dr. Bernard Kreissman, humanities librarian; Dr. Campbell R. McConnell, economics; Dr. Donald W. Miller, mathematics; Dr. Charles H. Patterson, philosophy; Myron Roberts, music; Dr. Carl J. Schneider, political science; Richard P. Trickey, art; Dr. Richard Videbeck, sociology; Dr. John W. Weymouth, physics; and Dr. Arthur Bruce Winter, political science.

And, finally, at the end only because tradition has made this the proper place to do it, my thanks to Prentice-Hall's editor, Paul O'Connell, and publishers' representatives, William Wing, George Crawford, and Ed Susanin.

NEALE COPPLE

Contents

1

The Reader in His Habitat

There he sits, magazines at his elbow, books within reach, possibly a cool glass within the same radius. The television flickers, his children clamor for attention, his wife describes the day's activities, and, if you are lucky, your newspaper is across his lap.

There is your partner—the reader—in his habitat, surrounded by your competition.

Against that competition, what can the American newspaper turn to its advantage?

The short but confusing answer is time, space, and solidity.

Take them one at a time. Speed works for television and radio, but time works against them. No matter how well these media might do with news, there are only 24 hours in a day. Of that 24 hours, only a few are good viewing or listening times. Television, for example, can expect peak audiences only between 6:00 P.M. and midnight. That cuts the time to six hours. Within those choice viewing hours there must be crammed a variety of entertainment. The news, on most stations, gets from a half-hour to an hour between 6:00 and 10:30 P.M. How much of that time is devoted to news?

On the average half-hour news show, after deducting time for commercials, about 20 to 24 minutes is devoted to sports, weather, local, national, and international news. Weather and sports take about nine minutes. That leaves 15 minutes for local, national, and international news in each half-hour news show. During the six-hour evening period about 30 minutes would be devoted to these

1

three areas of news. In almost every instance there is some repetition between the suppertime show and the 9:30 or 10:00 P.M. show. Ignoring the repetition, and assuming the announcer talks almost constantly, he has time to announce about 3,000 to 3,500 words. This would equal a little more than one-half page in an eight-column newspaper.

In other words, no matter how well television does with the news, it simply does not have time to do a complete job. In most instances, television can give the reader, at most, a half-dozen paragraphs from the top stories. This amounts to bulletin coverage. It amounts to something else, too. It often amounts to a teaser, just enough to whet the appetite, but not enough to quench the viewer's thirst.

The newspaper which deals in depth can turn television's capsule into a promotion for the news columns.

The Big Eye has another disadvantage. If, during the suppertime show Junior spilled his milk, mother and dad lose forever the part of the news show they missed while they mopped up.

The newspaper is at hand from the time it hits the front porch until it wraps the garbage. The newspapermen's goal, of course, is to lengthen the time between the two actions. They cannot, as did one successful Midwestern tabloid circulation manager, sell their newspapers to farm wives because it was the perfect size for lining shelves.

Radio has some of the same disadvantages as television. Time is the limiting factor, although modern radio can give just about as much time to a very hot news story as it wishes. Radio, however, chased out of the living room by television, has an audience limited primarily to those doing something else while they listen. Car radios get very high listenership. So do radios in kitchens and workshops. But, as many radio men frankly admit, this is listening in snatches, and it requires repetition in advertising and elsewhere to deliver the message.

Although magazines have more time to digest and organize their presentation of current topics, time also works against them. They cannot pretend to cover the breaking news or explain it in depth. They must work with deadlines, days and sometimes weeks ahead of publication. They must pick their depth coverage carefully lest it stale before delivery.

These, then, are the newspaper's three advantages—time, space, and solidity. Time—of the reader's own choosing to read his newspaper when and where he pleases. Space—to give the depth report on a story handled only in bulletin form by television and radio. Solidity—in that it can be put down when Junior spills his milk and picked up again when the mopping is over.

With these advantages depth becomes a potent weapon for the newspaper, providing, of course, the reader wants depth. Does he want it? Does he know what he wants?

Howard Allaway, former editor of *Popular Science Monthly,* and assistant Sunday editor of *The New York Times,* puts it this way:

> Most of all, research can't tell us how much our readers might have liked something that we did not print; even more, how much they might have liked something that they have never tasted at all because no editor has yet had the imagination to give it to them. We can research the hell out of our readers, but we can't find out what they don't know.

If the reader himself can't tell us what he wants because he doesn't know, then perhaps a study of this elusive creature in his native habitat may help. To find out how he occupies his time, let's look at the competition for it.

First, consider the magazines. In an age when such household familiars as *Collier's, American, Coronet,* and *Woman's Home Companion* have fallen, the magazine editor has become, by necessity, a person acutely aware of the reader's wants. Maybe his product can tell us something about changing reading habits.

One certain shift in the magazine business is from fiction to nonfiction. In such general publications as *The Saturday Evening Post,* the degree of the shift becomes evident in a study of a 20-year period. In 1940 *The Post* was running about 40 percent nonfiction and about 60 percent fiction. By 1960 the figures had almost reversed. In that year, *The Post* was running 39 percent fiction and 61 percent nonfiction.

In a way, *Reader's Digest* with its fantastic circulation, speaks for almost all of the magazine industry. Although the *Reader's Digest* does print condensed fiction, as sort of a back-of-the-book extra, its historic and successful emphasis has been on condensed nonfiction articles from magazines all over the world.

The trend to nonfiction—a trend that might indicate a desire for more solid facts—is even more apparent when you list the ten or 12 magazines with the highest circulation. Try it for any recent year. You will find that a majority of them publish nothing but non-fiction. In 1960, for example, seven of the top 12 dealt solely with nonfiction. The remainder gave emphasis to nonfiction.

Don't interpret this as an attack on fiction. We are discussing newspapers, which do not intentionally run fiction. We want to know what the reader wants. It seems logical to assume that if he wants more nonfiction in his magazines, he may want more facts. If he wants more facts, he may enjoy finding them in his newspaper.

While you are standing at a magazine stand, note the tremendous success of the news magazines—*Time, Life, Newsweek, U.S. News & World Report,* and *Look.* In some instances, these magazines base their popularity on the reader's desire to take in capsule form a week's supply of the news. The capsule is skillfully prepared, easily taken, and leaves a good taste. Two of these magazines, *U.S. News & World Report* and *Look,* make a different diagnosis of the reader's wants.

Look picks subjects of current interest and handles them with depth and dexterity, not to mention complete illustration. *Look,* however, does not try to keep up with the current news. Its depth stories deal with subjects of general interest which frequently are not tied to the news "last week."

U.S. News & World Report, on the other hand, does worry about last week's news, but does it in a very selective way. Certain subjects are picked from the major continuing news events, and these subjects are dealt with in depth. For example, if there is a crisis in the Near East, *U.S. News & World Report* can be expected, while the crisis is still hot, to deliver to its readers a complete story. That story will include background, analysis, and illustration in the form of attractive maps and charts.

More evidence of what the reader wants can be found in another communications medium—television—which deals at least part-time in the business of giving out information. Choice and expensive evening time is allotted to news shows. While many of these shows, which run about a half-hour, give the viewer only from 18 to 24 minutes of news, weather, and sports, many millions of American families end their day with the television report of the news.

Some of TV's documentaries, such as those on the population

explosion, have been successful and have helped bring TV of age. The skillfully, intelligently, and tastefully told story of the world's alarming birth rate was so popular that it was lengthened and reshown.

And educational TV is a strange infant bringing some gratifying results. For example, the National Broadcasting Company must have been a little surprised itself when some quarter of a million people across the country started getting up at 6:30 five mornings a week to watch a TV course in physics for the atomic age.

The figures on adult education also tell a story of Americans who want more information. In 1960, there were an estimated 2.5 million Americans enrolled as part-time students. This included those taking correspondence courses offered by universities, colleges, the armed forces, and industries. Many universities which offer correspondence courses have since 1950 been flooded with enrollment increases of more than 300 percent.

Of course, with the rise of all kinds of education, the textbook business has also boomed. So, as a matter of fact, has the trade-book publishing business.

At that same newsstand where you noted the success of the news magazines you also saw a large selection of paperback books. Not all of them were mysteries and Westerns whose covers were decorated with seminude girls. Some of those paperbacks were works by Plato, Aristotle, Freud, and Shakespeare.

Much of this evidence of a growing reader desire for more non-fiction, more facts, and more depth has been based upon the competition to the American newspaper. From magazines, from television, and from books, examples have been drawn of what some editors hope is a cultural explosion in the nuclear age.

Now, let's look at our newspapers.

Although the magazine editors may be more active and the television producers of documentaries more obvious, some newspaper editors are fully aware of a changing public demand.

As these men watch magazines invade the field of giving depth to current news, as they see television take an hour's costly time to document the population explosion, as they observe Americans going to school and going back to school, they are wondering about some of the old rules of thumb which should have long since been banished from the newsroom.

They wonder if they are really editing a paper for a reader with a sixth-grade education. They look around and wonder how so many sixth graders got loose when most state laws require education at least through the sixteenth year. They wonder where all the sixth graders come from when an acquaintance with less than a high school education is a rarity. They look at the bulging enrollments in universities and colleges and wonder how all the sixth graders got left behind.

Some of them are saying, "Baloney," and are editing their papers for a better-educated reader. A few of them already have this tradition. *The New York Times,* for instance, assumes its readers can read through the entire text of a presidential address and form their own conclusions. *The St. Louis Post-Dispatch* spends hundreds of thousands of dollars to hire and pay the expenses of men who do nothing but depth reporting. This newspaper did not worry about the "sixth-grade" education of its readers when it had General Maxwell D. Taylor write a story about the massive retaliation doctrine. Nor did it assume it was writing for an uneducated audience when it examined public ownership of mass transportation in Los Angeles and other cities. Nor does *The Wall Street Journal* think it is a waste of time when it assigns a valuable writer to spend six weeks to produce just one story.

The awareness of a better-educated reading audience is not confined to the metropolitan newspapers. *The Corpus Christi* (Texas) *Caller-Times* assigned the late James Greenwood to do a job on taxation. The editors of that newspaper gave Greenwood help and all the time he needed. He produced depth stories on taxation that won a Political Science Association Award for 1959.

The Caller-Times is a medium-sized newspaper. Some smaller dailies, and the weeklies also, are showing an awareness that their readers might like a little depth. One of the students in the University of Nebraska depth reporting class found this out, although it was not his intention. His intention, just before the state legislature met, was to give the reader some perspective about the biennial battle to broaden the tax base. He wanted to assemble the history, the problems, the arguments, the perspective—in short, the facts—in one bundle. It took a series of five articles, each a thousand words long, to do it.

The result was not entertainment. It was not simple reading for simple readers. It was adult information, well organized and clearly written for an audience of taxpayers. Most of the state's editors were delighted enough to shake up their papers five weeks in a row to find space to run the series.

For almost all these newspapers, the prospect of allotting two columns of space to one story involved a major editorial decision. However, that series ran in more than 500,000 circulation of the state's total of 850,000. Daily newspapers ranging from eight to 12 pages devoted two columns to the tax series. Weekly newspapers with only ten to 12 *columns* of reading space also ran the tax series. In some instances the story was started on page one and jumped to the editorial page where it took up all the space normally allotted to editorials. The Nebraska editors who made the decision to run this series also assumed that they were not printing their newspapers for sixth graders.

Indeed, as the nation's thinking editors review the situation, many of them know they would not be in the newspaper business if they thought they were merely providing primer level information for a primer level audience. This could hardly be called a challenge to the intelligent men who carry the burden of the nation's press.

Evidence has piled upon evidence. Magazine editors are directing their efforts toward an audience they believe hungry for the background and depth behind current news. Television producers are devoting tens of thousands of dollars to produce a one-hour documentary based on relatively current news. And the nation's best newspaper editors are busily tossing out rules of thumb that dictate the preparation of their newspapers for an audience of sixth graders.

It would be convenient to go a step further and conclude that most Americans are spending most of their off-work, out-of-bed hours thirsting for more knowledge—information in depth. This would, of course, be a surface, rather than a depth, assumption.

Sociology, one of the tools of depth reporting, can provide some information about what Americans do with their spare time. The sociologists point out that the amount of spare time has increased steadily since the industrial revolution. They assume the 40-hour work week, anticipate the 37½-hour work week, and predict the 35-hour week. But, they also point out that the demands on this new-found spare time are almost endless.

As part of America's urbanization (an often neglected subject by the nation's press), the move to the city has been countered by a move of city dwellers to the suburbs. Life in suburbia takes time for lawns, rose gardens, and neighborhood projects. And in suburbia the American male has been encouraged to be, and has become, a part-time playmate of his children. It's probably good for him and the kids, but he couldn't do otherwise unless he wants to fight the sociologists, the educators, the PTA, his children, and his wife.

Along with spare time has come a rising popularity in participation sports—bowling, golf, boating, hunting, and fishing. "Do-it-yourself" has become a household phrase and fact. The Big Eye in the living room, the family room, and the playroom, and sometimes in all three, has made its inroads on time.

In short, when the sociologists' comments on the short work week are added up, they come out with a shortage of spare time. Americans, as always, are a busy people, and not all that busyness is devoted to thirsting for knowledge.

What might a profile of this American reader look like? He's busy—at work and at home. However, he is buying an increased fare of facts and information. He looks at television documentaries and news reports. He signs up for part-time education.

All this should indicate that the newspaper is in a perfect spot to cash in on what some call a "cultural explosion." If that is a bit much for a business whose professionals are trained in skepticism, then call it simply a growing hunger for more information. The question is, "How do we satisfy that hunger?"

I believe, without reservation, the answer is reporting in depth.

It would be wonderful if, by simply believing it and saying it, the job would be done. But the newsmen who deal in depth and the students who are learning to do it know this is only lip-service. Depth is hard work. It is creative. It is demanding research. It is careful organization. And it is the most beautiful writing American journalists have ever produced.

2

Antidote for a Lively Corpse

In a hotel room in Kansas City, Missouri, a group of newsmen worked quietly and steadily with just a touch of haste. Reporters wrote, copy editors edited, and artists worked with drawings, maps, and pictures. A makeup man put together pages and planned for the art.

Not far away, in the offices of an engineering firm, other newsmen worked, collecting information, talking with the highway engineers, and planning as they moved.

Earlier, back home in Des Moines, Iowa, aerial photographers had flown above the city. On the ground, news photographers had shot pictures of every major building inside a mile-wide strip across the city.

In Kansas City, the Des Moines newsmen worked with those aerials. They were so sharp, so clearly defined, that any given resident of any given block could find his home. These men in the Kansas City hotel room were nearing the end of a one-week job to produce one major news story. The city editor of *The Des Moines Tribune* had been pulled from his desk to direct the operation. Now, with the job completed in Kansas City, he took his men— reporters, artists, copyreaders—back home. There printers were handed small bits of this big story. Extra engravers were called back to work.

That was Monday. On Tuesday morning, the State Highway Commission met to announce the route of a freeway through the city, and *The Des Moines Tribune* was ready. That evening, its readers received with their regular newspaper an eight-page special section giving them the complete details, cause, and effect, of the biggest change in the face of their city for many years.

The Des Moines Tribune was not the first to announce the news. Minutes after the Highway Commission acted, radio and television broadcast bulletins. But *The Des Moines Tribune* did something more important than get there first with the barest facts. Its readers knew the complete details of the route of the superhighway through their city. Any individual reader whose house was in the general area of the freeway could find his specific house in his specific block. He could tell exactly how he stood in relation to the gigantic road-way. *The Des Moines Tribune* had done *a great deal more* than give the barest facts—it had given its readers the story in depth.

These Des Moines newsmen and others scattered over America are also giving a solid answer to the critics who are busy burying the "late giant of the communications industry." The men who deal in depth are proving the nation's newspapers can be the live-liest corpse upon whom anyone has ever tried a funeral march.

The answers to the critics come not only from newsrooms. Look now into a classroom of a Midwestern university. A half-dozen students relax around the rim of a scarred copy desk. The atmos-phere is informal. The talk is intense. Here, too, they deal in depth.

These youngsters know what it means to put a hundred hours into a story, to dig until there's nothing left to find, to write a lead a dozen times, and to rewrite a story a half-dozen more. These students also know this kind of work brings both self-satisfaction and results. They know, too, that depth can give substance to any section of the newspaper with the possible exception of the comic page. They know that:

Local governmental news needs depth—

One student story put the state's tax problems into perspective. As the state legislators prepared to meet, the student polled every one of them on their views toward change. The resulting series was called by several editors "the most complete and understandable story ever written about the subject."

Farm and industrial news needs depth—

Another student, as the Kennedy administration prepared to launch its farm program, took on the awesome subject of surpluses.

He confined that much-written-about but seldom understood national headache to the problems of one Nebraska county. Editors outside the corn belt asked for copies of the story so that they might try the technique on their own particular brand of farm surpluses.

Sports needs depth—

A student dug out for the first time all the figures on athletic scholarships in the Big Eight Conference. He then compared them with the team standings. He found that in college athletics you apparently get what you pay for. The story had a circulation of some three million in the Midwest. The sports editor of a metropolitan paper said, "Tell him it's a fine story. I'm only ashamed that my own staff didn't dig it up."

And depth can take the newspaper into the high school classroom. To find out just how thoroughly they could cover one big story, a University of Nebraska depth reporting class took on the nation's only unicameral legislature. They talked about the weaknesses and strengths of the system with state senators, committee chairmen, speakers, lieutenant governors, governors, party leaders, political scientists, and historians. They probed its efficiency and its economy. They described, through the eyes of those who had seen it happen, the battles and beginnings in 1937.

The results were published in Sunday magazine format. Requests for it came from California to Israel. Editorial writers praised it. A state constitutional convention asked for copies. A farm leader from the Northwest said this was the information he had been trying to get for a quarter of a century. Perhaps most important of all, hundreds of requests came from high schools. The social science teachers wanted to use this product of journalism as a classroom supplement. Those concerned about the newspapers' prestige were delighted to see a newspaper product become required reading in all those classrooms full of future subscribers.

The point of all this can be summed up in one of those accumulative sentences that are the delight of childhood nursery rhymes:

College students, who can combine broad academic background with professional journalism, must join the newsmen who deal in depth to answer the critics who are trying to bury the American newspaper.

There's no doubt that the critics have a case. Past the half-way mark in the twentieth century, America's newspapers are in trouble. Any journalist who does not believe that has his head buried too deeply in his own product.

Competition for the advertising dollar is the greatest in history. And the competition is getting its share. In 1935 newspapers carried 45 percent of all advertising. Twenty-five years later the figure was 30 percent.

There was a time when the newspaper assumed that one-fourth to one-third of its income would come from national advertising. Today the small daily expects eight to ten percent from national ads, and the medium-sized paper from 18 to 20 percent.

But don't let all this shake you. Just let it jar you a bit. Advertising linage has climbed steadily. The dollar income from national advertising climbed some 500 percent between 1950 and 1960. The percentage losses have been partly recovered by increases in the local display and want-ad departments. Nonmetropolitan dailies used to count on five to six percent from want ads. Today the want-ad figure is more like 24 to 26 percent. And newspapers still get more advertising dollars than anyone else.

Then, what's all the fuss about?

For one thing, the fuss is about production costs. They are up on the newspaper at least 400 percent since World War II.

That brings us to profits—the difference between income and production costs. The smaller and medium-sized papers may bring in a comfortable, safe return of three to four percent. Many of the giant metropolitan newspapers would be delighted with such a margin. Although they may report several hundred thousand dollars, a half million, or a million, they may be talking about the return on an investment of from $90 to $100 million. Figure out the percentages on that and realize that it was at a time when gilt-edge stocks might bring five percent without the headaches of owning a newspaper.

Circulation, like ad linage, is at a new high. But that, too, is deceptive. In many areas it has not kept up with the increase in population.

"So what?" you may say. "The population increase is in youngsters."

That's right, they are youngsters, many of them in colleges. And how well do they read the newspaper?

A survey of the Big Eight schools of the Midwest showed that one paper was sold for about every eight students. That was giving them every break. The married students were the subscribers. Sororities and fraternities with from 40 to 60 students averaged 2.5 papers for the lot. Dormitories with from 100 to 500 residents averaged 7.5 newspapers.

Actually, it does not make much difference how many newspapers we sell unless they are read. How well do newspapers do on that score?

The television surveys may be a little bit long in their estimates because television sets can be on when no one is looking. The TV surveyors believe the average family has its TV set on from four to five hours a day. The newspaper estimates may be a bit short, because they do not multiply by the number of the members of a family who can read. Most surveys give the newspaper a daily average of from 20 to 30 minutes—and that's to read the equivalent of a short novel.

Finally, there is the question of influence. Do the readers believe what newspapers tell them?

There is no question that newspapers still wield editorial influence at the local level. But nationally the majority of the press has backed only one presidential winner since 1928. Although that may not be very significant, it is a point in which the critics delight.

Yes, those critics have some points, but there also are answers.

"TV," the critics cry, "is killing you."

"No such thing," reply the men who deal in depth; "TV can only whet the appetite for what we offer."

"Radio," say the critics, "beats you with the news every hour of the day."

"Let them beat us with surface reports," reply the depth writers. "If you miss it on radio, it's gone. You can read our stories in depth anytime you want to pick up your paper."

"Millions of Americans," say the critics, "are getting their news nicely digested each week in a magazine."

"They can't digest our local news," reply the depth writers, "and we can give them the complete story every day, not weekly."

Honest newspapermen do not deny that the prophets of doom have some evidence. It is true, for instance, that no high-speed rotary press can be as fast as the uttered word or a picture transmitted through the air. Technocracy has stripped the newspaper of a big gun—the *scoop*. This word, so much a part of the American newspaper, has become a part of its history.

T. C. Harris, executive editor of *The St. Petersburg* (Florida) *Times,* puts it this way:

> The old-time extra with the flash and the streamer headline is passé—radio and TV killed it.

But Harris, speaking for a good many American newspapermen, is writing no obituary. He has more to say:

> Superficial reporting is moribund, too. This means that we have to report in depth if we are to make our paper interesting.

Harris's key word is *depth*.

3

The Noblest Word

Why depth? Why not background, orientation, interpretation, analysis, or any of the other words which a few newspapermen and teachers have been preaching on semi-deaf ears for a couple of decades? Because depth is a more complete concept, and because many of the other words have been corrupted by a lack of understanding and too much lip-service.

If it pleases you, call it "pie-in-the-sky reporting," so long as you mean the best that American colleges and newspapers can produce. And *best* should be synonymous with *depth*. There are hazards in putting the word *depth* in front of the word *reporting*. It can sound like a highly perishable miracle drug. It also becomes a trifle upsetting when an antiseptic begins "protecting in depth" and radio stations begin calling their two-minute spots "the news in depth." But these, too, will pass, and it really does not make much difference what word we use so long as we agree on a definition.

No good reporter likes to slow the pace of a story for a long definition. But later in this book you will find a great to-do about reporters who have a love affair with the English language. In these affairs, like the more conventional kind, the trick is using the right word at the right time.

Right now is the time to decide what is meant when the word *depth* is placed in front of the word *reporting*.

Happily, none of the journalists who talk about depth reporting see it as a brand-new idea—a fad, a magic phrase—that will snatch readers from their television sets, their radios, their magazines, their motorboats, their lawnmowers, their kitchens, or their women's clubs to sit glued to the news columns.

James S. Pope, former executive editor of *The Louisville Courier-Journal* and *The Louisville Times,* makes the point with a minimum of hedging. He believes that "publishers' deficiencies may be to blame even more than slack editing," and he adds: "I do think it is important that newspapers which have done superficial jobs, do not get the idea that the simple solution is to add something called 'depth.' It sounds like a commodity the syndicates will be putting out and you can buy at so much a week, like comics, and save work."

Pope, in something resembling a journalistic semantic wrath, cries for a revival of the word *reporting.* He says:

> Actually, what we all mean is better reporting. . . . I think "reporting" is one of the noble words of our language. It has been used to embrace the sheerest tripey nonsense. A reporter may have to meet a deadline with an incomplete story. But he will not stop there. I object somewhat to "depth" reporting because it implies there is such a thing as shallow reporting which is at times acceptable. But if it's shallow, it's not reporting.

At a time when the word *reporting* appears to have degenerated as much as Pope indicates, it may be necessary to add the word *depth* to spark a reporting revival. If so, what does it mean?

Ben W. Gilbert, city editor of *The Washington Post,* describes it rather bluntly as a story "which tells the reader what the fuss is all about."

Depth, as R. L. Crowley, former managing editor of *The St. Louis Post-Dispatch,* points out rather simply, is, "of course, by definition, the opposite of surface reporting."

The words that mean breaking beneath the surface into the depth explanation of a shrinking and steadily more complicated world are unending. Some mean something specific. Others mean what the writer wants them to mean.

Backgrounding was probably the earliest of the antisurface words. To most newsmen, it means adding information to the surface news. Sometimes it is history, ancient and modern, that gives the reader perspective. Usually, backgrounding is limited to the subject at hand, rather than becoming an effort to tie the current news peg into a total picture. Too often it has come to mean "go to the morgue and get the clips on Joe Jones, who just died." Getting the clips on Joe Jones is simply a part of good, solid reporting. Backgrounding Joe's death might explain that he died in an accident at a blind intersection where five others have been killed in the past two years. Backgrounding would explain that requests for funds to correct the blind intersection had been cut from the city budget three times in three years. The reason given each year by the city council was "economy."

Humanizing is simply one of the words that means bringing the story into the reader's environment. It does not mean writing down to the reader. It means making the story mean something to him. For example, *The Wall Street Journal* in its rapid climb through the circulation ranks has proved the success of writing business news in terms of the reader's pocketbook. Humanizing touches the depth story with life, making its subjects live for the reader. Humanizing Joe Jones's story would make him a cigar-smoking mechanic who spent his Saturdays helping kids build safe soapbox racers.

Some might call this feature writing or featurizing. But there is a word that has been giving city editors and teachers trouble for years. All they have to do is mutter the magic word, "feature," and the reporter changes hats.

Suddenly, his imagination comes alive. He works at being interesting. He writes brightly. He writes lightly. He writes humanly about human beings. Ask yourself if that's not the way every decent story should be written. If featurizing means making a story readable, then it is part of all well-written stories. If it means making human beings out of the people in the news, then substitute it for "humanizing" and let's get on with it. Humanizing or featurizing is a tool of depth reporting.

Interpretation is one of the most controversial of the beneath-the-surface words. In its purest sense the word means to give super-definition to a subject. Webster puts it this way:

"To explain, tell meaning of; translate, elucidate. To construe in the light of an individual belief, judgment of interest; as to interpret a contract."

Some newsmen, such as managing editor Turner Catledge of *The New York Times,* use *interpretative reporting* and *depth reporting* as synonyms. However, during the past 20 years, for some journalists the word *interpretation* has acquired a connotation of personal opinion.

Catledge does not mean opinion. He says quite clearly:

> From his training and experience, the able reporter knows what weight should be given each detail. He knows as well that his own opinions have no validity; if a reporter does not know this canon, the editor is there to see that he is made aware of it.

When interpretation means reporter opinion, editors of repute denounce it. " 'Interpretative' reporting," Pope says, "has become a pretext for news column editorials. I think a paper should inform and inform so thoroughly that every reader can become his own interpreter, his own editorial writer."

Yet, to many reporters, interpretation means license to use their own opinion. These newsmen believe that they have become so expert in their fields that they may use opinion without attribution or qualification. It is difficult to reconcile this viewpoint in a world so complicated that persons spend an entire lifetime studying one small part of one subject.

Correct interpretation of Joe Jones's story might pick up where backgrounding left off. Taking the background facts, interpretation would explain where the money requested for the blind corner was used, and why. Interpretation would explain that there are ten such intersections in the city, and correction of all of them is part of a ten-year plan proposed by the city engineer. Interpretation would explain also that augmentation of the ten-year plan is being held up for lack of funds.

But true interpretation would not allow the reporter to write, "A malingering city council and stingy taxpayers have cost five lives at the corner of 20th and Washington Streets." That is opinion and the job of an editorial writer.

There is confusion about interpretation, observation, and opinion. Interpretation is superdefinition. Observation involves description of facts. Opinion involves personal findings from those facts. Observation and interpretation without opinion are certainly legitimate parts of depth reporting. Observation, in the case of Joe Jones, would have involved a description of the blind intersection and the accident.

Investigative reporting is almost self-explanatory and can apply to any subject. Usually it describes the writing that results from digging out facts beneath the surface. There is no opinion in truly investigative reporting. It resembles a scientific approach. Fact is laid upon fact. No conclusions are drawn until the facts themselves form a conclusion. Such newspapers as *The St. Louis Post-Dispatch, The Kansas City Star,* and *The Portland Oregonian* have years of experience and numerous Pulitzer prizes to prove their adeptness at investigative reporting. It is a valuable tool of the depth writers.

Investigation of the Joe Jones story might have taken several days to find out exactly where current city street funds were going, exactly who decided priorities, and, in the opinion of the experts, if the system of priorities was in the best interest of the public.

Orientation adds depth to all the words used to describe beneath-the-surface reporting. When a reporter orients a story, he fits it into the reader's world. A depth story, well oriented, puts a new federal tax into the reader's budget.

Orientation of the Joe Jones story would put this accident into perspective with the entire city street problem. Orientation would tell the reader if one of the blind intersections was on his route to work. It would have made the bad corner, which the reader understood easily, a take-off point for his understanding of complicated problems of his city street system.

Now, in violation of all the rules of definition, it is fairly easy to say what depth reporting is *not*. It is *not* opinion. It is *not* primarily an effort to influence, although influence may frequently be a by-product.

Then, what is this thing called depth reporting?

"There is nothing mystical about it," says *The New York Times*'s Catledge; "the word *reporting* is complete in itself. It requires that a reporter and his newspaper give the reader accurate information as fully as the importance of any story dictates."

Although Catledge wipes away any mysticism about the phrase, it is difficult to define briefly anything quite so broad.

"We regard depth reporting as telling the reader all the essential facts about the subject, the whys and the wherefores of it, as many sides of it as we can get, and plenty of background," explains Harris of *The St. Petersburg Times.* "We try to spell out to the reader what it means to him. Depth reporting, in my opinion, is simply good, solid, substantial reporting as against the superficial reporting that so often graces today's news pages."

Both Catledge and Harris make an important point. The modern concept of depth reporting must include much of what was considered in the past as pure reporting—the best a newsman could do with his professional training. However, depth writing in a modern, complicated world against tougher competition for the reader's time adds responsibility to the concept of pure reporting.

To meet the complicated world, the depth reporter of the future must be the most avid student who sits in a college class in political science, history, sociology, psychology, and almost any other of the myriad courses that will become his launching pad for writing in depth.

To meet the competition that did not exist when the publishing world had a monopoly on informing the public, he must be better prepared professionally. He must learn how to use the tools he acquired in background courses. He must be able to write better than his predecessors and many of his contemporaries. If he is to write in depth, he must be a pro.

In this light, depth reporting becomes a many-faceted thing. Crowley, of *The Post Dispatch,* defines it in three phases, but, before doing so, lays the background for his own definition. He points out that depth is an extension of surface reporting—the development of the facts covered in a news story which in itself merely told what had happened in a given situation. Then he adds:

> In order to achieve reporting in depth, it would then be necessary to interpret the news already covered to:
> 1. Give the reader the full background of the events which resulted in the news story.
> 2. Tell what the facts and circumstances meant, perhaps at the time of their occurrence, and what would most likely develop in the future as a result of this set of facts and circumstances. That is interpretation.
> 3. Analyze the facts and situations described in (1) and (2). That is analysis.

All this adds up, of course, to reporting in depth. The editor and the writer must never be satisfied, therefore, with a plain recital of the facts which make up a story if they are interested in depth reporting.

Since depth reporting by its very nature is not a simple thing, none of the respected editors in America today try to define it simply.

For instance, Robert Bottorff, executive editor of *The Wall Street Journal*, starts with the simple statement that depth reporting in his newspaper "tries to tell the reader everything he needs to know about a given development." However, Bottorff has more to say:

> Assume the reader knows nothing about the development. . . . Sift out material only in the news sense . . . as a part of news judgment. . . . Answer these questions—what has happened and why it had come about.

Edward M. Miller, assistant managing editor of *The Portland Oregonian*, spells out yet another facet of depth reporting.

> Reporting in depth provides the background to make the day's spot news intelligible. . . . Reporting in depth also takes cognizance of situations that have developed slowly and without the emphasis of spot news happenings.

The "humanizing" element of depth reporting itself becomes alive when Frank Eyerly, managing editor of *The Des Moines Register and Tribune,* talks about it:

> Reporting in depth is, in our viewpoint, the exhaustive, almost encyclopedic coverage of a news event that is significant and can be related to the lives of the reader. Every family with a child in school, in this period of much attention to family life and juvenile delinquency, is interested in and affected by the strange case of the youthful killer. Every family in this city has been and will be affected in some way by the routing of a wide highway right through the heart of the city.

A sharply digested version of all these definitions sounds a bit stuffy and is a trifle guilty of lack of depth itself, but it could read quite simply:

> Depth reporting is telling the reader all the essential facts in a way that brings the story into the reader's environment.

What does depth mean to the story of Joe Jones?

It means that a five-paragraph obituary about a mechanic who was killed in an automobile accident became a story that informed a city. Joe became a human being with whom the readers could associate themselves. The corner where he died became a launching platform for an understanding of the entire city street system.

Every one of the words that helped get beneath the surface of the news contributed to the story. A writer capable of depth applied all his professional training to produce a story so well written that it attracted the attention of the readers despite the competition and left them well-informed.

Any newsman or journalism student knows that words and definitions are simply semantic exercises if they don't bring results. Newsmen like Barry Bingham, president and editor of *The Louisville Courier-Journal* and *The Louisville Times,* believe there must be results. Bingham realizes that the need for this kind of reporting "grows more insistent week by week, and the newspaper that tries to ignore it will do so at the risk of its survival."

Bingham's newspaper and a number of others over the nation are already proving that they are no part of a communications corpse.

The New York Times, for instance, with a century of reputation for telling the complete story, would not imagine depth reporting as a new concept. However, in recognition of its growing importance, *The Times* has made changes. Following the organization of a public affairs reporting team, managing editor Catledge said:

> Inception of the public affairs team was primarily an attempt to build a cohesive group; it did not mean that *The New York Times* suddenly awoke to the need for depth reporting. This is as much a tradition on the city desk as it is with the national and foreign staffs.

The Minneapolis Star and *The Minneapolis Tribune,* newspapers with relatively small staffs, orient their coverage in favor of depth. Breaking news is covered, but after that, much of the attention and money goes to the complete story of significance. A man may be pulled from the staff for such an assignment as "Go to Central America and find out why they don't like us."

The Milwaukee Journal, with a reputation for saturating its area, still finds need for depth. A sports editor is relieved of his duties to devote full time to an explanation of conservation. An editorial writer is given carte blanche to learn about reclamation, water, and power problems. A business writer takes all the time he needs to write Pulitzer prize-winning stories about Canada.

The Washington Post, which has reorganized its local news staff into two staffs—one for regular beat coverage and the other to go beyond the news—has made depth a part of its daily diet. Thus, while the regular beat reporters give protection on spot news, the depth reporters do a series on poverty and crime in the capital city.

The Des Moines Register allows a veteran city hall and state-house reporter to set up a state-wide municipal beat. In a day when growing cities have many problems in common, *The Register* covers urbanization.

Perhaps the most telling example of all can be found in *The Wall Street Journal*'s jet-propelled climb since World War II. The circulation figures tell the effect. From a mere 50,000 circulation, this fastest-growing national newspaper in the country reached more than 800,000 by 1962. The cause can be found in the editorial policies of those who run *The Wall Street Journal*. These men print a newspaper "for everyone interested in making a living" and they do it in depth. Through *The Journal*'s efforts five days a week, complicated business activities become personal pocketbook stories for the readers.

There is a sentiment among some newsmen that depth reporting is a luxury to be afforded only by the metropolitan press. However, a number of medium-sized and small papers refuse to buy the theory that without metropolitan status they can have no part in the future of American journalism. For instance, a reporter on the *St. Petersburg Times* could explain to the readers the road problems, no matter how large his paper. He could tell them why country roads cost more to maintain and build than city roads. He could do his part for what his paper calls "Building a Better Florida."

Or, *The Lincoln* (Nebraska) *Evening Journal* could pull its city editor from the desk in the midst of an academic hair-pulling contest at the University of Nebraska. The fight over how to train the state's public school teachers had the campus in an uproar, and the readers were lost in a barrage of academic gobbledegook. *The Journal*'s city editor was told to find out what was going on and tell the readers, no matter how much valuable news space was eaten up. The resulting 12,000-word series broke the letters-to-the-editor record for such a subject.

These newspapers, from the smallest to the largest, are the answers to the prophets of doom. In their newsrooms the word *depth* placed in front of the word *reporting* is the key to the future.

Introduction

This section of this book is devoted entirely to the depth reporter, his imagination, his planning, his research, his organization, and his writing.

It is not an effort to bind with new rules these rare reporters whom we need so badly. It is an effort to free them so that their minds, not somebody's rules, will work for them. It is not an effort to turn reporters into editorial writers, columnists, interpreters, or analytic experts. It is an effort to show young writers that within the revival of the newspaper as the main source of facts and information lies the greatest writing challenge in history.

Some of the best reporters in America have contributed their thoughts and stories to this section. There are student contributions, too. At the end of each chapter in this section on writing, there is a case history of a depth story. Many of the examples within the chapters are from professionals—the best professionals. But the case histories are student work. Student stories were chosen for these end-of-the-chapter spots because this book is primarily for advanced students and young professionals. They know what the masters can do. They need to see what they themselves can do.

First, to set a mood for this section, read what the Associated Press's word-master, Saul Pett, has to say about writing. Mr. Pett and I might appear to disagree. I don't think there is any such thing today as a feature story. If feature means writing a more interesting story, a more readable story, then it should be part of

25

every story. Actually, Mr. Pett and I preach the same sermon. Mine simply does not include the word, "feature."

A Feature Writer Defines His Art

by SAUL PETT (AP)

I'm supposed to tell you something about feature writing.

I feel about as comfortable as a condemned man called upon to lecture the firing squad on marksmanship.

Everything I say can be held against me. There are no rules about writing I can think of that I don't break—even my own rules. There are no generalizations about writing that are foolproof, except the one I just made.

Now let me generalize.

All sermons on writing that inhibit the writer are worse than the sins they're trying to correct. Before it's finished, good writing always involves a sense of discipline but good writing begins in a sense of freedom, of elbow room, of space, of a challenge to grope and find the heart of the matter, of an invitation to say it differently if the thing needs to be said differently but never just to be different. Good writing begins with the impetus of one individual, the writer. The good writer does not write for the reader or the bureau chief or Gallagher or the writing committee, he writes for himself. Good writing is self-expression. This above all, to thine own self, etc. If you want to get pompous, you can call it integrity. But it is a practical matter. If it isn't self-expressive, it isn't fun, it isn't good, and why not go into another racket and make more dough and sit back and laugh at these poor tormented slobs trying to write?

Good writing is torment and anybody who is ashamed of it, who says that torment isn't professional, who cringes from the word "creative" as if it were a horrible tag applied only to queers and poets and not to rough, tough newspapermen, is in the wrong century.

Remember how it used to be the mark of a professional to whip through a feature like he was blowing it out of one nostril, to march across the street, have a drink and then brag about how he knocked off those 500 dancing words in 14 minutes with only three facts to begin with?

Well, you and I know that we're all in another league now or should be. The reader wants more today—and I suspect he was never that stupid to begin with, anyway—and the woods are full of competitors ready to give him more.

We can no longer give the reader the fast brush. We can no longer whiz through the files for 20 minutes, grab a cab, spend 30 minutes interviewing our subject, come back to the office, concoct a clever lead that goes nowhere, drag in 15 or 20 more paragraphs like tired sausage, sprinkle them with four quotes, pepper them with 14 scintillating adjectives all synonymous and then draw back and call that an incisive portrait of a human being.

Today the reader wants more in his features. Over his second or third Sunday cup of coffee, he wants to be drawn by substance. He wants meat on his bones and leaves on his trees. He wants dimension and depth and perspective and completeness and insight and, of course, honesty.

After 500 or 1,500 or 2,500 words, the reader wants to know more about a man's personality than that he is "mild-mannered" or "quiet" or "unassuming." . . . Willie Sutton, the bank robber, is mild-mannered, quiet, unassuming. So is Dr. Albert Schweitzer.

How can you write about a man without knowing what others have written about him? How can you write about a man without knowing what others think and know of him? How can you write about a man without interviewing him at great length and in great detail and in such a way that he begins to reveal something of himself? How can you interview him that way without planning a good part of your questioning beforehand?

How, when you've collected all you're going to collect, how can you write about a man without thinking long and hard about what you've learned? How can you write about a man without writing about the man, not merely grabbing one thin angle simply because it makes a socko anecdotal lead and leaves the essence a vague blur?

How can you write about a man simply by telling me what he says without telling me how he says it? How can you write about a man simply by telling me what he is without telling me what he is like or what he'd like to be? How can you write about a man without telling me what he is afraid of, what he wishes he could do over again, what pleases him most, what pleases him least, what illusions were broken, what vague yearning remains? How can you write about a successful man without telling me his failures or about any man without somehow indicating his own view of himself?

How can you write about a man without being there? I don't simply mean being there in the reporting, but being there in the writing. For our purposes, when a huge tree falls in the forest and there is no one to hear it, there is no sound. For our purposes, a story about a man without the writer being in it is a story about no man.

Feature stories without the writer in them are as meaningless as a rimless zero. You cannot capture the feeling of a man without reacting to him. You cannot tell me about him without telling me your reactions and impressions and you can't do that until you think hard and add it all up.

Without a viewpoint, the writer's separate little facts, his quotable quotes, his stubborn statistics, his bouncy biographical data, his clever alliterations, his flashy touches are all so much trivia, strung together without purpose, without shape, without effect.

It makes no difference what you're writing about—a man, a town, a country, an administration, an issue, a team of jugglers, a school of piranha. Put yourself there, buster, and take me with you.

All good stories, all good writing, are but two sides of the same coin. How is this man different from me, how is he like me? Me, me, me. Me, the writer. Me, the reader. Don't just tell me how much the circus midget earns a week. Tell me about his difficulties in living in a world built for taller people like me—how he reaches up to the box to mail a letter, how he makes the high first step of a bus.

Give me the extraordinary and give me the ordinary. Does the richest man in the world have everything he wants? Does he bother to look at the prices on a menu at all? That strange, remote, isolated little village way up in the Canadian bush. Don't just tell me about the polar bears and the deer. Tell me, buster, how do they get a suit cleaned there?

Tell me the large by telling me the small. Tell me the small by telling me the large. Identify with me, plug into my circuit, come in loud and clear. Don't give me your high-sounding abstractions about foreign aid. Tell me, buster, what's it going to cost me? Will it help me sleep better—can I worry less about the big bomb, will it mean, maybe, my son won't be drafted, or at least, his son?

And, of course, don't leave me gaping through holes in your story. You know, I think the worst phrase ever developed in the newspaper business is "well, write around it." In other words, there's a big hole in our information, let's fudge it, let's throw some grass over it, let's obscure it and quickly get on to the next thing.

This phrase and attitude may, of course, be necessary in some spot stories. It should rarely be necessary in preparing a good feature. If we don't have the missing fact, you can bet somebody else will.

Don't tease me unless you can deliver, baby. Don't tell me the situation was dramatic and expect me to take your word for it. Show me how it was dramatic and I'll supply the adjective. You say this character is unpredictable? When, where, how? Give me the evidence, not just the chapter headings.

All of this, of course, takes time, and time is what you and your staff have least of. I can't help you there. Go see Gallagher or the chaplain.

But I do have a nasty suggestion. Want to separate the men from the boys? Give a man a good feature assignment and then take away all of his alibis in advance. Tell him he has all the time he needs. Tell him if the first two interviews don't do it, he can go back again. Tell him all we want is the best story he can do.

This, of course, is a dirty thing to do to a writer and leaves him utterly defenseless at his typewriter. Anyway, it's worth a try. You might find some good feature writers that way. You might also find that a writer stripped completely of his alibis will beg to go back to spot news, never more to stray.

But the larger point I'm trying to make is this. The fully dimensional human viewpoint cannot be matched by any machine. The eye of man is still sharper than the eye of a television camera because it is linked to a brain and a heart.

4

Guide Line to Depth

"Now here's a story that needs the full treatment. It's important, but it's so complicated that nobody understands why. It needs backgrounding. It needs to show the reader how he fits into it. It needs to sing like a combination of Hemingway and Sandburg. You may have to read a couple of books before you get started. Then you may have to interview 15 or 20 people. And, oh, yes, today is Wednesday; we'll run the story on Sunday."

There is an assignment designed to leave the average reporter with his mouth agape, his eyes slightly glazed, and frantic thoughts running through his mind. He blinks his eyes and wishes to heaven, or elsewhere, that someone would provide a good, old-fashioned murder yarn to take the boss's mind off this foolishness.

It takes a well-trained reporter to close his mouth and go about such an assignment. There are such writers in the business and a few are beginning to come from colleges. Very soon now—yesterday would be about right—there must be many more reporters who can close their mouths and go to work on what might be called a hurry-up depth assignment. That doesn't mean for the next edition, but it may mean within a couple of days. And that is not very much time to turn out the equivalent of a polished magazine article.

Depth does not always mean take all the time in the world. It often means background and perspective for today's news—and just as soon as possible, for depth in most cases is simply complete, quality news writing.

Critics of the depth approach often say, "This stuff is all right, but just how many times can you write about the problems of education?"

Their complaint stems from a surface knowledge of the philosophy of the complete news story. Readership is low, and deservedly so, on just another series on education, taxation, slum clearance, and what have you. That is not what we are talking about.

The subjects for depth stories are just as multitudinous as the news itself. Depth can be part of a breaking news story. It can be the breaking news story. It can put the breaking news story into perspective while it still breaks. It can explain complicated news while it still is confusing the reader's fickle mind. No, the problem is not finding subjects. It is recognizing, selecting, and refining them. The trick, of course, is picking the right story from the hundreds of perishable items that flow into the newsroom every day.

For example, the highway deaths of four teen-agers near Hampton, Iowa, was tragic, but routine, until *The Des Moines Sunday Register* sent George Mills to do the story. Normally, two to three hours of work would wrap up such a story. Mills spent 18 hours just interviewing residents of Hampton.

The newspaper had already carried the routine story four days before Mills's story ran. Then why send him 110 miles to Hampton to spend 18 hours interviewing?

So that he could reconstruct the lives of every one of the victims for three hours before the crash. Not so that he could get a "feeling" and do just another mood piece on an accident. So that he could collect more facts than had anyone else, and having collected and organized them, let those facts tell a story of suspense and meaning. This was not just another safety-on-the-highways story. Here are the first nine paragraphs of Mills's story as it appeared in November of 1949:

Hampton, Ia.—Eighteen-year-old Francis Elwood plowed all day on the Heilskov farm where he was working southwest of town.

After a supper of wieners, he went up to his room to write some letters. He was tired. He planned to go to bed early.

He didn't know that he had a date with death in three hours.

In northeast Hampton, big George Kibsgaard also didn't know he had only three hours left to live. George, 18, had helped his electrician father move a meter in a house that day.

After supper, George took his 1936 Oldsmobile and went uptown, just as he always had done. It was so routine that he didn't even say good-by to his parents.

In west Hampton, little Russell Jensen, 19 and young-looking for his age, washed up in the little backlot house where he lived with his father.

Russ polished cars that day in the Ford garage. Now he was going to have a bowl of chili at the Skelly lunchroom where the teen-agers hang out.

Russell similarly had no realization of the fact that the end of his life was only hours away.

Lloyd Casey, 18, a big likable redhead, went home from the *Hampton Chronicle* where he was working as a printer apprentice. He also thought he would drop over to the Skelly lunch after the evening meal. The march of events was to claim Lloyd's life, too, very soon.

It does not matter that *The Register* ran a story four days late. It matters only that Mills's four-column story told his readers far more than a dozen routine death-on-the-highway stories.

The story came about because someone with imagination— Mills, his editors—took time to think. Having thought, having created an idea—yes, "created"—they let the facts, all the facts, take over.

Mills's hurry-up depth piece came after the breaking news. Sometimes depth comes before the news break. Then it prepares the reader for what he might not understand in the heat of a fast-breaking story. This was the case when *The Wall Street Journal's* Ed Cony went to Havana, Cuba, in December of 1958.

The Journal's Pulitzer prize winner wrote a story of Batista's Cuba. Read the first three paragraphs:

> Havana—"The Cuban economy has deteriorated badly in the past month. The situation is now very serious. The Batista government right now is weathering the storm. But if Cuba's economy continues to weaken for another 30 days—anything could happen."
>
> So says one of the best informed economic experts in Cuba who, like many another observer of this island's business life, has witnessed its surprising previous success in remaining healthy during two years of increasingly bitter conflict between President Fulgencio Batista's government forces and Fidel Castro's rebels.
>
> But during the past few weeks, Cuba's economy has faltered noticeably, and the chief reason is the stepped-up offensive by Castro's increasingly powerful guerrillas.

Two weeks after Cony's story reached his readers, Batista fled, leaving behind one of the major news stories of a decade. Because of Cony's depth-in-advance his readers better understood the rise of Castro's Cuba.

It didn't take a crystal ball to predict the need for Cony's story. It took a reporter and editors with imaginations. With the facts of Cuba's economic decay before them, they had an idea. It led to a news story before the breaking news.

Of course, there are depth stories that may be assembled over a period of weeks. This variety, improperly done, leads to the just-another-series complaint. And it should. It takes no brains to order, "Give us another series on the lousy shape of the public schools. You know, no money, too many kids, all that stuff."

Most readers know "all that stuff" and a good deal more. If you are going to take the time and space for a series, then, for the readers' sake, get to a point.

If Johnny can't spell, is it because there isn't enough money or the way he is taught? If Johnny can't read, is it because there are too many kids in his room, or because of what he reads?

Those questions are simply ideas in the form of questions. As ideas, there is very little chance that they will ever appear in the newspaper in exactly their original form. Few good ideas do. They are simply starting points. The facts usually change the original idea, but those same facts also usually lead to an even better depth story. And, if the original question—the original idea—was provocative enough, the chances are slight that the results will be "just another series about education."

Phil Meyer of *The Miami Herald* did not know when he started out on an idea just where the facts would lead him. They led him to a story about school insurance premiums by patronage. He did not worry any more than usual about how long it took him to stack fact upon fact. There was no time peg on this story—until he broke it. Then Phil Meyer's facts made page-one news. Read the first few paragraphs of his series as it appeared in September of 1959 and see how it fits your news judgment:

> A total of $59,000 in school insurance commissions is being handed out this year to local agents who never lift a finger to earn it.
> The money is passed out to 181 agents, chosen by School Board members under a time-honored plan of political patronage. Estimated total cost to taxpayers: $200,000 a year.

The system, inherited by the present School Board from an earlier era when the insurance plum was much smaller, has resisted more than six years of efforts to dislodge it.

This year, the School Board is paying $314,886 to insure its $92 million worth of school buildings. According to Metro experiences with competitive bidding, the figure is about $200,000 too high.

Under the patronage system $59,000 is going to agents who prepare no policies, collect no premiums, service no claims. The only thing required of them is to endorse their checks which range from $49.40 to nearly $3,000.

These insurance men were the major source of campaign contributions for three School Board members in last year's primary, and an important source for two others.

That story won for Meyer an American Political Science Association award for local governmental writing. He deserved it. He started with an idea, a hint about school insurance. He dug until the facts told the story. But, remember, it started with an idea, a reporter's idea, which editors had enough imagination to see. The fertile germ of every decent depth story is the idea—the product of the ability to imagine, to dream, to create. It all starts with the idea, the product of educated imagination. When you began learning to write, someone told you the lead was the toughest part of a story. That is not so. The hardest part is getting the idea—something that must take place long before the first tap of a typewriter key.

For too many years, too many newspapers and schools of journalism have failed to tackle head-on the problem of ideas. They have clung to the notion that this idea business is kind of ghostly. It slips from your grasp if you try to pin it down. Furthermore, they have rationalized, we cannot even cover thoroughly all the news that breaks every day. The result too often is frantic writing and editing under the pressure of the day's news. When pressure rather than thought controls writing and editing, we become set-ups for the competition. We write briefly and frantically and are happy if the paper comes out with a little bit of everything. Then, we go home and turn on the evening television newscast.

"There," we say smugly, "they had nothing we didn't have in the paper. In fact, we had lots more items they didn't touch."

That smugness is badly misplaced. We didn't win any battle against the competition. We lost.

If we had little more of the major stories than television, the competition won. It is easier to watch the Big Eye than to read. If we think we won because of those extra, less newsworthy items, we lost again. If our only margin is minimal news, we are like the car dealer who believes he beats the competition because he sells the same number of $3,000 cars plus an extra ten jack handles. It took time and money to sell the jack handles, too. He probably lost.

To come out ahead the car dealer must sell more $3,000 cars, not more jack handles. To beat the competition the newspaper must carry more really important news, not more minimal stories. The difference, of course, is ideas, imagination, creativity.

The newsman must ride on top of the news. His imagination must not suffocate under its pressure. He must have time to pick and choose from all the news that which is most important. He must have time to pick what should be expanded in order to leave the competition in the bulletin business and to put him back in the business of giving all the important news. To do this he must have ideas. He must see the need to send a George Mills to Hampton, Iowa, for 18 hours of interviewing. He must see the need to let a Phil Meyer have all the time it takes to dig out all the facts about public school insurance. He must see the need to send an Ed Cony to Havana before the bottom drops out of Cuba's economy. These men ride on top of the news. They do not struggle frantically simply to keep up with the competition. And, again, the difference is ideas, imagination, creativity.

These three servants of depth do not work in a vacuum. They have to be educated. An idea doesn't just happen. It may seem to pop into its creator's mind. It doesn't. It is born because his mind has all kinds of launching platforms for ideas.

He knows enough about a dozen, or several dozen, areas of human activity to recognize an idea when it gnaws at his imagination. Later in this book there is a whole section devoted to building mental platforms in many academic areas. At the moment just think about the importance of the educated hunch—the idea.

Advertising men are fond of saying that nothing happens until somebody advertises. They may be right, but if they think a little further, they will know that nothing happens on any American newspaper until somebody in the news department has an idea. Advertisers buy readership. News departments with ideas create readership.

Of course, the idea is only the start. Think again for a moment about that reporter who has been told, "Give me the whole story, make it sing, and turn it in the day after tomorrow." As he stands there with his mouth open, he thinks, "But where do I start?" Yes, there's the rub—where does he start?

The reporter and his editor at this point are in much the same position as huge corporations sometimes find themselves. It is not uncommon for a corporation to ask one of its own experts or an outsider for an analysis. Having stretched the corporation out on the couch, the expert invariably starts with one question:

"Just what is it you are trying to do?"

The obvious answer is, "To make money." But that does not answer the question of how and why.

Business experts say that a sure way to upset most boards of directors is to reply, "Yes, everyone wants to make money. But you tell me how you want to do it—and tell me in one sentence."

This approach may be upsetting, but it is not a game. The businessman who can reduce his objectives to one simple clear-cut sentence has something upon which to base the planning for his entire business. It can serve as a guide for his instructions to his executives. It can serve as a guide for the executives to supervise those under them. It is a guide line for the whole operation.

The guide line is what the depth reporter needs once he has his idea. Getting the guide line may require long creative thought both by him and by his editor. Ideas are just a start. Usually they are far too general. In this unrefined state they would result in just another series, or just another long story gobbling up valuable space.

However, if the idea for depth treatment is a good one, it usually does one of three things:

1. It expands and puts into perspective a breaking local story, and does it well beyond the competition's limitations.
2. It develops a local story that has gone unwritten for any number of reasons—often neglect.
3. It gives local perspective to a national story.

A good idea may involve none of these areas, but it may help you judge any idea if it fits one of these three categories. It also may help to ask this question: "Why can I write this story better here than somewhere else?"

Students with their refreshingly broad horizons frequently want to write about such subjects as "that stock market situation. Someone ought to deal with that in depth," they say quite seriously. They may be right, but then they must answer the question, "How can I write better about the stock exchange in Butte, Montana, than someone else can on Wall Street?" Such a question can wreck an apparently good idea, but it also can help avoid a dry run.

All of this self-interrogation is part of the reporter's and editor's search for the gimmick, the peg, the guide line, for an idea. Take the time necessary to find that guide line. Hasty decisions at this point can result in later waste of time, money, and news space. We do enough of this now in the classroom and newsroom. This also may be the time for a little bit of togetherness.

Note, we said a *little bit* of togetherness. There is little room in the job of creating a depth story for the overworked, modern concept of togetherness. An editor, a reporter, a photographer, a rewriteman, and a copyreader can, as a group, refine an idea into a guide line. They can, as a group, plan the over-all story. The reporter can do the research. The photographer can take the pictures. The reporter can write the story. The rewriteman can rewrite it. The copyreader can edit it. And the editor can coordinate the whole business. But if they try as a group to do every step they, like the committee, may put together a camel instead of a horse.

They all can, and should, help refine the idea into a guide line. Although the research may change it, it gives them all a roadmap with a destination in boldface caps.

Let's see how it works. Check the following guide lines for depth stories by top professionals:

Does the boom in licking and pasting trading stamps make economic sense?—Louis B. Fleming, *The Los Angeles Times.*

Four teen-agers had a date with death.—George Mills, *The Des Moines Sunday Register.*

The economic decay of Batista's Cuba may mean Castro victory.—Ed Cony, *The Wall Street Journal.*

The use of insurance premiums as patronage in public schools.—Phil Meyer, *The Miami Herald.*

The strange odyssey of the $100,000 bill with an $80,000 price tag. —Morton Mintz, *The Washington Post.*

These reporters may not have started with exactly these guide lines. The facts may have changed their original ideas. But when the research was complete and the facts assembled, these guide lines could serve as a life preserver for any reporter writing any of these stories. Does a real professional need a life preserver?

No amount of experience eliminates the need for something to hang onto as you wade through the sea of facts turned up by most depth reporting assignments. The beginner certainly needs it, and it is helpful to the editor.

It is easy to tell a reporter to go cover a fire. He can hear the sirens, he can smell the smoke, and he can see the flames. It is a good deal more difficult to tell him to explain to the reader the status of the city's fire insurance rating in view of the lack of money for new equipment. It would help the editor and his reporter to agree on a guide line.

It also helps the instructor and the journalism student. Let's see how it worked with Hal Brown, a depth reporting student at the University of Nebraska.

He announced that he wanted to do a story about "isolationism." At first glance, that idea had only one qualification for depth treatment. It certainly could be better written in the center of the so-called isolationist Midwest than in, say, New York City. Beyond that, the idea seemed almost hopeless. Several million well-chosen (and otherwise) words had been produced on the subject. None of them had really settled anything. It did not seem likely that Hal Brown, a senior who was having trouble passing his science requirement, was going to settle anything either.

But, unless you are totally insensitive, you are not going to discourage a potential reporter with as much drive, desire, and savvy as Hal Brown has. So, you settle back, relax, open your mind and let him talk. Now and then you throw in a question. Then you listen some more.

It may take an hour. It may take more. This time it took almost two hours for Hal Brown to travel from a vague idea about isolationism to a story guide line. That guide line—"The so-called isolationist Midwest has become the front line of defense for the Western world." This time the original guide line held up all the way through the research, organization, and writing of the story. A case history and the story are at the end of this chapter.

Look again at those three words—idea, imagination, and creativity. They belong in the newsroom just as surely as do the writers you will meet later who talk about the ring and rhythm of the words they use. Hal Brown had an idea. He used his imagination to refine it into a workable guide line. He used creativity, too. But this was just a start. He would use it later as he researched, organized, and wrote.

Case History of a Story

Student: Hal Brown.

Idea: Isolationism.

Guide Line: The so-called isolationist Midwest has become the front line of defense for the Western world.

Sources: Brown went first to history and political science where he tried to locate a definition of isolationism. He found that the definitions were multiple, as were the opinions about the existence of isolationism in the Midwest. With help from these two areas, he then read the background of isolationism in the Midwest. With the help of the head of the state historical society he localized his readings to isolationism in Nebraska. He examined, for example, the viewpoint of the late Senator George W. Norris.

Legwork: Armed with a launching platform from which to ask questions about isolationism, he went to the small towns near missile sites in Nebraska. Here he talked with the people about their viewpoint on isolationism. Finally, he went to the missile sites themselves and to the headquarters of the Strategic Air Command just south of Omaha, Nebraska.

Organization: Several outlines for the story failed to write. Finally, when he decided to start on Main Street of a small town near a missile site and to tie his story to a period of extremely cold weather, the story began to take shape. After three drafts, the fourth went together as you will see below.

Results: This story ran in Nebraska newspapers the day after an explosion at the Mead missile site. It was judged first in the Hearst Foundation news contest. The judges, Roger Tatarian, general news director, UPI; Hubbard Keavey, Los Angeles Bureau Chief, AP; William Ruggles, former editorial page editor of *The Dallas Morning News*; and Basil (Stuffy) L. Walters, newspaper consultant and former executive editor for the Knight newspapers, picked the story unanimously, even though much of it did not deal with breaking news. After it won, the story was widely reprinted.

The Story:

"We just never give much thought to the missile site. We realize it's there, but we don't think about it. We just go about our business."

That was Roy Carlson, a garage owner in Mead, Nebraska (population, 428). Yet not a mile from the spot in which these calm words were spoken was the scaffolding for a silo unlike any other silo in this farm community.

For this silo would hold not silage, but an Atlas missile with a deadly nose cone destined for an enemy target.

These two scenes eloquently illustrate one of the strangest contrasts in Nebraska's history. One, the quiet, calm main street approach paints a word picture of the detached viewpoint, sometimes called isolationism, for which the Midwest has become noted. The second, that deadly silo, presents physical evidence that this same part of mid-America has in fact become the front line of defense for the Western world.

It was cold that day on Mead's main street. Bitterly cold, in fact. Nebraska was nearing the end of two months of near-Arctic weather. On at least 16 days during December and January, the thermometer had dropped to zero or below.

On the farms around Mead where the ordinary kind of silo is the rule, work had all but halted. Frigid temperatures and biting winds had chased the farmers indoors, or at least to protected repair work around the farmyard. But at the missile site, work had continued without a slowdown. In fact, Strategic Air Command spokesmen at home base south of Omaha announced that no slowdowns in the massive missile program had been caused by weather. They pointed out that there had been some brief stoppages, but none of these could be laid to the chilling temperatures that had brought much of Nebraska to a halt.

Elsewhere in this state, often called isolationist, some schools had closed. Some towns had practically shut down because of gas shortages, and normal construction had often come to a frozen halt. But over the state near many little towns like Mead, work went on in the effort that was fortifying this as the center of our national defense.

Those few who drove the lonely highways on cold nights may have seen the lights at the missile complexes and wondered:

Is this Nebraska? Is this the Midwest where we have approached any business but our own with caution?

They asked a question that has been argued in Nebraska for decades:

Is this state isolationist?

Perfectly proper is another question:

If it is isolationist, is that bad?

You will not find agreement on the answers to either question.

Some historians say Nebraska never was isolationist. They point to the role played by the Mississippi Valley in the early shaping of America's dealings with foreign powers. Parts of this great section of mid-America have existed under five flags, they point out. They also refer to the large number of immigrants who settled in Nebraska.

But at least one historian says this immigration was a factor in making this state isolationist. Richard W. Van Alstyne, writing in the *Mississippi Valley Historical Review,* says:

"After the Revolution, New England isolationism which I take to be indistinguishable from nationalism, seems to have focused on animosity toward the British as competitors and oppressors on the high seas.

"Isolationism in the Mississippi Valley must have drawn heavily on the New England inheritance, but the remoteness of the interior from the seas is believed to have emphasized cultural as well as political separation from Europe.

"Furthermore, political animosities which link isolationism with Anglophobia (dislike for the English) were reinforced in the Mississippi Valley by the introduction of non-English emigrant strains, in whom inherited prejudices from the Old World were poured into the new mold of American nationalism."

Other historians, such as Dr. James C. Olson, chairman of the University of Nebraska history department, say Nebraska is and always has been isolationist.

Olson, who defines an isolationist as one "who believes in

unilateral action and wants to work out his own destiny without reference to outside forces," points to the voting records of Nebraska Congressmen to back up his stand.

Beginning with the late Senator George W. Norris who in his later years was not considered an isolationist by most, Nebraska Congressmen have generally opposed war, mutual security, and foreign aid, this group of historians points out. They add, however, that the Nebraska Congressional delegations have generally supported the Trade Agreements Act of 1934 and the extensions of the act.

An examination of the voting record of Nebraska's Congressmen does back up this viewpoint. While in some instances votes have been split on bills generally considered internationalist in nature, in the majority of cases, Nebraska representatives in Washington have voted against foreign entanglements.

Perhaps George Norris, who in his later years was considered by many to be somewhat of an internationalist, best makes the point. In World War I days he was one of six who voted against entry into the war. Twenty years later he was considered by many to be in agreement with President Franklin Delano Roosevelt on many internationalist points. However, an historian even at that time quotes him as saying:

"In spite of world tensions even greater than at the start of World War I, the U.S. should have no interest in so-called collective security. Our business is in America."

Today, historians who say Nebraska is less isolationist than in the past point to (1) the Cuban refugees who have been accepted into Nebraska, (2) development by the state of survival rations such as the Nebraskit and the milk bar, (3) the University of Nebraska's cooperation in founding and maintaining a university in Turkey, and (4) the foreign student programs that are gaining momentum on many of the state's campuses.

None of this answers totally the question of whether we are isolationist, or not. Nor does it tell us whether isolationism, as such, is good or bad. But it explains why this part of the country has been called "the isolationist Midwest."

And with that tag our steadily growing importance as a defense center makes us another paradox in national history. That the

Midwest is the front line of defense for the Western world is easily established. There is physical evidence.

It started, probably, during World War II when temporary air bases and training centers were set up in Nebraska. However, these were temporary and they were several steps removed from the front lines.

Nebraska moved into the front lines of the cold war after World War II when Offutt Air Base near Omaha was selected as headquarters for SAC in the spring of 1948.

From a total assigned strength of 1,100 men, SAC headquarters has grown to a strength of more than 10,000 in the past 14 years. What was once an army outpost is now headquarters for one of America's biggest businesses with a payroll topping 224,000 men and women, scattered on 70 bases on four continents.

It is from this building and its almost unbelievable underground control centers that retaliatory weapons would be fired if the United States should be attacked. For all its reputation, its red phone to the president, and its second-by-second world-wide contact, the building itself is not conspicuous. It seems to nestle down in the middle of Nebraska farmland and cattle feeding country.

The Offutt Base was joined by the Lincoln Air Base later, as LAFB became one of the larger SAC bases from which first line bombers flew. And then came the period of the missile.

This, to a degree, changed the focus of world-wide attention on Nebraska. As SAC spokesmen explain, their headquarters were located in the Midwest originally as part of the dispersal from Washington, D.C., and because of the central location. Geographically Offutt Base became the center of the world for retaliatory purposes.

However, the speed of missiles, many times faster than manned bombers, has eliminated some of the advantage of the central location, they explain. The warning time on an attack has been drastically cut, they point out, with intercontinental ballistic missiles traveling several thousand miles an hour.

Even so, the red phone is still in Nebraska, and in or near many small Nebraska towns, such as Mead, those deadly silos are under construction.

Have Nebraskans resented the monsters being installed in their backyards?

Generally not, say SAC spokesmen. In fact, they continue, the reception has been good. In only a few instances have there been problems.

Men working on the missile sites have found a welcome in nearby towns.

As for the presence of the missile itself, there seems to have been little change in attitude by the people. If Mead is typical, most residents of small communities feel the installation has had little or no influence on their lives. Most take the attitude that it is there, so what? They admit that little thought is given to the fact that their town may have become a prime target area.

Most of those interviewed felt the missile work had done little to increase their interest in world affairs. There has been no sudden interest, they explain, in fall-out shelters, for instance.

From Mead to the other little towns with their strange silos, to SAC with its red phone, the questions about isolationism may still be unanswered. But over the same route there could be no question that the Midwest, sometimes called isolationist, was the center of defense for the Western world.

5

Reporting by Research

Those who write in depth might call their line of work exhaustive reporting. In fact, more descriptive than depth reporting might be the term *research reporting*.

For at last, the word *research* has an honorable place in the American newsroom. In the journalism classroom the word has had a place for some time. However, even there it has often applied to research into the profession, an examination of its performance, its problems, its influence on public opinion. Certainly every profession needs this kind of professional research, and the journalism school is the right place to do it.

Research, however, has an even more direct application in learning to write a depth story. Remember Mills of *The Des Moines Register* and his 18 hours of interviewing? He spent several hours of planning questions before he even started. In fact, Mills considers this such an important phase of his reporting that he watches for signs that his keenness may be dulling as he prepares questions.

"If I get punchy trying to concentrate on questions," he says, "I turn my mind away from the problem for ten minutes or so. I listen to the radio, maybe. Then I start again. Such a break often is very helpful in getting your mind to think of other angles that have been overlooked."

What are Mills's hours preparing questions but preparation for research? Those questions guide the hours of digging that follow.

45

And those hours are nothing more than research for a complete news story.

Here research becomes a step in producing depth. First the reporter has an idea. Then he refines it into a guide line, which is nothing more than a solid news reason for writing the story. At the conception of the story—the idea and guide line stages—imagination plays the important part. But remember, the reporter is dealing in news. He must substitute facts for the educated opinion involved in the idea.

The facts may change the idea. They may even kill it, though more often they will suggest an even better idea. The modern reporter, just as did the more illustrious of his predecessors, must go where the facts take him. That route is research, the next step in writing a depth story.

Right now understand that this is not an effort to build a new set of rules. From personal experience, experience of students and young reporters, and the experience of some of the best professionals, we are suggesting a skeleton. Around that skeleton it may be easier to put the flesh and blood of a depth story. Use the bones of the skeleton that are applicable to the story involved.

Think about it as a launching platform for a complicated story. Beneath the platform are the time-tested ethics of the business. For example, writer opinion belongs on the editorial page, not in the news columns. The steps suggested here are simply the countdown check points. They do not bind your mind. They encourage its use by helping to get it organized. Without organization the depth story can become the most disorganized thing in a business that has been called "organized chaos." Research is a vital step in that organization.

Read what some professionals say about research:

The Wall Street Journal editors tell reporters working on the complete story:

> The reporting must be thorough and must have depth. Major questions shouldn't be left unanswered. Interesting and important side angles shouldn't be left unexplored. Background, analysis, interpretation should be there. The specific should replace the general. The precise should replace the obscure.

Now listen to Louis B. Fleming, reporter for *The Los Angeles Times*:

Exhaustive, tireless research is essential in any yarn looking at a subject for the first time. It is terrifyingly easy to come up with the wrong answer if you short-cut on preparation.

The Wall Street Journal editors and Fleming were getting at the same point. The depth story is made or broken in the research phase. Here facts replace opinion. Facts make the difference between an idea and an honest-to-goodness news story.

So far as the reporter is concerned, the research step of a depth story is probably his greatest departure from the routine of a one-dimensional news story. Suddenly, he has at least hours instead of minutes to get the facts. If he is lucky, he may have days and weeks. But he is only fooling himself if he thinks that research is a soft pitch—an easy out from the routine of the city desk. Research, the depth writers will tell you, is the hardest kind of work.

An editor appraising the qualities of a good reporter, if the reporter in question really is good, sooner or later, says, ". . . and that man can dig. He can dig and dig until he gets *all* the facts." Digging is just a synonym for research—a quality with which no one comes completely equipped. It has to be learned.

Reporter Robert Wells of *The Milwaukee Journal* gives good advice on learning to both reporter and student when he says:

> The point is that what a newspaper man needs from college is, primarily, some practice in doing research fast, and coming in a poor second, a little background in as wide a selection of subjects as possible. It is impractical to know something about everything, although that would be the ideal preparation for your career. But if you know enough to ask the right questions about as many topics as possible, you're doing pretty well.

Mr. Wells puts it mildly. If the reporter knows the right questions to ask, he has an unbeatable edge on the competition.

But even when he knows enough to ask the right questions, a good depth assignment will probably send him scurrying for the reference books. The day is gone when a reporter with his nose in a book was a reporter reading a mystery novel out of sight of the city desk.

However, it is important to go scurrying to the *right* reference books. It is so important, in fact, that a later section of this book is devoted entirely to locating the right references from many of the academic disciplines, which are really only reporters' tools as far as we in the newspaper business must be concerned.

At the moment, assume that the reporter knows which reference books will help him most with his subject. Now, he must read them. If this sounds childish, examine how *The St. Petersburg Times*'s Lowell Brandle went about doing an offbeat series that qualified very handily as one kind of depth.

Brandle, a Nieman Fellow, was not concerned at the moment with taxation, segregation, or any one of a hundred more serious subjects he has handled. He, as a good citizen of Florida, was interested in the moon. He set out to learn if the moon, besides its tourist value, really had any other effects on the human race.

He went to the city library and read two books on the subject and a couple of magazine articles. He also wrote to the American Medical Association. That was a start. Now, in Brandle's words, follow him on the trail of the moon over a six-week period:

> In preparation, I talked to an old police captain, the hospital administrator, a clinical psychologist, two medical researchers, and six psychiatrists.
>
> I had one of our staff, whose brother is a teacher at Johns Hopkins, write to him for any information he had.
>
> I went to the police station and spent two days going through the thousands of complaints, moving traffic violations, and arrest files for the past year. . . . (Laying the foundation for future follow-up stories on the same story, I asked one of the medical researchers to check in *Index Medica* to see what research has been done in recent years on the subject, all over the world, and to order relevant research papers for me from the Library of Congress. He was happy to do so.)
>
> Obviously, this preparation was spread over six weeks, and I did other work in the meantime, while the material was coming in. The actual writing took about one day. I worked with our art department, suggesting illustrations and charts which would accompany the story. The color printing was scheduled far in advance. . . . The series was successful in that it created widespread interest in the community for several days during and after publication. My spies reported that it provided a discussion topic for one whole evening at the Medical Society and at several parties. [And the following was the compliment supreme to Brandle's effort.] I heard the men in the composing room discussing it also. And the elevator operator was anxious to talk about it with me.

What did Brandle find in this series that stirred so much interest? Certainly it wasn't world-shaking, possibly not even significant, but for three days running, *The St. Petersburg Times* entertained its

readers by posing some big question marks about the influence of
the moon on mankind. Brandle's research revealed that arrests
increased during the full moon. Psychiatrists told him that patients
were more disturbed when the moon was shining brightly—but
the doctors didn't know why. Other medical evidence indicated
that hemorrhaging is more likely during the full moon.

Yes, Brandle and *The St. Petersburg Times* entertained their
readers and gave them ready-made conversation pieces for at least
three days. Maybe that was enough, but because Brandle's research
was so thorough he did something for himself, and the newspaper,
too. He handled "moon madness" in a way that gained rather than
lost respect for him and his newspaper in medical circles.

A lot of research for a trifling subject? It depends upon your
viewpoint, but how many hours did it steal in reading time from
the competition?

Sometimes what seems to be trivia in our busy world may turn
into something important under the scrutiny of a depth writer. Any
man who has cleaned out his coat pockets, any woman who has
cleaned out her purse, any janitor who has swept up the floor is
aware of one of America's biggest retail sales promotions—the big
business of trading stamps.

Louis B. Fleming, reporter for *The Los Angeles Times,* was assigned to look into this sticky subject. What he produced was no
free advertisement for either the trading-stamp people or the re-
tailers who dealt with them. It was a significant story on everyday
pocketbook economics.

For this household business, about which very little is known by
the general reader, Fleming could use no reference books.

This is the way he went about it:

> I started out with interviews with top executives of all trading stamp
> companies and any group that had been concerned: service station
> owners, for example. This gave me the statistics and the economics
> from the stamp company viewpoint.
>
> I interviewed the merchants using them, also. There was an article
> in *Fortune* magazine which had explored some of the ground from the
> national angle and was helpful mainly in supporting some of my
> independent conclusions.
>
> The story, for our Sunday finance section, was written with a conclu-
> sive lead: "Los Angeles area housewives are collecting, licking, and
> redeeming a record number of trading stamps in a boom that makes
> increasingly less economic sense."

The story that followed enlightened the collecting, licking, and redeeming housewives on a subject they accepted as part of their daily lives. Fleming's facts posed some provoking questions, but it made no difference whether the story came out for or against trading stamps. All that mattered was that Fleming provided the readers with the facts. And Fleming, like many good newspaper writers, drew some barbs as well as flowers for his efforts.

It is terrifyingly easy to come up with the wrong answer if you short-cut on preparation. In the trading-stamp story, for example, we trampled a few toes of major advertisers who were sharply critical. We were able to answer all questions completely because the homework had been done in advance.

The examples cited from Brandle and Fleming indicate extensive use of reference material in Brandle's case, and personal interview in Fleming's effort. There are many kinds of research—as many as there are subjects, probably. But a very common form in the newspaper plant is use of the newspaper itself. Not only are the newspaper files perhaps the best source in tracing the flavor of local history, but they also can supply the only running account of a story that has been given to the readers piecemeal over a long period of time. It actually takes a very short time for the facts of a running story to become distorted. This is particularly true when the readers' emotions are involved in a controversy.

A reader may miss one of the running stories. One day it may be played on page one, and the next on page 13. There is no time in the routine rush of covering the breaking news to recapitulate what has gone before. Soon, individual readers are trying to decide whether each day's story is for or against them. They find it impossible to realize that not every story in a controversy can give both sides, but an aggregate of all the stories does this fairly. The newspaper finds itself accused of unfairness only because it is covering the breaking news. That is the time for depth. Don Holm of *The Portland Oregonian* reached this point in a story he was covering.

As city hall reporter for *The Oregonian,* he covered an entire controversy over the battle of the Ash Street ramp. Every experienced reporter has run into local stories of this kind. The Ash Street story involved what might have been a routine city building project. After accidents had occurred during a celebration in the

Ash Street area of town, the City Council had made what could have been a routine move to help eliminate traffic congestion and thus prevent accidents. A ramp (viaduct) was to be built. The action became a good deal more than routine and developed into a city-wide controversy when city planners and others interested in beauti-fication objected. They did not want a ramp in an area of town which they hoped both to preserve and to rebuild as an example of the "red plush" days of Portland.

Experienced newsmen know how such an apparently routine story can rage as a community controversy. These newsmen do not sneer at such a story as the essence of insignificance. They know that this story involves their city which is made up of people who are their readers.

The Ash Street debate raged in Portland for six months. When it was over, Don Holm and his boss, Assistant Managing Editor Ed Miller, believed there was still a job to be done. The battle of the Ash Street ramp had to be put into perspective. Here is the way Holm tells what followed:

As city hall reporter, I covered the entire controversy with day-to-day stories; after the battle was over, Ed Miller suggested a depth piece to wrap up the whole ball of wax, to put things back into proper perspective with a thorough analysis. We discussed this piece at length. Then he told me to go ahead and write it the way I saw it and take as much space as I needed. Right here I would like to emphasize the importance of a good editor to the writer. Any writer who thinks differently is only kidding himself.

To give you a little background, as this controversy gained momentum, it turned into a bitter fight all out of proportion to its importance. From the start, I simply called the shots as I saw them.

. . . As the battle developed, a lot of the bitterness spilled over onto me for not defending city hall. At one point, I was taking so much abuse from city officials . . . that I had to complain about it to the desk. This is beside the point, but I wanted to make the comment that this piece, written afterwards, put me back in the good graces of everybody on both sides of the fight, although it wasn't intended to softsoap anybody.

Since I knew the subject intimately, the first thing I did was to collect all the clips of the stories I had done on it. Then, after tempers had cooled, I went around and interviewed all the principal characters in the act—just talked to them off the cuff, looking for reaction, signs of bitterness, and to see how the scars were healing.

When I had absorbed all of this, I thought about it for a few days and sat down and wrote it at one sitting. It ran long, but Ed Miller read it and said, "Don't cut anything." And that's the way it ran.

How was Holm's "ball of wax" received? In his words:

> The reaction was terrific from readers. My phone rang all morning—calls from people who had been on both sides of the fight. All of them liked it, and, more important, I could sense that people were getting back a sense of humor. The point is that the piece must have been extremely well read in spite of its length, judging from the phone calls, mail, etc. received not only by us, but by many of the characters in the story. This ought to prove that some people still like to read as well as sit in front of a picture box.

Holm's experience illustrates two points: (1) a kind of depth story and (2) a kind of research.

His kind of depth story is something we call a "recap," a recapitulation of a running story. Newsmen do not agree that this is always a good thing to do. Students get totally confused about it. They tend to recap a breaking story so often that the reader has trouble finding the new news. The students' confusion illustrates the newsmen's doubts.

We cannot recap every running story. Someone has to sit back, think, and decide when a recap will really serve the community. The team of Miller and Holm of *The Oregonian* resulted in the valuable kind of recap story.

Assistant Managing Editor Miller saw the need and reporter Holm did the research. His research materials were in his own plant. They were the clippings and files of his own newspaper. Far too many students and professionals fail to check the history of a story as it has been unveiled in their own news columns.

No matter what kind of research the reporter does, if it is complete, he ends up knee-deep in facts. Those facts can make gray out of black and white. Actually, the depth story reveals that gray is the true color of many controversies. *The Los Angeles Times*'s Fleming found that out:

> My biggest pitch, however, is directed at those gray shades between black and white. When we went to work on the recent Civil Defense section in *The Times* . . . our investigation raised all the doubts that truly exist. We prepared a section which included a firm statement that there is no clear answer to the problem, which emphasized its complexity.

We may have lost some readers, and confused others, but we did not mislead them with oversimplified data.

Take it from Fleming, a thorough research job often does reduce an idea from black or white to gray. It is the old problem of the cracker-barrel philosopher: Too many facts can louse up a good story.

This discovery is often traumatic, particularly for the student facing his first depth piece. He starts with a beautiful idea. It is sharp. It is clear. It will make a significant story. Then he researches and facts begin to cloud the original idea. At this point, his first reaction is to say, "There is no story." Of course, he is wrong. His story is just beginning to develop.

Stephen Lough, a University of Nebraska student, was ready to throw in the sponge at this point in his first depth assignment. He saw gray instead of black or white when he tried to find out if college students were becoming more liberal or more conservative in their political outlook.

It started because Steve grew tired of reading apparently factless accounts of changing student political views. His research problem was staggering. He first tried to find references to define liberal and conservative. Of course, he found gray. Then he wanted to interview every one of the elected heads of every student political group on eight Midwestern campuses. He wanted to talk with chairmen of Young Republicans, Young Democrats, conservatives, and socialists.

It was when he tried to get the names of these campus leaders that he almost gave up. He discovered that national party headquarters seemed to have little or no factual information about these college groups. In some cases state party leaders were equally ignorant of their campus counterparts.

Student reporter Lough ran his hand vigorously through his fuzz cut and complained loudly that the story could not be had. Of course, after a half hour or so of guided contemplation, he realized that he already had part of a story.

He solved his problem by contacting the campus newspapers. Their editors quickly supplied names and background. That was only the start of his research. For a full account of it, see the case history of Lough's story at the end of this chapter. He, like Fleming of *The Los Angeles Times,* researched until he was flooded with facts.

Fleming's search that led him to the gray between the alleged black and white of Civil Defense, took him a long way, literally. He gathered information in California, New York, and the nation's capital. He read dozens of reports and books.

When the research was done, he reduced all the material onto small pieces of copy paper, one fact per page. As he said, "They were not unlike cards used by undergraduates for term papers."

Reporter Fleming and student reporter Lough had reached the end of their research and were looking for a way to organize what they had found. That, of course, is the next step in producing a depth story. Somehow, all those results from all that research have to be organized.

Case History of a Story

Student: Stephen Lough.

Idea: Student political activity.

Guide Line: Are college students becoming more conservative or more liberal?

Sources: Twenty-two young political leaders on eight college campuses, 300 student members of campus political groups, and 21 professors, considered accurate observers of student political activity on the eight campuses.

Legwork: The student political party members were surveyed by questionnaire. The professors and student leaders were interviewed in person where possible and otherwise by telephone. In this case, experimental funds were available to cover the long distance telephone bill of approximately $150. The point is not that $150 was spent, but that it may be necessary, if we are to teach depth at the college level, for these kinds of funds to be budgeted for student research. Many newspapers would have considered this a relatively small price to pay for a major, significant story.

Organization: Compilation of the questionnaire results on charts with pertinent student comments typed out on separate pieces of paper. All the quotes from the interviews were typed out on separate pieces of paper. All this was then arranged—several times—in the order it would appear in the story. Particularly difficult was the organization of the summary lead this kind of story requires.

Results: The story was widely run throughout the Midwest. Student newspapers picked it up and gave it prominent play. Off-campus newspapers also gave it the complete makeup treatment. Its circulation was somewhere in the neighborhood of one million. It was later chosen in sixth place nationally in the Hearst Foundation investigative reporting contest.

The Story:

National political leaders all claim him. Party spokesmen woo him. It's the rage to write about him.

Who?

The fledgling voter on the nation's college campuses. In the Midwest much attention focuses on the Big Eight—Colorado, Oklahoma, Oklahoma State, Kansas, Kansas State, Nebraska, Missouri, and Iowa State. What is the political profile of this future voter of mid-America?

Interviews with his campus political group leaders, a survey of the membership of his organizations, and the opinions of his instructors indicate:

1. Conservative activity is on the rise with the organization of at least five conservative groups on Big Eight campuses within the past year.

2. There is increased political activity on the campuses, but not necessarily an increase in numbers. As one professor put it, "more noise from the same people."

3. Students will accept a political label—Republican, Democrat, Conservative, Liberal—but most of them won't accept all of the philosophies for which that label is generally believed to stand. For example, 30 out of 35 members of two conservative groups were for low tariffs.

4. A majority of the students contacted seem to inherit their politics, despite the often-popular theory that Junior comes down to college and switches political parties. But, though they may inherit their party, most of them don't inherit straight tickets.

5. Grown-up politicos at the national level don't seem to know much about their budding counterparts at the campus level.

Young Republicans on the campus are not even organized nationally, and the Democrats at national headquarters confess to lack of such specific information as names of campus Young Democrat presidents.

These indications are the result of:

—Interviews of leaders (22 in all) of every Big Eight campus political group that could be discovered and contacted.

—Interviews with most of the heads of political science, history, and economics departments on all eight campuses. Because of varying departmental organization, the total was 21. In some instances the department heads referred to other professors in their department whom they felt were more informed.

—A survey of more than 300 students, most of whom are enough interested in politics to belong to a campus political group.

The leaders and professors were contacted in person or by telephone. The survey was conducted by mail with student leaders passing out questionnaires to their group members.

Those were the sources. Their opinions could not add up to answers in clear-cut blacks and whites. But their answers could provide indications—indications that help answer questions being asked about the future voter on Midwestern college campuses:

Is there an increase in political activity among the students?

Apparently, yes. A majority of the professors and student leaders indicated that they felt there was an increase in political activity. Most thought the increase was slight at the present time, but would pick up as the elections move nearer.

However, those at Kansas State University disagreed. Both student leaders and professors feel there is a general air of apathy towards politics. Philip M. Rice, chairman of the department of political science and history, said, "Students at Kansas State are unpolitical-minded."

What is the cause of this increased political activity?

Those who feel there is an increase think that the students have a greater awareness of the issues than they have had in the past. They attributed this awareness to the gravity of the international situation.

Is this increase in numbers?

Carl Schneider, acting chairman of the department of political science at the University of Nebraska, answered the question this way:

"There is more discussion, but I don't think that it involves more students."

A majority of the others interviewed echoed Schneider's sentiments with the exception of those at the University of Colorado. All the individuals interviewed there feel that the increase is in numbers as well as activity per capita.

Membership figures obtained from some of the 16 Young Democrat and Young Republican organizations support the view that there is no increase in numbers. Of the membership figures available, only the Young Republicans at the University of Colorado show an increase. That organization had 169 members last year compared with 258 for this year. The Young Democrats at the University of Nebraska and Oklahoma State have maintained a steady membership the last two years.

Other figures are:

	1961-62	1960-61
Kansas Young Democrats	202	350
Kansas State Young Republicans	over 400	over 600
Missouri Young Democrats	200	500
Colorado Young Democrats	60	196

Most of these groups had records that go back only for a year which was a presidential election year. Therefore, observers point out that membership would naturally be greater last year than it is this year.

Is there increased conservative activity?

Definitely, yes. Within the last year, at least five conservative groups have organized on Big Eight campuses. Iowa State, Kansas, and Kansas State have organized Young Americans for Freedom (YAF) chapters. Missouri now has a Young Conservative Club. These clubs have between 25 and 50 members. Bruce Vanderburg, one of six students organizing a YAF chapter at the University of Oklahoma, says he expects to get 1,000 members in his organization.

Nearly all the professors and student leaders interviewed feel there is an increase in conservatism. They feel that the presence of Senator Barry Goldwater, the recognized leader of the conservative movement, was largely responsible for the activity and that opposition to policies of the Kennedy administration also added coal to the fire.

Is there liberal activity?

Glenn B. Hawkins, chairman of the department of political science at Oklahoma State, said, "I think students are far more liberal than they were 10 or 20 years ago on almost every issue." Hawkins can find support at every Big Eight university that there is more liberal activity but not in large proportions.

Most professors and students feel that there is an increase in activity on both the conservative and liberal sides, but the liberals are not as pronounced in their actions and are becoming active only because they must combat the rising tide of conservatism.

Two groups whose title includes the word "socialist" were reported. One was a Fabian Socialist group at the University of Missouri. The other was a Young People's Socialist League (YPSL) at the University of Colorado. Thomas Milstein, president of the YPSL at Colorado, said that his chapter is the second largest west of the Mississippi River. He estimated he had 50 to 60 members.

Do students follow the general stereotype of a liberal or a conservative philosophy on issues?

Apparently not. In every case a majority of the members of four conservative organizations voted in favor of low tariffs. Low tariffs are generally recognized as a liberal approach.

In the Young Republican organizations a greater number of students favored low tariffs over high ones. Several were satisfied with the present tariff or didn't give an answer.

As many Young Republicans favored more federal aid to education as opposed it. A few were pleased with the present aid. A large share of the conservative groups had no objection to extended social security provided it was done on a voluntary basis.

In every case a majority of the members of the Young Democrat organizations were consistent with the policies of the Kennedy administration. However, there were many students among these organizations whose answers were inconsistent with the label they had given themselves. For example:

A Missouri Young Democrat tagged himself a liberal Democrat

but he wanted less federal aid to education, less power for the executive, and less coverage under social security.

Another liberal Democrat at Missouri wanted high tariffs, less executive powers, and was against federal medical care for the aged.

A liberal Democrat at Oklahoma State wanted less executive power, less social security coverage, and was against federal medical care for the aged.

A Young Democrat at Kansas State tagged herself a conservative but voted straight liberal ticket on questions about tariffs, federal aid to education, executive powers, social security, and federal medical care for the aged.

Many other students who tagged themselves as conservatives voiced liberal opinions on three or four of the issues.

A Young Conservative at the University of Missouri said that the entire social security program should be abolished—then added that Kennedy's federal medical care for the aged was a good idea.

On a visit to the University of Nebraska, Senator Barry Goldwater was asked to comment on these statistics. He said that these students simply were not what they called themselves. He said he failed to understand how anybody could abolish social security and support federal medical care for the aged.

The students contacted didn't seem to have a pat definition for Republican, Democrat, conservative, or liberal. A student at Iowa State and one at Kansas State defined the Republican party as liberal and the Democratic party as conservative. A student at the University of Nebraska called the Democrats conservatives and the Republicans reactionary. Several students said both parties are liberal. Another defined both as reactionary. The president of one Young Republican organization in the Big Eight said, "Our organization definitely follows the conservative trend. We are followers of the George Norris philosophy." The late Senator George Norris of Nebraska might not have agreed. He wrote an autobiography entitled *Fighting Liberal*.

Will students cross party lines when they vote?

Seventy-seven percent of the students interviewed in all political groups combined said that they would split their ballot in a general election if they did not like their own candidate.

Do students inherit their politics from their parents?

In every political group, with the exception of the Young Republicans at the University of Nebraska, a majority had the same political philosophy as their parents. Every professor and student leader interviewed agreed that students inherit their politics.

Where do the campus political groups fit in with the senior party?

The Young Democrats on the campus claim to be a part of the national organization. But a telephone call to the college director at Democratic National Headquarters in Washington, D.C., produced the name of the president of only one Young Democrat Club in the Big Eight. The respective clubs on each campus carried on no correspondence with each other. The president of one club did not know the names of any of the presidents of the other clubs. However, the Young Democrats do appear to be in the organization of the party within each state.

The Young Republicans on the campus don't even claim organization on a national level. They extend only to the state level. As was the case with the Young Democrats, the Young Republican leaders did not know each other and apparently carried on no correspondence.

The only way campus leaders of any political faith could be found was through the campus newspaper at each school.

What do these students feel is the political philosophy of their parents?

There were no surprises in the answer to that one. It made no difference what the professed political faith of the student. Of those who had a clear-cut opinion, they believed by a whopping, top-heavy majority that politically mom and dad are—

"Conservative."

6

Organize That Chaos

Those of us who could never quite master it are glad the day of the triple-folded copy paper is passing. Whenever I see a reporter arranging his notes taken on the traditional triple-fold, I think of the lesson in map folding the Air Corps gave fliers during World War II.

The object was to keep the map in a neat little rectangle. Then, according to the instructor, you could turn it and fold it very logically along your route. This was supposed to work under any conditions—fighter attack, an antiaircraft barrage, or while you ate a sandwich.

Somehow, I was never even able to fold the map into the proper little rectangle. Because the stubborn thing would always blossom into a huge, blowing sheet, I was utterly sympathetic with a navigator friend who gave his pilot a ten-degree correction to the right as they returned alone from a combat mission.

"Are you sure you don't mean ten degrees to the left?" the pilot asked.

"Oh, ten degrees left, ten degrees right," replied the navigator. "I don't know where I am."

This could be the beginning depth reporter as he completes his research.

He has read all the clippings. He has read all the references. He has asked all the questions. (Well, maybe not quite all of them. No one ever does.) He has taken notes in some fashion. They may be on pieces of copy paper. They may be on cards. They may be in a stenographic notebook or on the reporter's traditional triple-fold. They may even be on tapes.

Now he has it all, or at least enough to start. It spreads over his desk. It may even be laid out on the floor. Some of it is still running around in his head. After all this preparation to get ready to write a story in depth he now faces a period, if not of panic, at least of frustration. While he has worked, the story probably has been trying to form itself in his mind, but few minds can hold the organization of a complicated story.

Actually, his viewpoint on the story now is probably in that area of gray rather than black and white. He is not unlike the story teller in that old joke probably made most popular by Irvin S. Cobb:

The teller of a good story is deep in the vivid details of his tale, when he is interrupted by a listener who says, "That's not the way it was. I was there."

To which the story teller responds, "There's always some blankety-blank eyewitness to ruin a good story."

The reporter with all his research may feel that he is the eyewitness and the story has suffered from too much information. In some way or another he is going to have to get organized, and since this is the newspaper business, next week won't do; nor, probably, will the old inverted pyramid style.

That approach, taught to beginners in the classroom and in the newsroom, works fine for a fast-breaking story. Beyond that, many news writers feel it is probably overdone, even in the handling of what we call straight news. At the risk of committing journalistic blasphemy, as far as depth writing is concerned, pyramids, inverted or otherwise, are for the Egyptians. And the ancient ones at that.

The inverted pyramid represents an upside-down, backward way to tell a story. It makes it easy for the beginning writer to learn an organizational style and little else. It makes it easy for the reader to skim his newspaper.

Although no one is advocating the complete abolishment of the traditional inverted pyramid approach, perhaps newsmen should think for a moment about how closely this parallels the skimming TV and radio approach to news.

This is no effort to run down television and radio news offerings. It is about as simple as this: They have stolen the newspapers' scoop on a breaking news story. It makes little sense for the newspapers to try to beat them at what has become their game.

Newspapers, whether they like it or not, are now in a position to use television and radio. While the electronic media provide the surface, they can promote our depth. Properly educated readers will be sent by the newscast capsule to our newspapers for depth. While the reporter organizes his story he must remember that he is not getting there first, but he is getting there with the most.

While the average newspaper writer has been involved with getting that day's news written and into the paper, magazine writers and a few depth reporters have been more involved in getting the reader into the story. While the news story had to be banged out in minutes on the typewriter, the magazine writer was spending hours, maybe even days, plotting his yarn so that it would trap the reader, and hold him while the whole story was being told.

To plot a yarn means simply to organize it, to outline it, and that is what the modern reporter also must do.

Newsmen and university instructors have tended too often to sneer at an outline. Their sneers were apropos when our speed was king and we were there first with the news, but in the age of depth writing, the sneers are cynical rather than wise. Every good newspaper man who deals in depth does some kind of planning before he writes. Perhaps his reluctance to make an outline a routine part of his writing stems from his public school approach to the technique.

Remember that English teacher in high school? When she introduced outlining, she did it with a note of reverence. It wasn't her fault that the real use of an outline may have been lost somewhere in the decades—even centuries—that the subject has been taught. Proper outlining, she said, helps to organize your thoughts. She was correct. This is the true and proper use of an outline.

However, then came the detailed explanation involving Roman numerals, Arabic numbers, capital letters, small letters, parentheses, double and triple parentheses, and on and on. It went on so far, in fact, that soon the real meaning of an outline was lost for most students.

As a result, when students reach the college classroom they have a kind of awed respect for the sacred outline. That hard-working English teacher in high school did not want that to happen, but many of her colleagues at the university level not only do little to discourage this attitude, but they may go to great lengths to encourage it.

What many teachers and students seem to forget is that an outline is only a guide to help organization. It is not a crutch. It is not inviolate. In fact, it is just the opposite. It is simply an outline and having done it, the writer can do with it as he pleases, including throwing it into the wastepaper basket if it doesn't work. Every writer who has outlined at all has had the pleasure of throwing an outline into the wastepaper basket and doing another that works.

For the sake of emphasis, let's be redundant for a moment. Outlines are guides, not crutches. But outline the reporter must, in some fashion. If the depth reporter, floundering in his mass of facts, can put those facts into an outline, it will help him solve his problem. He may want to use that beautifully organized combination of Roman numerals, Arabic numbers, and the alphabet. That's fine, as long as he remembers one important fact. He mustn't get lost in the beauty of his outline. He is a writer, not an outliner. And the reader will read his story, not his outline. But no longer need he blush if the boys in the city room find him outlining. He is only doing what the men already practicing depth are doing.

Let's see how these men organize a story. Let's see if they have any peculiar twist to the old-fashioned outline.

George Mills of *The Des Moines Register* likes to type out a play-by-play résumé before he writes a depth story.

But Fleming of *The Los Angeles Times,* makes notes on cards or pieces of paper. His outlining may consist of simply stacking these in the order they are to appear in the story. This is an especially expedient type of outlining since it is quite easy to reshuffle the cards if the outline doesn't lend itself to writing.

Or the reporter may, as time allows, simply jot down a few notes. This is the observation of *The New York Times*'s Pulitzer-prize winning Anthony Lewis:

> In writing any serious story, I think about the whole story before writing it, at least to decide what points I should cover and in what order. If there is time—which there frequently is not—I may jot down an outline. I probably would do so for a Sunday piece, for example.

It probably doesn't matter much what the reporter does, the

important thing being that he plan his story with a good deal of
forethought. He may, and probably will, have some trouble simply
deciding his outline's arrangement. He may have difficulty deciding
just how best to tell this story. The oldtimer will undoubtedly be
planning it in his mind as he goes, but even he may have a planning gimmick or two. For instance, Rod Van Every of *The Milwaukee Journal* doesn't outline as such. He makes "a couple of
notes of points to cover" and then uses his own technique for organization.

> I have found that often a story is told more easily and interestingly
> if you just sit down and let her go as you might tell the story to your
> wife, without referring to notes, exact quotes, etc.

Van Every is suggesting another approach to organization which
also has been too often forgotten in classroom and newsroom. *The
Wall Street Journal* has long since revived it in its newsrooms, and
according to its editors, it works. A reporter may be required to tell
his story orally before he starts to write. *The Wall Street Journal*
also advocates outlining. Reporters are told:

> Organize the story and write it naturally. One of the biggest prob-
> lems is the spiral story. It is one which winds back where it was
> originally and then starts covering the ground again in slightly different
> language. To avoid this and other disorganized writing, reporters are
> urged to make themselves an outline before starting to write.

The spiral story against which *Wall Street Journal* writers are
warned is, of course, just a complication of the inverted pyramid.
But we are spiraling away from the point—this business of talking
to yourself.

Society looks with suspicion on this practice. Could it be that
society is wrong? It could be that at the moment the reporter finds
himself the most interesting person to talk to. It could be he is
preparing to write in depth.

Try talking to yourself. Sit there, or better yet, lean back and tell
the story to a girl friend, a wife, the boys at coffee. You may be
amazed at how naturally this easy exercise of the larynx organizes
a story. I doubt that you will be surprised to discover that it seldom
will end up as an inverted pyramid.

Once a reporter has tackled a half-dozen depth pieces he loses some of his stage fright and finds that the story may be organizing itself in his mind as he researches. Lowell Brandle of *The St. Petersburg Times* describes this natural approach:

> Each story is an individual thing with its own identity, its own tastes, its own vocabulary, its own architecture. As I acquire the material for it, it gradually assumes its own proportions and characters, and then my job is simply to introduce it to the reader and let it tell itself in its own way. That may sound confusing, or it may appear that I am avoiding an answer. It's just that I think every story organizes differently. It has its own distinct fingerprints.

If Brandle is right about the fingerprints—and, fortunately he is, or we would all be bored to death—none of the planning systems we have examined so far will work perfectly for the beginner. A play-by-play résumé of the story, a stack of cards or papers, and the high school English teacher's careful outline all help, but only in getting the facts in order. For the Lewises, the Millses, the Flemings, the Van Everys, the Brandles of the business, that may be enough. They are experienced depth reporters. The young professional needs to do more than organize his facts. He needs to plan in advance how he will fit them together.

What he needs is a very special kind of an outline. It must be complete enough to let the brain think about the vital job of putting words together, but it must not bind. It must make sure that the reader gets the information, but will not be bored to the point of putting down the paper. It must, if possible, make sure the story will be interesting, but will not entertain at the expense of facts.

Although the reporter can devise an outline that will do all these things, he cannot devise anything in this business of depth reporting that will eliminate the need for thinking. However, it is possible for the beginner to use his brain in advance of the writing so that he can use it later solely on the writing itself. Look over the following outline for a depth story. See if it would not help on almost any tough assignment.

You are never going to escape it; the first thing you have to worry about is your lead. You should have been worrying about it from the moment you got the assignment. It should have shifted in your mind a dozen times as you researched. Reporters are writers and everything they do should be overridden by the plaguing thought that this eventually has to get down on paper for the reader.

As the first item in your outline, try writing the lead. It may not be the one you finally use, but assume that it is. Work on it until you are satisfied that if the story will write this way, this will be the lead. Don't be satisfied with the first paragraph. Later you will find that many depth stories lead with several paragraphs. So, write the first few paragraphs. Do not consider this an exercise. Try to make this lead the last lead. If you do, you know where your story starts. Now, you can try to organize the rest of it.

Now, remember that guide line? Write it down in front of you. Keep it right there so that it will remind you that this is the point of the story from now until it goes into the newspaper. With the guide line in front of you, jot down the major points you think the story has to cover. As you do this, with the lead and guide line to help you, the organization of the story—the natural organization of it—may start to fall into place. It may not, too. You may end up with 10 or 12 notes that are completely out of order.

If this happens, it is time to start talking to yourself or to someone else. How would you tell this story to include these major points? Forget for the moment that you have to write this story. Just sit there, ignore your notes, and tell the story in your own words. City editors seldom have time for this in the newsroom. Teachers seldom take time for it in the classroom. But I suspect both had better take time for it if they expect to produce depth.

Take student Sharon Olson, for example. Her assignment was nonpartisanship in the Nebraska Unicameral Legislature. There were two reasons for writing it. The Unicameral was approaching its 25th birthday. At the same time there was a revival in what has been a periodic effort to return to partisanship. Leaders of both parties had demanded the change. Editorial writers were taking sides. It was time for some facts.

When Miss Olson completed her research this is what she had: Statements on nonpartisanship from 68 senators (most of them chairmen or past chairmen of major committees or speakers of the legislature), history, political theories, and charges and counter-charges. She also had an almost overwhelming job of organization on her hands.

It was such a job that she had no idea where to start. Listen in as Miss Olson, with the help of an instructor, talked herself out of her problem:

Instructor: Do you have a lead that kind of wraps up what you found in all this research?

Miss O.: It's almost impossible. Nobody agrees and there's no middle ground. You are either for nonpartisanship or you are against it.

Instructor: What do you mean, "you are either for it or against it"?

Miss O.: You either think it is the greatest thing about the Unicameral, or you think it's a joke.

Instructor: Would that make a lead?

Miss O.: Would what make a lead?

Instructor: Either it's the greatest thing in the Unicameral or it's a joke.

Miss O.: Say, it might make a lead at that. But then where do I go?

Instructor: What's your guide line? What's the over-all impression you have from the story that your reader should get?

Miss O.: Well, I'm amazed that after 25 years of nonpartisanship we still are not sure whether it is right or wrong.

Instructor: Do you think the reader knows that?

Miss O.: No, I think that most of the readers think that since we've had it for 25 years it probably is working out just fine.

Instructor: Then, maybe that's what you want to be sure to tell your reader. Do the facts back it up?

Miss O.: Oh, sure. There are plenty of pros and cons, and most of them are pretty hot about it. Most of the legislators like it. Most of the Democratic and Republican party leaders don't like it. You should hear what the GOP chairman said . . .

Instructor: Yes, what did he say?

Miss O.: Oh, it was just kind of funny. He is kind of upset about it. When I said that most of the senators like it, he said, "A guy with a full house doesn't ask for a new deal."

Instructor: Pretty cute quote. Let's get back to it in a minute. But, now, how did we get this nonpartisan business?

Miss O.: The historians say that George Norris insisted that it be part of the Unicameral Amendment.

Instructor: How so? I thought the late senator was a Republican.

Miss O.: Oh, he was elected originally as one and ran as one, but later he was practically an independent.

Instructor: Do you know the political theory behind it?

Miss O.: Sure. I've talked with the political scientists about both nonpartisanship and partisanship.

Instructor: Could you explain that to your reader?

Miss O.: Easily. They made it quite clear, although you understand they don't all agree.

Instructor: Nobody seems to sometimes. Maybe your reader needs to know both viewpoints. Do you have the charges against nonpartisanship?

Miss O.: Yes.

Instructor: Do you have the answers?

Miss O.: Yes, and you should see the way some of the party leaders and those senators talked. They were pretty hot about it.

Instructor: Let's get back to the way they talked in a minute or two. Now, where do all these comments seem to end up, besides in a fight?

Miss O.: Mostly they seem to get to leadership . . . whether it develops under nonpartisanship or not.

Instructor: Maybe that is where you should end up, too. Do you think you can organize your story now?

Miss O.: What do you mean?

Instructor: I mean you have outlined a pretty fair story while you were talking to me. You have a lead. You have an ending to tell you where you want to go. You have the historical background and the governmental theory. And you have the pros and cons of a darned good fight. I believe almost anyone would call that a news story.

Miss O.: I do have a story, don't I? But what about those good quotes we were going to talk about?

Instructor: Well, what about them? Do you like them?

Miss O.: Of course, I do. They kind of tickle me.

Instructor: Then put them in at the right places. They might tickle your reader, too.

That is the way Sharon Olson organized her story on nonpartisanship in Nebraska's unique unicameral legislature. It took a little relaxation and a little guidance. See the end of this chapter for the case history and the story.

What did Miss Olson's talk-session produce in the way of an outline?

She found a lead. She found the major points in her story and she found an ending. She also discovered that she had some good anecdotal material that would make the story live and brighten up some dull spots.

The following procedure worked on Miss Olson's story. It will work on almost any story:

1. Note your guide line and don't bury it. Your story fails if you write around, but never make, this point.
2. Write a lead with which you can live.
3. Note the important points you must make.
4. Talk to yourself until you are sure you have them in an order in which they will fall naturally.
5. Find some ending. The copy desk may chop it off later, but it will help you to write if you know where you are going.
6. Write the ending, if it will help.
7. Check for the climax of your story. Make sure as you write that you do not allow your story to drag on after the major point is made.

(There are other new points on this most flexible of outlines. Let's make those points and then examine them.)

8. Check for the dull spots. See if you have anecdotal material that will brighten the dull spots and make good examples.
9. Check for the places that are going to need transitions. In a complicated story, if you lose your reader for lack of a good transition, you might as well have not written it.

Dull spots, anecdotes, and transitions need to be discussed at the same time. Anecdotes often solve the problems created by dull spots and difficult transitions. These problems are so important that you will find whole chapters devoted to them later. However, they do have to be considered in the outlining stage.

As the depth writer outlines, he'll do best if he plots his transitions. He must make sure that he is going to lead his reader logically and quickly from point to point as he builds toward the climax and the end of his story.

As the outline grows, it may also grow dull. The major job of the newspaper writer is to give facts to the reader. Fact upon fact upon fact tells the story, and tells it exactly. But, in dealing with facts, the writer needs to remember that he must also be malicious. He must also hang onto that reader—or better yet, make that reader hang onto the story.

News writers too often forget the great value of the anecdote that tickles the reader, holds him to the story, and moves him easily into the next subject. Maybe anecdote is the wrong word. What the depth reporter wants is almost anything that gives the reader a light touch and keeps him interested. *The Christian Science Monitor*'s William H. Stringer describes this and makes outlining seem simple when he says that he organizes a story "simply by passing out new and interesting points as the story continues." And he adds, "Be lively all the way through."

I, as you may have guessed, lean toward the little-piece-of-copy-paper or five-by-seven-card technique of outlining for the long involved story. It helps me be malicious with ease.

Once, when faced with the assignment of writing a centennial history, I ended up with notes on 10,000 five-by-seven cards. I had the facts, but I also had confusion, frustration, and a deadline.

My cards helped solve the problem. I divided them into chapters. Then I spread out the cards as I prepared to write each chapter. Spreading out, itself, presented something of a problem when some chapters involved 500 cards. This was solved by simply scattering them all over my basement floor. Then, I walked among them placing them in their proper order. When that was done, I exercised a little malice. I walked back through the cards, spotting weak transitions and dull spots. Then I turned to a private card collection of anecdotes. And, Mr. Historian, please forgive me, I put those anecdotes where they would relieve dull spots and provide lively transitions. (Note, for example, how this chapter opened.)

You don't have to cover your basement or newsroom floor with five-by-seven cards. You don't have to do any of this outlining, which some students call "Mickey Mouse" stuff. But, if you want to compete with those who want your reader's time, and are willing to give them everything from sin to symphonies, you are going to have to plan. And you are going to have to do it with facts and well-organized, beautiful writing.

Organization—outlining—is the most important step leading up at last to that beautiful writing. Because, once organized, you must now, if you'll excuse the melodrama, commune with your reader.

This is the way Bob Wells of *The Milwaukee Journal* describes that relationship.

> I use reader, not readers, advisedly. Writing, like sex, requires exactly two people—the writer and the reader—never more. And never less, either. A fellow sitting at a typewriter turning out words no one but himself will ever read is not a writer.

Case History of a Story

Student: Sharon Olson.

Idea: Nonpartisanship in the Unicameral Legislature.

Guide Line: After 25 years of nonpartisanship, we still are not sure whether it is right or wrong.

Sources: Sixty-eight senators, most chairmen or former chairmen of major committees, or speakers of the legislature. State history books and state historians. Political science references on nonpartisanship, and political scientists. Leaders of both political parties.

Legwork: Interviewing the senators in person or by mail and interviewing in person all other sources.

Organization: As described earlier in this chapter.

Results: This story proved to be the lead story in the major section of a publication on the Unicameral Legislature. It was used to lead into a series of stories about the problems and success of the only one-house legislature in the United States. The publication itself has been used in high schools as a supplemental text in newspaper format, in constitutional conventions as resource material, to spark at least one drive for a unicameral legislature, and to serve as reference material for many of the country's political writers and editorial writers. Miss Olson's piece, in particular, has been widely reprinted in newspapers, and the facts in the piece have been used by many editorial writers either attacking or supporting the nonpartisan approach to legislation.

The Story:

"Nonpartisanship is probably the strongest advantage of the Unicameral."

"Nonpartisanship is a joke."

These two statements made by senators with long experience in Nebraska's Legislature represent the extremes in viewpoints about nonpartisanship. That word—nonpartisanship—has been wed to the Unicameral Legislature since the campaign in 1934.

Those who favor it and those who oppose it, both with equal vigor, admit that there is nothing peculiar about nonpartisanship that makes it a necessary part of the one-house legislature. It could be, they point out, a part of a two-house system, a part of a city council, or a part of any lawmaking body.

However, in Nebraska, nonpartisanship was firmly attached to the Unicameral Legislature by the men who fought for its approval in 1934. With George Norris as the leading spokesman for this aspect of Nebraska's new legislature, the proponents made nonpartisanship a major provision in the plan to give the state a one-house system.

Their arguments and those opposing them have echoed throughout Nebraska during the nearly quarter-century the state has had its unique system of legislation.

However, the senators who have made laws within the system generally seem to have found a preference for nonpartisanship. Of the 68 senators participating in this survey, a large majority of them said nonpartisanship was a strength rather than a weakness in the system. Their viewpoints varied from absolute backing, to lukewarm approval, to absolute opposition. Even so, the large majority of them had their answers to the critics of the system.

What are the criticisms? What are the answers?

Here, from the survey of Nebraska senators, are the criticisms and the answers:

1. Nonpartisanship leads to buck-passing.

(There is just as much buck-passing between the two houses of a bicameral system.)

2. Nonpartisanship weakens the two-party system, which is a part of American political life.

(Although nonpartisanship does not strengthen the party system, the advantages gained in independent legislation outweigh this objection.)

3. Nonpartisanship cannot separate an office-holder from his politics.

(There have been few instances in the history of the Unicameral Legislature where partisanship was obvious.)

4. Nonpartisanship eliminates the normal development of leadership.

(The lack of party control allows leadership to develop on its own merit.)

5. Nonpartisanship makes it difficult for a governor elected on a partisan basis to coordinate his program with the Legislature.

(A large majority of the senators participating in the survey felt that this liaison was not a problem. However, Nebraska governors, who also were interviewed, felt that problems of liaison had arisen during their administrations.)

6. Nonpartisanship leads to a lack of responsibility and subsequently a lack of legislative action.

(The Unicameral Legislature has produced enough legislation to govern Nebraska, and, in some instances, more good legislation than bicameral, partisan legislatures in other states.)

These, as the senators saw it, were the criticisms and the answers. While the majority of those taking part in the survey backed nonpartisanship, in several instances men strongly in favor of the unicameral system departed from their support to criticize this aspect of Nebraska's legislature. The history of the Unicameral Legislature and the replies to the survey by the senators bore out the notion that partisanship versus nonpartisanship has long been a lively subject in Nebraska political circles.

The theory of nonpartisanship differs from partisanship in one major respect: In a nonpartisan situation, a candidate is elected on his own personal integrity and convictions without a party label. In a partisan system, however, a candidate accepts the party stand and is backed by his party before, during, and after his campaign and election.

There is a "naturalness" in the two-party system, according to two University of Nebraska political science professors. There are always at least two sides to every issue. The clash of opinions and competition between the two parties results in better decisions, they say.

Yet, as indicated by the operation of the Unicameral Legislature, there may be more than two sides. Instead of a two-sided disagreement, there is sometimes a 43-sided argument which in most cases is resolved into one legislative bill.

R. D. Sloan, Jr., assistant professor of political science at the University, explains that when an issue comes before the public in a two-party situation, the parties assume responsibilities by making certain promises. Responsibility can thus be pinpointed and much buck-passing can be eliminated.

The two-party system began with the disagreement between Alexander Hamilton and Thomas Jefferson on the question of a centralized government or a confederation of sovereign states, according to Dr. J. B. Shannon, chairman of the political science department. The Civil War widened the split resulting in the majority of the Northern states joining the Republican party while the South became staunchly Democratic.

"When there are two parties, there is constant criticism to keep the people on their toes," Dr. Shannon added.

Laymen, political scientists, and other states view Nebraska quite critically because it is the only state employing both a one-house legislature and the nonpartisan system. One answer for which they are all searching is: Has nonpartisanship worked in this state? . . .

A majority of the senators surveyed agreed with Dr. Adam Breckenridge on the apparent success of nonpartisanship. However, several who observed the earliest days of Nebraska's one-house legislature pointed out that nonpartisanship did not become a legislative fact of life overnight.

"In the beginning," one senator wrote, "the nonpartisanship feature was a weakness. There was no responsibility of any member of the legislature except to his own voters in his own district. However, the commonly accepted system of responsibility and leadership has developed. As a result, party lines have no effect on legislation and the governor is able to work in cooperation with the legislature."

Many of the senators praised the independence given them under the nonpartisanship system. One of them commented:

"I think this is part of the one-house. It allows each senator to be just what the people have elected him to be. A representative of all the people regardless of party. This gives the senator more incentive since it eliminates going to the party bosses with anything that he thinks will be good for all the people and told to lay off if it may make a few votes for the other party.". . .

This charge of buck-passing has been heard periodically since 1937. These critics said that the lack of party responsibility has made it possible for Nebraska legislators to ignore vital legislation. The survey, however, indicated that most of the senators themselves felt this charge was not borne out by the facts.

One senator said, "You can't keep partisanship out of a government man. I say the Unicameral boys still follow their politics."

However, this same senator added, "There's nothing to the buck-passing idea.". . .

During the 1960 state conventions, Democratic and Republican parties both spoke out against nonpartisanship and urged a return to party politics in state government.

Charles Hein, executive state secretary of the Democratic party, concurred, saying that he feels that although people are not apathetic toward state government as a whole party effectiveness is destroyed by the nonpartisan system. . . .

Charles Thone, state chairman of the Republican party, said the same thing in different words when he described the nonpartisan legislature as "43 leaders going in different directions.". . .

He said that members of the legislature are not willing to return to a partisan system because they can escape much responsibility. "A guy with a full house," Thone said, "doesn't ask for a new deal."

Note: Sections of this story were deleted from this reprint of it, but most of the points involved in the original outlining problem remain.

7

Substance with Style

How can you describe good writing? How can you describe the good sound that some bells make? Good writing is a personal liaison between the writer and the reader that takes a reader by the hand, willing or unwilling, and leads him into a new experience of emotion or thought. It may be a soft lullaby or a strident bellow, and he may cry, or he may laugh. It may be meaningful or absolute nonsense, it may be crude, or it may be highly polished verbal sophistication. But one thing, it holds that reader to the last echoing word.

Clarity would be the quality I'd put first in importance in newspaper writing. Too many stories on serious subjects are hopelessly confused and misinformed. Rhythm and color are desirable, too, of course. A good lead should sound right in one's head. I think any good newspaper writer should think about the rhythm of sentences as he writes; after a while this becomes almost subconscious.

Are these the words of lyric poets discussing their art? It wouldn't matter if they were, but these are comments on writing—style—by two proven newspapermen. The first is Lowell Brandle of *The St. Petersburg Times;* the second is Anthony Lewis of *The New York Times.*

Their talk of the sound of bells and the rhythm of sentences doesn't sound much like the journalese about which some English scholars love to complain. That's just as well, since it's time both the English scholars and the journalists begin to think and act about one thing—good writing—no matter who does it or where it is printed.

Brandle and Lewis are really talking about that ghostly thing

77

called style. If you try to describe it too anatomically, it slips from your grasp. But it is what frequently makes the difference between a good writer and the best writer. It is what keeps good reporters from ever becoming boring. It is what makes a reader stick with a story until the end. It does not submerge the major objective of news writing. Nothing must ever do that. Newspapermen cannot forget for the tap of a typewriter key that they have one all-important job—to inform the reader.

To do that job, the depth writer must remember from the moment he starts organizing until the last sentence is written that he is writing about one subject, one idea. Too often the beginning writer who takes on this kind of a story tends to write around the point. He loses the reader and the objective of his story in a maze of vague references and complicated logic.

Unfortunately, the young writer also may lose his reader because he strives for a writing style. He is like a young lover who gropes for the right words but does not seem to make his point. He uses them at the wrong time, the wrong place, and with the wrong emphasis. And he uses too many of them. The object of all his passionate prose has to figure out for herself what he means.

But the newspaper reader lacks the advantage of the young lover's sweetheart. She has centuries of feminine intuition to help her make sense of his love-locked tongue. If the newspaper reader had to depend upon that kind of intuition, the writer would be jilted before he read three little words.

The young writer, like the young lover, must not subordinate what he has to say to the way he says it. He must learn that style is simply a way of using words to best tell his story. It makes the facts come through, like Brandle's bells, more clearly, more smoothly, and often more personally. Style often means to come on out with it and tell your reader what the story is all about. Don Holm of *The Portland Oregonian* backs up this point very neatly when he says:

> Within the bounds of good taste and the almighty style book, a newspaper writer should strive to be original in his approach. . . .
> He should be bold in his writing, but not extreme in his statements. He shouldn't use weasel words and pussyfoot around the subject for fear someone might not like what he writes. If it's worth saying, it's worth saying in a straightforward way.

Holm and his colleagues are simply acknowledging their obligation to the reader. Style to these men is a means to an end, not an end in itself. "Good news writing must communicate without pretension, in clear and simple language, information and ideas," Louis Fleming of *The Los Angeles Times* explains. He then warns the writer against being too cute:

> It often speaks best if it is in the vernacular, but this cuteness and brightness must never confuse its essential object of communication. Simple writing does not in any way imply a limitation as to subject matter: the most complex problems, the most intricate scientific theories, can be communicated in simple terms. In seeking clarity and simplicity, the writing must not oversimplify the subject matter. Careful, disciplined attention must be given to the gray tones between the blacks and the whites.

These gray tones are facts, just as are the black and the white areas. As part of simple, straightforward writing, facts are the major ingredients. Read what one *Wall Street Journal* news executive tells his reporters.

> My own belief is that any one of you can be a good writer—at least by my definition. I mean a clear writer, who writes fact-packed stories —two solid facts to a line is about what I like. There is no substitute for information. . . .

There it is again—information. Facts, information, more facts. Yet alone they do not make a story. A list of facts is not a story. Although a list of facts may satisfy the journalistic precept that we get all the facts, that list alone makes no sense. The difference between a list of facts and a story is style.

Style is the way you use words to express those facts. Style is the way you explain those facts. Style is the way you put those facts into perspective. Style is the way you turn those facts into a complete, satisfying story.

Your style may differ from that of someone else because of your approach to the problem of putting words together. Now, follow this closely. Your approach is in part governed by the rules you have set up in your own mind about the kind of reader you are trying to reach.

This makes a difference, doesn't it? If you think you are writing for a dumbbell, your mental rules tell you to write in dumbbell English. In the newspaper business you may be told you are writing for readers with a sixth-grade or an eighth-grade education. This becomes one of those mental rules which help to govern your style. In following it you may be tempted to write down to your reader. And if you do, you have made a fatal mistake.

There is quite a difference between writing down to the reader and writing for a reader who lacks information. Bob Wells of *The Milwaukee Journal* understands that difference. He approaches it this way:

> I don't, when I am writing a story, begin by telling myself, "Now let's write this for Sam Schmidt, who has a duplex, and an IQ of 83, on North 47th Street." But I do try to bear in mind that I am writing for flesh and blood individuals who can, if I bore them, throw down the paper and turn on the TV. And they have every right to do just that if I bore them. So I try not to.

In one short paragraph, Wells helps destroy the sixth-grade-reader audience cult and strikes a blow for not only the writers but the readers. He believes that you can beat the competition by writing to a better educated reader:

> He (the newspaper writer) can delve more deeply into things—depth of reporting is the biggest asset the written word has over the spoken. He can, if his editor will let him, spend enough time to get all the story instead of part. He can quit trying to please the low IQ's among the newspaper's customers, because they'll be watching TV anyway. (They'll still buy the paper for the ads and funnies, but they won't read it. They never did read it, even before TV.)

Newsmen like Wells simply do not allow themselves to be trapped by an old saw that tells them their readers are a pretty stupid lot anyhow, so why worry about style? They know that writing style is really what makes the difference for the newspaper reader. Don Holm of *The Portland Oregonian* describes that difference this way:

> I don't think TV or radio can compete with these stories for depth, color, drama, and background. It would take an hour on TV to tell this particular story—and who would spend the money to sponsor it?
>
> A news story is dead for TV after a few hours of repetition. In a newspaper the story is still good as long after the event as people are still thinking about it.
>
> A newspaper writer can compete by approaching the subjects as a real life drama, telling a complete story and interpreting it out of his own background and experience, and bringing it to life for the reader.

If the writer is a reasonably intelligent person, skilled in his craft, and has really thought it out beforehand, he can do a job that TV and radio simply can't do. It goes without saying that people do like to read and like to be informed through reading. It's a form of intellectual stimulation that TV and radio can't match.

When a newspaper writer talks about stimulating writing, he is not talking about writing for a moron or about writing by formula. There is, as a matter of fact, an area of newspaper research which has been misunderstood by many newspapermen. The research is about this business of readership. It tries to answer such questions as: How does the reader read? What does he read? What does he read most easily? What would he like to read?

From this area of research there has come much valuable information. But it also has encouraged the development of another newsroom formula. That formula is the well known short-word, short-sentence, short-paragraph, short-story advice to the writers in this business. There is nothing wrong with the advice, provided it is not misunderstood and provided that it does not kill style.

Those who subscribe completely to the short-everything cult trade style for formula. As long as writers can use, but not worship, readership studies, the results of those studies are valuable.

Short sentences probably are more easily read. But short sentences can also get dull simply on the basis of their staccato pounding on the reader's mind. It may be a little like getting used to an air hammer in the street outside your bedroom window. For the most part, short sentences probably lead to the simplest and most direct writing. But good writers who use short sentences don't necessarily count words. For example, that twentieth-century master of the English language, Winston Churchill, writes in short sentences. His average is about 15 words to the sentence, but it is hard to imagine the British lion counting words. It happens that he simply tries to include only one idea in each sentence.

Other writers of the English language as it should be written use short sentences for contrast with long sentences. Ernest Hemingway, whose major contribution to literature is usually considered his style, delighted in this tactic. He pounded at your mind. Staccato sentences jerked at your attention. Action came alive. It moved faster. Emotions sparked your senses. And then Mr. Hemingway gave you a long, rolling, rhythmic sentence that soothed you and let you catch a mental breath before plunging on.

Anyone who has read Hemingway is aware that he did the same thing with words. He seemed to enjoy lulling the reader along in English that resembled the smooth, quiet flow of colloquial Spanish. Then suddenly came a four-letter, Anglo-Saxon word that made very sure the reader was wide awake.

Newspaper writers can and do use the same tactics, if they are real stylists. Wells of *The Milwaukee Journal* describes his efforts this way:

> You lead off with something that you hope is interesting or important or intriguing enough to grab the reader's attention. You try to arouse his interest without fully satisfying it until he has read the whole story. You make sure you have a good grip on him before you venture to include those things which are dull but necessary to the story.
>
> And every once in a while, if you can, you try to snap him awake and rekindle his interest by saying something unexpected. For example, you say something funny in an otherwise serious context. The copy desk may cut this out, on the theory that all newspaper writing should be the same shade of gray as adopted by the AP, but that's the chance you take.

Just as good newspaper writers have learned to use contrast to keep their readers with them, they have also learned that despite what they may have been told, there are times when repetition is not only good but highly effective. The day is slowly passing when the beginning journalist was told with finality in both the classroom and the newsroom that words must not be repeated lest they become dull. In general, synonyms may help make writing sparkle, but again if there is a rule here at all, it is here to be broken when necessary. The effectiveness of this is illustrated in the following example:

> The new infantryman soon learned that walking is not the only way an army travels. He discovered that it crawled. He crawled across obstacle courses. He crawled through sand. He crawled through mud. He crawled under barbed wire. He crawled in the dirt while machine guns fired over his head. When it was over, he crawled into bed, and next morning he was barely able to crawl out again.

Try substituting some synonyms for "crawled" in that paragraph and see what happens to it. For that matter, look again at the quotes from Lowell Brandle that started this chapter. Remember how he discussed style?

... it may be a soft lullaby or a strident bellow, and he may laugh, or he may cry. It may be meaningful or absolute nonsense. It may be crude, or it may be highly polished verbal sophistication. . . .

Mr. Brandle's writing sings even when he is answering questionnaires for book-writing professors. It may be that you can find synonyms for his "it may be," but it may be that you would be foolish to try.

There is another stylistic approach which newspapers have abandoned, perhaps too completely. It was part of what its critics called personal journalism. It was the part of personal journalism that let us use first- and second-person pronouns. We wed ourselves to *he, she, it,* and *they.* We thought we had divorced the reporter's opinion from the story.

By removing the *I,* we probably helped discourage opinion. By removing the *you,* we probably discouraged preaching at the reader. But by removing the first- and second-person pronouns, we also moved ourselves further away from the reader.

Our competition *I*'s, *we*'s, and *you*'s at the public all the time, and, in the case of TV, in person. There are times when an occasional *you* might help the reader identify himself with the story.

Bob Wells of *The Milwaukee Journal* also is worried about the lack of the personal pronoun in newspaper copy:

> Newspapers, unlike magazines, avoid the use of the pronoun "I." This I feel is a mistake—some stories would be better written if the old rule were abandoned. To make for greater informality and to encourage reader identification, I sometimes use "you" to put the reader into the picture. But this has to be done carefully and not overdone.

I am fully aware that there are rules in the newsroom and the classroom for very good reasons. They help guide the beginner. They lend uniformity to the copy. And they help produce a newspaper in an atmosphere of speed. But let me remind you that this is not a discussion for beginners. It is not a discussion of a straight, breaking news story. It is a discussion of writing in depth with the help of men who make their living that way. If these men are going to give newspapers the edge on the competition, they need to know that rules are only guides. They need to break them or bend them as is necessary to inform their readers. Without rules

84

there could be no uniformity. But without style we cannot exploit the difference between the newspaper and its competition.

Later in this book there are chapters about parts of style. The skillful handling of leads, endings, transitions, description, quotes, and anecdotes all help make up writing style. Even what you do not write and what you cut from a story are parts of your style. Style is really the craft, the technique, of your profession.

The word *technique* has led to confusion. It often means learning to write a simple inverted pyramid story. This is what can be learned in six months in the newsroom or the classroom, but it is not style. It is formula. Style comes from knowledge, experience, senses, taste, and disciplined ability. All that adds up to thought. It is with this thought process, rather than a formula, that depth is written. You do not learn it in six months or six years. You have started developing it now and will still be developing it when you quit the business, providing you write with your mind, not by formula.

It can be, by the way, the difference between you and the hacks in the business and all those millions outside of it who think they can write without learning the craft. That is what you are doing now—learning a craft, providing a basis, acquiring (if you use the term properly) techniques that result in style.

The basis for your style is the precepts of journalism. You learn that writer opinion belongs on editorial pages; that you must tell all the significant facts; that you must tell all sides of a controversy; and that you have an obligation to tell the reader the source of those facts. Of course you know these and other precepts in the profession's code of ethics. Do not tuck them too far back in your mind; they are part of a discipline that forms a mental base for your style. The rest of that base, of course, is an intimate knowledge of the language with which you work.

You must know English so well that you can make it work for you. This, too, is the end product of discipline. First you acquire the discipline of good grammar. Then, you start what must be a life-long love affair with the English language.

From this twin base—ethics and English—you develop your style. Students and young graduates too often ignore or forget the discipline of this foundation. When they do forget, the resulting style is structurally weak. It may entertain, lightly, but it will not inform in depth. It may preach, obviously, but it may try to sway by pure opinion instead of fact. These are not the goals of any kind of news, let alone news in depth.

Style, built on the right foundation, is part of every story you write. You do not acquire it automatically out of some vague thing called talent. Talent means only that you have an aptitude for recognizing style and an ability to build your own. You build not with a formula, but with your mind—word upon word with your disciplined, educated mind.

In this chapter you have glimpsed style in a rare look into the minds of good news writers. Appreciate it. You do not often get that chance. Real writers don't talk about it. They write.

"Words have to be molded just as a sculptor molds clay," Don Holm of *The Portland Oregonian* explains. Then he adds a concise summary of the job ahead of the writer when he sits down to his typewriter:

> I am not the least bit bashful about rewriting stories two or even three times. I just finished a think piece that started eleven months ago. I rewrote it at least six times, and finally boiled it down from a five-part series into one 1,500-word piece. It just never felt right to me, and I never knew just why. I hate to sound trite, but I don't know of any way to learn to write without sticking a piece of copy paper into the typewriter and pounding away at it.

Case Histories of Style

The student examples for this chapter depart from earlier procedure. Instead of one student story, there are excerpts from several.

Problem: Without style a profile of a public figure can be little more than a premature obituary. When the public figure is involved in public conflict, it is a perfect time to introduce him in depth to the public. However, unless style helps do it adroitly, the alleged profile may seem to the reader to be just a rehash of the running conflict. The result, no readership. Student Judy Harrington faced both these problems when she wrote a profile of the Democratic state chairman when he was involved in a battle over who was really running the party.

Solution: Style solved her problem. She used it to slip the reader easily along through the story. She brought into play description that was not obvious, anecdotes that made points, and provided transitions that held the broad story together without seeming to do so. She used quotes in chronological order to background the battle and with style kept up a rapid pace that carried the reader quickly along through the story. This story tied for first place in the Hearst Foundation news contest.

(An analogy quickly introduced the conflict and digested it.)

The party roster says it simply—Russell Hanson, state chairman.

But once in the field black and white answers about Democratic management turn into gray.

One thing is clear-cut, however, and that, as some political observers say, is that Democratic progress walks a tight-rope in Nebraska. They suggest that what is termed a party split has discouraged some potential election candidates and alienated a number of party members and that the forthcoming election can make or break the Democratic party in Nebraska.

Some recognize Hanson as team manager. Others suggest he's not in charge. And that decisions released from headquarters in Omaha are only those of Bernard Boyle, national committeeman since 1952. . . .

(Good description is loaded with facts that move the story along.)

As you near Newcastle on bluff-bordered Highway 12, occasional roadside signs announce the chairman's private business— Hanson Implement Company—a farm machinery and supply firm which he had bought from his father.

Most farmers and machinery are at a standstill, however, if you're in Newcastle (population 360) on a March winter day. Most of the snow on main street has been pushed to one side, but traffic is at a minimum. The bawling of cattle and songs of only a few birds can be heard.

If you're looking for Mr. Hanson, he'll be there, with quick fulfillment of a farmer's order and with frank answers about Nebraska politics.

If it's noon, and you can tell by the peal of the bell at the high school, Hanson may already be on his way to lunch—up the hill to the east to the Hanson home where his wife, Josephine, presides. This, too, will be quiet.

Two of the Hansons' children are away from home, Russ in his third year at West Point, and Jo Ellen, a sophomore at the University of Nebraska. The others are Kevin, a high school senior, and Paul, an eighth-grader.

After a second cup of coffee and a cigarette, Hanson will tell you legends of Nebraska's northeast and why he has stayed. . . .

(A chronology of quotes provided humor and gave a fresh picture of the man that only words could have painted.)

In a series of statements from 1958 to 1960, Hanson rode the backs of state Republicans. Most of the issues were short-lived, but rhetorical humor can still be found in newsprint.

Among them: Suggestion that Republicans were suffering from "Quinnsy, a glandular inflammation of the throat that made it extremely difficult to swallow, in this case to swallow the defeat of Vic Anderson (former governor)."

Lincoln publicity man John Quinn replied that he would rather have "Quinnsy" than painful "Boyles." (Bernard Boyle was national committeeman.) But he added that neither had anything to do with a correct counting of the gubernatorial vote (the election was contested).

In June, 1959, Hanson called Republican Attorney General C. S. Beck "the last trumpeting bull in the graveyard of the GOP elephant."

Beck's retort? "Ouch, I have been bitten by a white rabbit."

The exchange took place after Beck called Democratic governor Brooks's election a flash in the pan.

Words from Nebraska Democratic headquarters continued to flow, not unlike those expected from any political office.

A few hours after Lincolnite Charles Thone took over as state GOP chairman in 1959, Hanson said that Thone's response to a grassroots movement must have been heartwarming to the traditional few who made the selection. "While I have great regard for my Republican counterpart," said Hanson, "I doubt that he will be much more than a Thone in the flesh to victory-hungry Republicans."

Thone then mentioned how "capable Willard Townsend was dumped out of office in a power-laden, back-room, brassy move for power by brass-rooters Boyle and Hanson."

In December, 1959, Hanson and Boyle shifted to defense.

Fellow Democrat Clair Callan of Odell said it was time for Nebraska Democrats to decide whether they wished to keep Hanson and Boyle. He considered it essential to have responsible party leadership and said it was apparent the Democrats were not receiving it.

Hanson's reply: "The party now has more money in the treasury, more people working enthusiastically and the election of a governor, treasurer, and two Congressmen. We have had complete unity in our organization until Frank Morrison (Democratic governor) started to campaign."

Boyle's comment: "Merry Christmas."

Christmas came a little early for the party constituents.

Democrats Don McGinley and Larry Brock lost their placard in the U.S. House of Representatives to Republicans Ralph Beerman and Dave Martin. Elective positions in the statehouse, with the exception of the governor's office, were taken up by Republicans. . . .

Problem: The State Board of Education had chosen the word "disapproved" to describe its action when taking free high school tuition away from scholastically substandard schools. The action was an effort to force closure of the schools and encourage eventual consolidation. The word the board chose—disapproved—was confusing, since they gave it a very special meaning. Hal Brown, the student writer, had to find a way to define the word in its new sense, tell what it meant to the communities, and do it without slowing down his story.

Solution: The word was used to start off a series of paragraphs, actually adding drama to the story and providing a vehicle to quickly digest background.

This situation exists in Waterbury, a town of about 80 people in northeast Nebraska. But it could describe many other small towns in Nebraska where the State Board of Education has disapproved the school.

Disapproved—Citizens in 32 school districts across the state have heard that word in the past five years as the State Board of Education cracked down and placed these high schools on the nonapproved list.

Disapproved—A word that means different things to different people. To the State Board of Education, it is a tool to force schools with inadequate facilities to close. To the people of these school districts, it means problems, discussions, conflict, and in many cases, even heated arguments.

Disapproved—Citizens of one town may hear that word and decided to file suit to save the school from it. Another town may decide to operate the school on a nonapproved basis. Another may decide to close the school and either redistrict or merely send the students to another school. Those who decide to sue, such as Walton is now doing, are of primary interest to the State Board of Education in its attempts to move forward in reducing the number of high schools in the state. . . .

Problem: The search for an easy way to describe a man whose profession has a public stereotype is too often solved by using the stereotype and then quickly adding, "But he isn't like that." It is not only the easy way, but the tritest, dullest, and least informative. Student Larry Novicki needed to describe the president of a church college. The man's jobs provided two stereotypes—that of a minister and that of a college president.

Solution: He forgot the stereotypes. Here are two descriptive passages:

As a student, a Navy chaplain, a minister, and now a college president, Dr. Rogers, his colleagues say, has belittled more challenges and passed more goals than most men of forty-three.

This short, round sort of a man has been rolling along at a fantastic pace as president of Nebraska Wesleyan University.

But his tireless physical pace doesn't match the rate at which the wheels of his creative mind are spinning. . . .

An Army surgeon serving with Rogers in the South Pacific prophesied that the ever-slaving chaplain would work himself to death by the time he was fifty.

But at forty-three, Rogers seems to have enough energy left to carry him far past that age. He is in good physical shape; his smooth face doesn't tell the story of his trying daily schedule or his eventful life which has seen him in all parts of this country as well as in countries across both oceans.

He's built like a football guard and appears to be in good enough condition to don a uniform and crack an opposing center just as he did in 1934-35 during his days at Gustavus Adolphus College in St. Peter, Minnesota.

8

Psst—Readers!

Psst—Girls!

Could you ignore that?

The desire named streetcar lingers here.

Or that?

"Chickenless" Wednesday is one of the new benefits that Fidel Castro has bestowed on the Cuban people.

Or that?

Speak softly, for death is in our house. Uncle Tom is dying.

If you could ignore any of those quotes, put down this book and confine yourself to the comic page. None of this is for you.

Those quotes are leads of depth stories. The first and third were in *The Wall Street Journal*. The second is from *The Washington Post* and the fourth from *The St. Petersburg Times*. Later you will find out about the stories those leads start. Right now, while they are still making you think "I wish I'd said that," there is a misunderstanding about depth story leads to dispel.

This kind of journalism is no paradise for the sloppy writer who lazes into his stories because that is the easiest way to do it. This is still the newspaper business and leads are still leads—only their job is tougher and they have to be better.

The depth writer must produce a complete piece that sparkles as well as any prose anywhere. It is true that newspapers run a lot of lazy writing. But it is also true that day in and day out the best writing in America can be found somewhere in some of its newspapers. In the future, there must be more. The competition demands it. The story in depth may necessarily be long. Understand, there is no rule that says a story must be long to be in depth, but by its very nature the complete story may take a little longer in telling. The newspaper writer who would take part in the future of American journalism must face up to this fact and accept what really amounts to the greatest writing challenge in newspaper history.

Enough theory, let's do what any decent lead must do, get down to the facts. First, imagine again the other half of your writing team:

He sits there in his chair, magazines at his elbow, books also within reach, maybe a cool glass within the same radius, the television flickers, his children clamor for his attention, his wife describes the day's activities, and, if you are lucky, the newspaper is across his lap. There is your partner—the reader—in his habitat, surrounded by your competition. All you have to do is make him read a story in the midst of many stories and you may want him to stick with you for as long as ten or fifteen minutes. To realize just how much you are asking, remember that many of your readers spend less than a half-hour with the whole newspaper. But ask you must, and you must do it with your lead.

Despite the many volumes written on the subject, your lead is still the knottiest, the most exasperating, the most demanding job you do.

It should grab your reader, willing or not, by the lapels and haul him into the story.

It should tell your reader something.

It should tell him something quickly.

It should tell it to him honestly.

That's all a lead has to do. As Louis B. Fleming of *The Los Angeles Times* says, "The lead for depth stories is written with the regular news ideas in mind; what kind of a hook will it give the copy desk for a head? How will it summarize what's coming up? How can it tease the reader into continuing for at least a few more paragraphs?"

Here is a lead from *The New York Times*. It certainly does the job, and it does it in a depth approach to a breaking news story:

Stalin today has put the Marshall Plan through Congress.*

That is the way Richard L. Strout described the Congressional approval of the Marshall Plan after the Soviet take-over of Czechoslovakia. Mr. Strout certainly didn't refer to a series of rules on leads, nor did he ask himself into which category his lead might fit. He did the newsman's job of grabbing the reader, telling him something, doing it quickly, and doing it honestly.

Unfortunately for American journalism, certain techniques have been developed both in the newsroom and in the classroom for teaching leads. Particularly in the classroom, leads have been categorized in order to make the teaching easier and provide the student with a guide. There is nothing wrong with this, if it gets the job done; that job being to make the beginning writer work like the devil on his leads. But if this system simply makes it easy to write leads, then it fails after the writer has gained some experience. It fails because it tries to categorize something for which there are several million categories.

Almost every journalist, be he the product of the college classroom or the newsroom classroom, is acquainted with the category system. It goes something like this:

My young friend, leads fall into several categories. There are the five W's and the H leads. These leads can be recognized if they start by answering the questions who? when? where? why? what? or how?.

There are also subdivisions of these categories, which include the various parts of speech. For instance, depending upon the way your lead starts, it may be a participial lead, an adjective lead, a noun lead, a verb lead, and so on.

In addition, there are other categories which do not fall quite so easily into place. These would include the punch lead, the descriptive lead, and so on and on and on. . . .

Once the beginning reporter has been introduced to the category system and has become aware of the importance of leads, he should forget all about categories. Can you imagine an experienced reporter sitting there, poised before his typewriter, trying to decide whether to write a "who" lead or a "what" lead or maybe an "adjective" or an "adverb" lead? This may be slightly unfair oversimplification, but oversimplification may be necessary to make

---

* Copyright by *The New York Times*. Reprinted by permission.

clearly one point. That point is that no reporter, no matter how much his experience, can afford to write a lazy lead. This becomes more evident in the area of depth writing, but it is true everywhere as today's newspaper story must grab for the reader. This means that a writer must find the very best lead by using his brains, not a category.

If for the good newspaper writer every story represents something of a challenge—and every depth story must represent a challenge —then every lead must do the same. If some of the nation's best news writers are correct when they say each news story has its own fingerprints, then each lead, too, has its own fingerprints.

In fact, it is fun to think about a lead as a hand with its five fingers. It has not been too many years since good newspapers insisted on a six-fingered hand, one finger for each of Rudyard Kipling's serving boys. Remember?

> I keep six honest serving men
> (They taught me all I knew)
> Their names are what and why and when
> And how and where and who.
>
> —*Just So Stories,* 1902

Mr. Kipling, we love you, but today that just won't do. You see, our competition is tougher. We need your serving boys in our stories but not all of them in the lead. Those six-fingered hands may have been fine when the competition was other newspapers also leading with six-fingered hands.

Today the competition is a face, a voice, a slick, well-polished magazine, a woman's club, or a foursome for bridge or golf. The bulky six-fingered hand with its five *W*'s and the *H* has been forced into obsolescence by this kind of competition. Against it the hand and fingers need to be considerably more flexible.

A lead may be just a coyly beckoning index finger. Remember that lead at the start of this chapter—"Psst—Girls"? It beckoned readers into a *Wall Street Journal* story about how furniture dealers were using psychology to tempt customers.

A lead may be as highly sophisticated as the poised hand of a post-season debutante. It might read like this: "The desire named streetcar still lingers here." That led a *Washington Post* story about the impending end of the trolley car era.

A lead may be as direct as a hand with all five fingers spread, reaching out to grab the reader and haul him into the story. That was the intent of *The Wall Street Journal* lead: "'Chickenless Wednesday' is one of the new benefits that Fidel Castro has bestowed on the Cuban people." There was no question that that story was about Cuba's faltering economy.

Hands also can become fists. Although it may not appear so, the last lead among those that opened this chapter was a fist, velvet-gloved, but nonetheless a fist. A *St. Petersburg Times* story about the changing Negro attitude started with: "Speak softly, for death is in our house. Uncle Tom is dying."

Of course, grabbing the reader is not enough. The good writer doesn't dare grab him without telling him something. Cuteness for cuteness's sake is wasted verbiage, particularly in the lead, and there is no more space for waste in a depth story than in any news story. The lead must say something, and it must say something quickly. Good writers who labor over their leads labor even over the first few words of that vital opening sentence. Examine this lead:

> Cities, like people, make mistakes. A group of citizens is convinced that the biggest blunder in the history of St. Louis was committed when the city divorced St. Louis County in 1876 to free itself of a corrupt county political ring and the burden of supporting a poor rural area.

Harry Wilensky of *The St. Louis Post-Dispatch* used that lead to start a difficult story about the much-written-about city-county problems. He could have backed into it with something like this:

> Over the nation the problem of the county with a large city within its borders is a growing one. City planners puzzle over it. Citizens wonder just how much overlapping exists. County and city officials are not always sure which job is whose.
> These problems also exist in St. Louis and St. Louis County . . .

That is the way Wilensky could have backed into that long story. It was not. He jumped in at once, grabbing the reader, giving him some facts, and sailing into the background without any apologies. Wilensky avoided the trap into which all writers fall, but which most tempts those who deal in depth. They know their stories have a long way to go. They know that they have spent hours, days, even weeks in research. It would seem only fair that they could take just a little while getting into it. But they cannot. They must make those first few words reach for the reader. They

96

must start informing him at once. Look at this factual lead by
Morton Mintz of *The Washington Post:*

> This is the story of a Treasury bill that was bought for $80,000 on a
> day when the market price, published in the newspaper, was $99,933.
> Some have compared this with buying a dollar bill for 80¢.
>
> Why the twenty percent discount? Clues there are, but this is a
> mystery story that is still being written. An important chapter will be
> contributed soon in Federal Court in Baltimore at the trial of a civil
> suit.

Instead of finding that he has more time to get to the reader, the
depth reporter discovers, perhaps to his dismay, that he has less
time. There are times when he cannot even let his lead use one of
the best techniques for putting drama into a sentence—saving the
punch for the very end of the sentence. This technique, used unconsciously by some news writers, should get more attention from the
rest. Frequently, it will pump life into the most passive sentence.
But in the lead you may not even dare wait for the end of the
first sentence. Quickly run through your mind the first words of
some of the leads already cited in this chapter:

Psst—Girls
"Chickenless Wednesday" is one of . . .
The desire named streetcar . . .
Speak softly, for death is . . .
Stalin today has put the Marshall Plan . . .
Cities, like people, make mistakes. . . .

Do you find any wasted verbiage there? Look at your own leads
the same way. You may have good reason for wasting a word or
two at the start; there is no rule that says you cannot. Just make
sure that a few wasted words at the start of the story ring an alarm
bell in your mind. Look at them again. If the reason satisfies you,
forget it. If not, rewrite.

This is not a book for beginners, yet this discussion of leads may
seem quite basic. If it is, it is because no matter how great his experience the master reporter never stops working on leads. My only
concern is that if there are among those reading this book just a
few still leaning on categories, still reaching for a formula, they
need to understand that all they can really do is use their own
minds. All anyone can do for them is to provide a few basic disciplines with which to help judge leads.

There are three measures of a good lead: It must grab the reader. It must tell him something. It must do it quickly. There is one more: It must do it honestly.

Here, as in the area of research, it is sadly true that all the facts can certainly ruin what appeared to be a good lead. Honesty, where the lead is concerned, is just a short way of describing two journalistic commandments: attribution and qualification. It is not becoming pedantic nor necessarily semantic to point out that these commandments make honest women of leads. A lead which might confuse or mislead the reader may need attribution, despite the fact that it slows down and lengthens the first paragraph. A lead that needs qualification because of possible libel or questionable ethics has to be qualified. This is the price the good writer pays for his integrity.

The Wall Street Journal was faced with these problems when it wrote its story about the Nelson Rockefeller impending divorce. While some newspapers discussed the personal angles of who was at fault, and so on, *The Wall Street Journal* dealt directly with the public's interest. To do so fairly—honestly, if you please—it had to slow down its lead with attribution and qualification:

> The majority of topmost political professionals, Republican and Democratic, suddenly came to agreement over the weekend on one opinion: Nelson Rockefeller's hope of winning the presidency has been badly bashed by announcement of his impending divorce.

The story went on to give the varying opinions of Democratic and Republican leaders. The information had been carefully rounded up in detail, else the lead could have been dishonest. To belabor the point, the good writer dare not pick the most enticing bit of information for his lead if the body of the story does not back it up.

Beyond these simple requirements for a good depth lead, there are only two additional guides. One binds the writer, the other sets him free.

First, the binder. It goes back to that guide line that should be in front of you all the time you plan and write. Your lead must make the point of your guide line or get to it very soon. If you really have been able to summarize your story in one simple sentence, that guide line will help you write the lead. If your lead does not somehow pertain to it, you had better see if it needs rewriting. While it seems only right that the writer should try to make his lead pertain to the story, there is just as legitimate a liberation. He must be allowed to let his imagination take him in search of the perfect lead.

Nothing should inhibit him at this point. None of the guides suggested here would inhibit him, though a category or a formula most certainly would. He should not be told to count words. He should not be told not to use direct quotes. He should not be told to do anything but use his educated imagination.

He should range through his experience, his reading, and his education. He should not be afraid of a technique that works in a book or a magazine. Some magazine writers are among the best technicians in the business.

It is not surprising that depth reporters frequently are also free-lance magazine writers. It is a bit distressing, however, when they discover that some magazine editors are much tougher copy editors than their own on the newspaper. It is a little embarrassing, almost too personal, the way a good magazine editor will tear apart your copy in intimate detail. Now that more American newspapers are running stories as complicated as magazine stories, a little deliberate theft might be in line. Magazines have been in this long-story business considerably longer than most of us. The initial larceny might take place in a close examination of magazine leads—good magazine leads. Now, don't go overboard; just take what looks good and see if it will work.

For example, you know that magazine writers often use a flash-back to introduce their stories. The technique is simple and effective. The writer merely reaches into his story for an enticing episode. He puts it out in front, and then with the help of an adroit transition gets back into the story so that he can tell it naturally. Admittedly, the technique can lead to dishonesty. If the flashback episode is also the climax, there is little left for the reader in the body of the copy. If the flashback deals with something extraneous to the main theme of the story then the lead becomes a dishonest lady. But, the flashback can be used in the newspaper and it can fit well within the simple guides I have suggested for a good lead. Here is one from *The Christian Science Monitor*. Try your judgment on it.

Not long ago the president looked up to find that the senator who had been most influential in launching his successful primary effort in Wisconsin was dragging his feet on administration-backed farm legislation.

The senator is William Proxmire, who continually seeks to make the point that he is under obligation to nobody except the voters.

This time the unpredictable Mr. Proxmire has personally polled a large number of Wisconsin dairy farmers, only to find a crystallizing sentiment against government-controlled supply management. Also, it is said that the senator sensed some degree of growing GOP sentiment as he toured the state.

Thus it is the senator's contention that he is representing his state and the farmers in his state when he challenges the administration's move toward supply management, dairy industry quotas, production controls, etc. . . .

Note how the fourth paragraph provides a transition back into the body of the story. Note, too, that the whole lead took several paragraphs to develop. That brings us to our next raid on the magazine business.

Ed Cony of *The Wall Street Journal* speaks on the next subject for depth writers who have been justifiably a little cautious about saying anything concerning it too loudly. They keep remembering that time-honored journalistic precept about one paragraph at the top of the story that is supposed to do almost everything. It is particularly supposed to do everything for the transient skip-reader who wants to know everything without working for it. Cony and his cohorts know that while those opening words must sparkle and work, it is very handy at times to develop the lead over several paragraphs. Cony says simply:

One thought about leads: I don't think they always have to be short (although there is certainly much to be said for the pithy lead). In the "Roads to Riches" story, you'll notice the reader doesn't really get much of an idea of what the story is about until he reads the second graph.

Here is the lead to Cony's "Roads to Riches" story:

"I was thirteen when I learned that money has great importance—when you need it. My father had to have an operation. The surgeon wanted $250. It might as well have been $250,000."

The opening lines of a daytime TV serial? Not at all. It's a quote from Sydney Baron, a millionaire public relations man today, 27 years after his father went to a public clinic for his operation. As recently as 1949, Mr. Baron's net worth was only $25,000.

To make his million. . . .

Obviously, you, like many magazine writers, can take several paragraphs to develop a really good lead idea, providing your opening does grab the reader. Then it is quite possible that ensuing sentences will hold readers as you develop the idea. Actually, this technique properly used gives you several opportunities to interest the reader and hold him for the rest of the story.

One of Cony's colleagues, Robert D. Novak, used this technique when he approached a round-up story about politics on the nation's campuses:

> The college campus is slowly breaking the cocoon of political apathy and cynicism that has encased it through most of the post-World War II era. An undergraduate of a decade ago might have spent his leisure moments in panty raids or water fights. Today's student is more apt to be unleashing his excess energy in turning out conservative propaganda, picketing against racial discrimination or the H-bomb—or most likely, spending endless hours over coffee and beer thrashing out the state of the nation and the world.

It took Novak a while to do it, but look at the audiences he must have held along the way: the politicians, the conservatives, the liberals, the pacificists, and possibly even the prohibitionists— though he may have lost a few panty raiders.

To try to find all the techniques good writers use for writing good leads would be trying to do the impossible. There are literally millions of techniques—one for almost every good story. This discussion is designed to free you from categories and formulas and replace them with simple guides that will help your mind find the right answer.

There is, however, one more suggestion that might help. A depth story has not only to start, but it must get somewhere. It must carry the reader through to the end. This requirement can be turned to the reporter's advantage.

If he knows that his story must get someplace, it may help him write his lead. Good writers often plan both the lead and the ending at the same time, knowing full well that that ending must risk the hazards of the copy desk. Nonetheless, the advantages are worth the danger. Planned endings are the subject of the next chapter.

Case Histories of Leads

Problem: Students in the University of Nebraska depth reporting class researched and wrote an entire publication on the state's unique unicameral legislature. One of their greatest problems of coordination involved writing leads for some 30 stories that in some way dealt with the same general subject. Since these stories were to be published together in a Sunday magazine format, the problem was magnified. The leads had to avoid sameness, and assure the reader that each new story was worth reading.

Solution: Part of the solution, of course, was close coordination among the students. The rest of the solution involved reaching into each story for the lead that typified it, rather than the whole story of the unicameral legislature. Finally, of course, the solution was rewriting until the leads did do their job. Here are some of their leads:

(For the lead story:)

In January, 1962, Nebraska's legislative experiment will be a quarter of a century old.

For 25 years Nebraska will have been the only state with a one-house legislature.

How, many observers have asked, did the state of Nebraska ever come up with a unicameral legislature?

In many cases they meant "how," but in others they meant "why." It has been difficult for these observers to understand how a state not noted for dramatic change from the traditional way of doing things could adopt a one-house state legislative system.

Actually, the one-house state legislature is not a stranger. . . .

(To introduce the man who first thought about and fought for a unicameral legislature for Nebraska:)

Speaker: "The floor recognizes the gentleman from Polk County."

Then arose a man with a mission, a conservative looking man, in a blue suit, a white shirt, and a black bow tie. He was of medium build, about 5' 11" tall, 170 pounds, with dark hair. His voice was clear and low and he used it with confidence as he addressed the Nebraska State Legislature.

"I know of no proposition that can be more properly submitted to the people of this state than the question of a one-house legislature," the Polk County representative said.

That was a Thursday afternoon in March, 1920, and John N. Norton already had campaigned for a unicameral legislature in Nebraska for seven years. . . .

(To introduce the word artist, Senator George W. Norris, who sold the unicameral idea to the voters:)

"If I offered the Lord's Prayer as an amendment, they would fight it."

The speaker, George William Norris. The place, McCook, Nebraska, his home town. The time, November 6, 1934. The words represented a moment of discouragement in the life of a man for whom lonely political battles had been not the exception, but the rule.

These weary words spoken in 1934 came at the end of another battle. They were spoken on election eve when Nebraskans were pondering the fate of the proposed Unicameral Legislature amendment. . . .

(To introduce the first director of the Unicameral Legislature's Legislative Council:)

A pioneer in some respects . . . a Pied Piper when it came to collecting friends . . . a professor and a researcher by occupation.

This was Dr. Roger V. Shumate, first director of the Legislative Council, a research bureau engaged in problems of state government.

As the first Nebraska director and one of three or four others in the country in 1937, Shumate was a pioneer in . . .

(To introduce the leadership problem of a nonpartisan legislature:)

There is a shopworn phrase of the space age which involves the punch line of many jokes, that punch line being:

"Take me to your leader."

Questions not unlike this statement are frequently asked by visitors to Nebraska's Unicameral Legislature. The observer, looking down from the galleries, may ask:

"Who is the majority leader?"

"Who is the minority leader?"

"Where are the party whips?"

The reply to all of these questions is the same—there are none. . . .

(To introduce the problems of liaison between a partisan governor and a nonpartisan legislature:)

How does a partisan governor get along with a nonpartisan legislature?

The answer seems to depend upon which chair you are sitting in. If you are sitting in the legislative chamber as a senator in Nebraska's Unicameral Legislature, the chances are you probably would say, "Just fine."

If you were sitting in the governor's chair, the answer would apparently be, "Not very well.". . .

(To introduce a story on the problems the legislators themselves feel the unicameral system has solved and created:)

The word "unicameral" means one-house. And the senators who took part in this survey gave Nebraska's one-house legislature the kind of a landslide vote they themselves would like to have at the polls. . . .

(To introduce the problems of the strange job of lieutenant governor as a partisan official presiding over a nonpartisan legislature:)

The chief presiding office of the Nebraska Unicameral Legislature is held by a man who must be a part-time politician, a part-time nonpartisan, a part-time governor, and whose full-time job is almost always in private enterprise.

This description represents the paradox that is the lieutenant governor's job in Nebraska. While he is all of these things, he is also one heart-beat away from the governor's chair. . . .

(To introduce and explain the importance of legislative committee work:)

At 2 p.m. for several months during the legislative session, it is impossible to find all of Nebraska's 43 senators in one spot.

At that hour the legislators start doing what many students of government consider their most important job—committee work. . . .

104

(To introduce a round-up of the special sessions of the Legislature:)

The eight special legislative sessions held since the formation of the Nebraska Unicameral Legislature in 1937 have been called to deal with matters ranging from taxation to diseased pigs. . . .

9

Are They Expendable?

In my wife's family there is the tradition of *das grosse Buch*. When a grandchild graduates from the highchair but is too short for a regular chair, "that big book," one of those handy one-volume encyclopedias, is placed between him and the chair, thus elevating him to eating height.

In journalism there also is the tradition of *das grosse Buch*. If all that has been written about leads was brought together, it would at least rival *das grosse Buch*. But if all that has been written about endings was brought together, it would scarcely rival the paper napkin tucked under Junior's chin. Perhaps writers have ignored endings because they have been so expendable.

On most copy desks, the ending is the last thing to arrive and the first to go. Sometimes those endings should go, as should all excess verbiage. Sometimes they must go simply because there is not enough space. Sometimes, from the reporter's viewpoint, they go as a therapeutic sacrifice to the copyreader's desire to cut something—anything—out of a long story.

The first reason for cutting—excess verbiage—is always legitimate. The second—lack of space—is partly so, and the third—copyreader therapy—is false medication. However, to the reporter the reasons for amputation make no difference. He approaches the planned ending with serious misgivings. Even William H. Stringer, whose copy is handled on *The Christian Science Monitor* by some of the finest deskmen in the country, expresses the writer's natural apprehension:

I used to plan endings sometimes. Now, perhaps because of habit they seem to come along naturally. It would always help to save some punch line, or some punch fact for the end. (If you can be reasonably certain the story will run without being truncated.)

Yes, it is true even on the best of copy desks that the ending for which the writer strove so proudly may be neatly nipped off. There are many good reasons for the death of an ending. Frequently, the simple speed and necessary routine of the daily newspaper may offer up endings as a normal sacrifice.

However, when depth is involved, the truncating feared by Mr. Stringer and his colleagues the world over may seriously hurt the story. The depth reporter must take his reader by the hand and lead him through an often complicated story. If the ending is the victim of the copy desk's shears or the composing room's hellbox, the reader may never be sure that he finished the trip. The result is something like one of those open-face sandwiches so popular at teas and cocktail parties. They may be the social thing to eat, but usually they aren't worth a darn for filling the stomach.

The problem of avoiding the open-face approach to the depth story is often one of layout and is discussed as such in a later section of this book. Right now, it is a reporting problem.

The writer's anguish over the loss of an ending could simply have to remain part of the postbirth pangs, since it is a valuable tool in preparation of the story. Like a sandwich, the beginning (or lead) and the ending provide something to hold the meat in place. Experienced writers frequently plan their endings at the same time that they sweat out their leads. This provides the reporter with a place to start and a place to end and makes it somewhat easier to establish the route between.

If an ending only helps plan a story, then there is no need to write it into finished, polished copy. Under such circumstances, we could simply use the end idea to help in planning and let the copyreader get his therapy elsewhere. Please, understand that I have nothing against copy *editors;* it is paragraph-marking, scissor-wielding copy*readers* whom I abhor as much as the hack reporter. In a later section of this book, the copy *editor's* role in depth is discussed. First, however, the reporter must write.

And he must write endings. He must do it not just for himself, but for his reader. Don't expect to grab your reader, haul him into the story, lead him tenderly through the facts, and then, just when you have almost satisfied him, drop him flat. He, like your story, must get somewhere. You needn't bring out the brass band, but at least let him know he got home.

While a few top news professionals have, with some trepidation, been writing endings, the competition has been making a science of it. The magazine writer builds skillfully to the climax and then bleeds it for all it is worth in a quick anticlimax—an ending, if you please. Television builds to a climax and then pops in a commercial, knowing full well that the viewer will hang around for the ending.

Just because the competition does it is no reason we have to. After all, our business is largely informing. Theirs is largely entertaining. But, just because the competition does it, is no reason we should not. They, too, would like to inform, and they do it very well at times. As a newsman it annoys me to see a TV or magazine writer bring the reader the full route on a story while a news writer on the same story may simply let him fade away like an upside-down open-face sandwich. I am afraid it also annoys the reader.

We cannot give a story perspective, one of the major attributes of depth, if that story does not get somewhere and does not make sure the reader knows it. It is time that paper napkin under Junior's chin was at least thick enough to be a chapter in *das grosse Buch* under his seat.

One advantage in learning about endings is that there are no ready-made categories.

The facts and the organization of a story dictate the ending. In other words, like a good lead, a good ending requires thought. A few questions tucked not too far away in your brain are about the only help you can get in your search for the right ending.

See if the following questions would help:

Does the ending really end the story? (If this is the kind of story which is complete, which can be told in its entirety, then the reader needs to realize that he has come the full route.)

Does the ending really satisfy the reader? (Paraphrasing what they say in show business—always leave them laughing, crying, or, at least, feeling something.)

Does it end honestly? (Many stories simply bring the reader as far as they can and end up in that gray area where there are still questions to be answered by later developments. The reader needs to end up knowing what it is that he cannot yet know.)

Finally, does the story need an ending at all? (It may be that the facts themselves create a logical ending. If so, there is no need to clutter it up with your lovely prose.)

Consciously, if you are a novice at quality writing, and unconsciously, if you are a veteran, you need to put the foregoing questions to the end of your story. One of them will help you make the end of that story do its job.

Let's see how some veterans put endings to work.

Bob Wells of *The Milwaukee Journal* describes his approach to the "closer" of a story this way:

> Do I plan an ending? Generally, yes, if the deadline isn't too close. It's a cliché to say that the beginning and end of a story are the most important parts, but it's true. When it isn't necessary to strain too hard to do so, I like to construct an ending that will bring the reader around full circle, giving some kind of a twist to the same idea used in the lead. This makes for a neat package.
>
> Let me give you an example. The lead on a 1957 story of mine out at Plainfield, Wisconsin, said that the murders and graverobbing activity of Ed Gein "might have been revealed long ago if only people had taken the little man seriously."
>
> The ending quotes a neighbor:
>
> "The kids talked about him and his haunted house and his shrunken heads," Diggles said. "We just thought it was foolishness, the kind of thing kids say. I guess this is one time they knew better than we did. I guess this is one time we all should have listened."

Phil Meyer of *The Miami Herald* also brought his story on patronage and insurance premiums the full route. Meyer had to do it over a three-part series. Remember, he started the first in the series like this:

> A total of $59,000 in school insurance commissions is being handed out this year [1959] to local agents who never lift a finger to earn it.
>
> The money is passed out to 181 agents, chosen by School Board members under a time-honored plan of political patronage. Estimated total cost to taxpayers: $200,000 a year.
>
> The system, inherited by the present School Board from an earlier era when the insurance plum was much smaller, has resisted more than six years of effort to dislodge it.

When the series was completed, Meyer had made the complete cycle. He started with the school board, patronage, and campaign contributions. He ended like this:

> Diestelhorst, on the other hand, sees the issue as a question of "deciding whether we want to do what's good for the county or what's good for the insurance men."
>
> Though he recently banked a check for $858 as his share of school insurance patronage, he thinks the Board would be better off with competitive bids.
>
> It could save still more by buying deductible policies and increasing the deductible amount each year while building up a self-insurance fund, he said.
>
> School Board chairman C. Raymond Van Dusen, whose election campaign was managed by Diestelhorst, agrees with this principle, even though recipients of school insurance patronage provided more than half his campaign contributions last year.
>
> "I've been trying for years to get a self-insurance program going," he said. "I will vote for it if it comes up again."

The show-business tactic—leave them feeling something—requires the careful planning of a good comedian's gag line. There are writers who are honestly afraid of the nearly perfect lead. They fear that once a really sharp lead has put them on the razor's edge, they must tread its fine line clear to the end. If they fall off, they fear, their story will flop, like the comedian's ill-timed gag line.

David F. Francis, writing for *The Christian Science Monitor*, took a terrifying subject, wrote it with sparkle, started it with a laugh, and ended it with a chuckle. His subject, tariffs. Can you think of a more deadly one? Probably not, but when Francis had finished with it, he had completed the cycle. This is the way he led it:

> Various industries are picking sides for the coming tariff battle.
>
> For a while, business observers here [New York] were like the apartment dweller who has heard one shoe drop—the free trade one. They were nervously waiting for the other shoe—the protectionist one—to hit the floor.

With a start like that, Francis placed himself right on the razor's edge. A thing like this happens, whether you know it or not, almost every time you write a lead that gives your artistic sensibilities a touch of tingle. Francis trod the razor's edge and ended his story like this:

So it goes. More and more industries can be expected to let their shoes—free trade or protectionist—fall to the floor. Congress will note which makes the most noise.

But its decision must also take into account those in the U.S. who have no trade shoes to drop.

Francis's ending left them smiling, at least, and also illustrated those stories that must leave the reader with questions yet to be answered in the future. For another look at that kind of story— it is a common one—let's go back to the announcement that the Nelson Rockefellers were planning a divorce. The reporters knew it would take years to unveil all the political implications of the announcement. The honest story had to end up in the gray area. You have seen how *The Wall Street Journal* and *The Christian Science Monitor* handled the lead. Now look at the endings:

A minority view, but one strongly espoused, holds that Mr. Rockefeller can take his trouble and use it to advantage. They argue that if the governor can win a respectable victory in New York State with its large Catholic block, it will be taken as evidence throughout the nation that divorce is no great handicap to a good candidate. A comparison is made with Mr. Kennedy's primary election victory in Protestant West Virginia last year which was cited as evidence that his Catholicism was no handicap.

This theory holds that in fact Mr. Rockefeller should have no trouble in producing such evidence—since New York is a "sophisticated" and "liberal" state where thousands might vote for him just to prove their lack of bias.

—*The Wall Street Journal*

Perhaps the one implication, which most seem reluctant to accept, is that Gov. Rockefeller is as forthright in meeting his personal crises as he is when the political chips are down. The separation is reported to be amicable. It ends 31 years of marriage—a condition not easily overlooked, and which, in itself, indicates the soberness of the decision.

When placed under the political lens, nevertheless, the development indicates either that the Rockefeller political ambitions end in Albany, or that a bold decision has been made to clear all decks and get ready for an all-out bid for the prize political post of all, with three years of time to soften the blow before ballots are cast for president in 1964.

—*The Christian Science Monitor*

Neither of those endings play rhetorical games with the reader. There are vast political questions to be answered on such a story. The reader deserves to be told forthrightly that he has been given the background to understand, but now he must wait and see for the final results.

Despite this plea for endings, it is now necessary to blunt your enthusiasm for them at least a trifle. *The Los Angeles Times*'s Louis B. Fleming dulls the edge this way:

> I seldom plan endings ahead of time. I scramble like mad through my notes. When I get to the last paragraph of a long depth piece I try to come up with something useful. If it isn't obviously available, I let it cut off sensibly without stretching for a grand finale.

Fleming, rather subtly, issues a very basic warning to every writer. While the beginner should not ignore planned endings, as does veteran Fleming, he does need to listen to the warning. No matter how much his experience, there comes a moment of weakness toward the end of the long grind that produces a good depth story. You have dug out the facts. You have sweat out the writing. And now, it seems only fair that you be allowed to play Aesop— as in Aesop's Fables—for "just one measly little paragraph."

Surely, no one can object if just here you draw a moral, and put a little of yourself into the story.

Unhappily, someone can object, and that someone is mighty important—your reader. The moral, the author's little sermon, can turn corny something that was near-perfect—a complete job of reporting that simply does not need a tagged-on ending.

Somehow, I did not want to end this chapter that way, but I was fearful lest I preach one of those little sermons that I have just finished denouncing. So, I cast about for another way and found among my research notes a quote from Lowell Brandle, that word artist on *The St. Petersburg Times.*

Remember his lead on the changing Negro attitude? "Speak softly, for death is in our house. Uncle Tom is dying."

After quoting Negro leaders who saw a growing pride in themselves and their race, he ended like this:

"My people," said the Negro matriarch, "my people are standing up."

Now, Mr. Brandle, what was it about those endings?

> I do not plan endings with the same care as I do leads, for the purpose of the two is so different. The lead must get them into the tent. Then you put on the show—you tell the story. The ending depends on what kind of a show you put on. Sometimes the best ending is to turn

out the lights and yell "Fire," which doesn't have much to do with
the show, but at least it gets them out of the tent.

Case Histories of Endings

(Note that the first sentence or two of the leads of these stories
has been repeated as well as the ending.)

(Sometimes, good quotes bring the story full cycle. Here, the
problem was telling the part John Nathaniel Norton, a former
Congressman, played in establishing the Nebraska Unicameral Legislature.)

Lead: Speaker: "The floor recognizes the gentleman from Polk
County." . . .

Ending: And the gentleman from Polk County left Nebraska
a special legacy—he was perhaps the first to dream of and then
actively promote a system of legislature that he believed would
"save time, talk and money."

(Here, the problem was the same, only this time the subject was
the late Senator George William Norris—a most quotable man.)

Lead: "If I offered the Lord's Prayer as an amendment, they
would fight it." . . .

Ending: On the Senator's centennial year, 1961, a plan was
proposed to turn the Norris's McCook home into a national
shrine.

"Mrs. Norris wants George William to have all the recognition
he deserves," said Harris.

It would be a shrine to a man who thought of humanity and
once said, "I lie awake at night thinking of what I may do to
help, but no matter what I may say, it all sounds like a voice
in the wilderness."

(Sometimes the writer's own words skillfully bring the story full
cycle. Here, the student reporter was trying to describe the multiple
duties of a multipurpose lieutenant governor.)

Lead: The chief presiding office of the Nebraska Unicameral
Legislature is held by a man who must be a part-time politician,
part-time nonpartisan, a part-time governor, and whose full-time
job is almost always in private enterprise.

Ending: Poet, editor, Indian-fighter, lawyer, farmer, business-man—these many jobs represent the full-time work of Nebraska's lieutenant governors. It is perhaps appropriate that their part-time job—lieutenant governor of Nebraska—is a mixture of presiding officer, nonpartisanship, partisanship, and executive duties.

The foregoing were leads and endings from a student-written report on Nebraska's Unicameral Legislature. The writing problem was intensified because all of the stories dealt with the same general subject.

The following examples are taken from individual student stories.

(Here, a student had the problem of painting a word picture of a very colorful and outspoken State Fair manager just before this annual fall extravaganza.)

Lead: "Hang onto this damned scooter, and I'll show you around."

Financially, what you're about to do is take the cheapest ride at the Nebraska Fairgrounds, but you'll be rich if you share the driver's enthusiasm for what you're about to see and hear.

The husky gentleman encouraging this small electric scooter along roads and ruts alike is Ed Schultz. He'll tell you that. Annually, he's responsible for the success or failure of the Nebraska State Fair. He'll accept this with some reservations. And he's Nebraskan through and through. You'll be able to tell that yourself.

What 63-year-old Ed Schultz does not like to talk about is the strain of his job and his necessary retirement as secretary of the Fair Board.

Ending: The yellow scooter is urged up over a curb and purrs to a stop in front of the secretary's office. If he hasn't bounced you off the passenger seat by this time, you have heard the big fellow tell you of his life here. You may conclude that because Schultz is a native Nebraskan, has farmed the land, and helped write the statutes, that he has developed a "Nebraska reflex" and can sense what Cornhuskers want at their biggest show of the year—the State Fair.

But the ride and the story are over now, and Schultz blasts himself back into the building, issues a half dozen requests to

Helen, and settles down to cure any slight colds the upcoming Fair may have developed by this time. He has booked Dennis Day, Emmett Kelly, Jr., and the Peter Palmer orchestra, among others. "It'll be the biggest show since Roy Rogers was here," he assures you.

The details are done now, for as the big man says, "Once you unlock those gates in September, the Fair is in the hands of the gods."

(Here, the difficult problem of Americans and poetry—built around the profile of a Pulitzer-prize-winning poet.)

Lead: Books and anthologies of poetry are regaining their places on the book shelves of homes in this country after an entire generation of Americans turned their reading attention elsewhere.

People are even spontaneously interested in the works of a new generation of poets who look upon their art as entertainment as well as work, a breed of poets writing for the eye and ear of the general public rather than only for intense study by other poets.

Ending: And for these people, the Shapiro pen is far from being empty. He now is working on a book of poems, and is considering writing "a novel of a kind."

Many artists, critics, and poetry-lovers throughout the country will be happy to know that this "poet for people" has not approached the period or even semicolon of a life built around something as commonplace as most of the subjects of his poems —words.

(Here, to get readership for a very long sports story, a calculated insult to start and a calculated compliment to close.)

Lead: To the outsider—the non-Nebraskan—the Cornhusker football fan may appear to be some kind of a super-loyal nut.

Under normal circumstances, the Cornhusker football fan probably couldn't care less about what an outsider thinks. But this week after almost two decades of football drought, Nebraska is in the process of picking a new athletic director.

What does the new regime face?

Ending: The Cornhusker football fan may well be some kind of a super-loyal nut. He may be conservative in his politics, but he is radical about his football. He may be pessimistic about Nebraska's future at times, but he is always optimistic about the Cornhuskers. He may rant. He may rave. He may scream for a win. But the Cornhuskers are his, and he is always there to watch them.

10

Meanwhile, Back at the Ranch

Any number of twentieth-century comedians include in their repertoire a line that is always good for a laugh. During the laughter the audience is carried to another subject. That multipurpose line, "Meanwhile, back at the ranch . . ." is simply a caricature of a transition. It does for the modern comic what a full-time job did for the old-time minstrel show.

In the heyday of the minstrel show, it was everybody's job to get them into the tent, but one man's job to keep them there in the normally vacant spot between acts. That gentleman, known as an interlocutor, carried the show from act to act, mood to mood, and scene to scene. While the performers paused between acts and prepared for the next, Mr. Interlocutor kept members of the audience from remembering that they sat in a flapping old tent instead of the Palace Theatre.

He was the glue that held the show together. His was the magic that made a whole thing out of something that was basically a series of parts. His job is now old-fashioned, but his writing counterpart of today certainly is not. His writing counterpart is only sadly neglected by too many newswriters and too many newspapers.

I sometimes wonder if the style of the inverted pyramid did not somehow creep into the English classroom where that sweet old high school teacher fully intended to discuss transitions, but somehow never quite got the point across. Indeed, if she did make her point, it seems to have been forgotten by college days, and totally obliterated by the time America's young journalists take to the typewriter.

The inverted pyramid is a useful tool, has been an absolutely necessary tool in journalism's history, and will continue to be part of the business in the foreseeable future. However, it is a little like the before-dinner glass of wine that encourages the appetite. If the glass becomes a bottle, you never get to the dinner. Most American newspapers have been so long at the bottle that they are a bit afraid to turn away from it and get on with the dinner.

The inverted pyramid must have a place in any discussion of transitions, because it is the creature that has helped destroy them. By its very nature, it makes it possible to tell the story without transitions. In fact, the method of telling a story this way is one great big transition in itself. When the story starts with the most important, most recent, or most startling fact and works steadily downward to facts with less of each of these qualities, the reader is pushed along as far as he cares to go. Without the inverted pyramid the reporter has no recourse but to honest-to-goodness transitions. Let's put transitions into perspective with the rest of the approach to the depth story.

The reader is grabbed by the lead, held by the writing, led by the transitions, and satisfied by the ending. Without every one of these, the depth story would better have been written in the inverted pyramid style with some assurance that the reader would get at least part way.

This discussion of reporting in depth has so far been one for professionals or near-professionals. However, since the transition is so badly neglected almost from the day a future writer meets the English language, let's get very basic. There are editors in America crying for a return to good, thorough reporting. Let's hope they are also crying for a return to good, thorough writing, including transitions.

What does a transition do for a story?

It glues the lead to the body of the story. It carries the reader from subject to subject, from fact to fact, from time to time, from place to place, and from person to person. And all that time it is the major connecting thread between the two-man, writer-reader team. There is no way to discuss transitions except to look at them and see what they do. For the writer who remembers what his high school or college English teacher may have said about transitions, there lingers some vague idea about such words as *meanwhile, but, then, on the other hand,* and a few others. These, however, may be the least used by the skillful writer. A transition doesn't have to be a word. It may simply be a quote mark that tells the reader the same person is still talking. It may be a simple attribution—*he said,* or *he added*—that keeps the reader with the person doing the talking. It may simply be the repetition of the subject of the story so that the reader is easily sure you're still talking about the same thing. It may be the whole idea of the story so skillfully woven into every paragraph that the idea itself is the glue. It may be simple punctuation after a forthright sentence, such as "Observers described the events this way:" This is the technique illustrated in the writing of Rod Van Every of *The Milwaukee Journal:*

> I have always believed that the reader has the easiest time if you lead him through a story chronologically. So, as soon as possible, after getting down a lead and the major points, I flash back and give it to him just as it happened. Attribution slows down a story terribly, so wherever possible, I'll give the source full sway as "John Brown gave this account:".

Van Every likes chronology, but it will not always work. For those many exceptions—they are probably the majority—you can find help from something you did at the beginning of your work on a depth story. That something is the ever-present guide line. If you doubt whether your reader is still with you, look again at that guide line. Have you strayed too far from the whole point of the story? Will some reference to the guide line reassure your reader? "Meanwhile, back at the ranch" represents the minority in the family of transitions employed by a skillful newswriter. From the moment he starts putting the story on paper, he makes sure his reader is with him.

Earlier, it was pointed out that some of the nation's best writers plan their lead and ending at the same time. This, they say, tells them where they are starting and where they are going. These same men, consciously or unconsciously, also plan their first major transition to get them from the lead into the story. How do they do it? Let's see how *The New York Times*'s John A. Osmundsen wrote a high key lead and then slipped the reader easily into the body of the story.

> Martinis for breakfast and insomnia for lunch are just two examples of the sort of thing that the tourist and traveling business man have to

put up with in these days of high-speed, globe-girdling transportation. In addition, victims of the 707 and DC-8 frequently feel dopey when everyone else around them seems to know the score or feels raring to go when others want to call it a day.

That is where the trouble lies. What the tourist calls mid-day (according to his "own time") may be mid-night or late afternoon or very early in the morning for the natives of wherever he happens to be traveling.

Difficulties of this sort from the nature of modern travel have now become the subject of scientific investigation. They were discussed here recently at a conference on biological rhythms held by the New York Academy of Sciences. At the outset, the conferees admitted that little is known about these phenomena.

For example, it is not too well understood. . . .*

The italicized words in this excerpt from Osmundsen's story show the transitions he used to carry his reader from a good lead into the story. Incidentally, his lead illustrates what can be done with a story that would have had minimal readership without it. How many readers would have read about a conference on biological rhythms unless they thought it had something to do with sex? But Osmundsen found a way to attract lots of readers, and having done so, knew that he dared not lose them with a poor transition into the body of his story.

This transition from the lead to the body may be a word, a few words, or, as in Osmundsen's case, several sentences. It is not simply written to carry the reader along, but like every other part of the story, must impart information and do it quickly to give the reader perspective.

Read the opening of the following story by *The Wall Street Journal's* Ed Cony:

The most common building material in this city is neither steel nor concrete, brick nor wood.

It is graft.

This at least is the conviction of many contractors, architects and engineers who are putting up new structures or remodeling existing ones in the nation's largest city. "For seven years I haven't been on a job here where we didn't have to make payoffs to city employees," says a veteran construction superintendent who watches over about 20 jobs a year in New York City.

---

* Copyright by *The New York Times.* Reprinted by permission.

The New York State Commission of Investigation spent ten months recently looking into the administration of building regulation in the city. Its finding: A pattern of corruption is saddling New York's construction industry with extra costs. These costs add millions of dollars annually to building outlays, now running at a rate of $1.4 billion a year. And by and large these costs are passed along to the consumer— the apartment dweller, the business firm renting office space, the manufacturer who builds a new factory, the retailer who remodels his store. *Who gets paid off?* "Almost everyone," the Commission said. "Clerks, plan examiners, multiple dwelling examiners and plumbing inspectors."
Other large cities apparently are similarly tainted. Says a major Chicago contractor: "I suppose it's possible to do a profitable contracting business in Chicago without greasing anyone's palm. But it wouldn't be easy and I don't know of anyone who's willing to try.". . .

The italicized paragraph illustrates the transition from the lead to the body. Other italicized sentences illustrate skillful shifting of subject and scene.

Sometimes a good lead that teases the reader simply because of its different approach requires that the lead and the transition into the body of the story be almost one. Robert E. Bedingfield of *The New York Times* had this problem when he made the annual meeting of a corporation come to life through the examination of its new president.

Perhaps the most ritualistic of big business rituals is the organization meeting of the board that follows the annual meeting of a corporation's stockholders.
If there is any fighting to be done, the stockholders' meeting is the place for it. After the fight, the victorious directors meet and pick their own slate of officers and the losers go off to, in effect, lick their wounds. Where there is no controversy, there is little or no news, *ninety-nine times out of a hundred.*
The hundredth time turned up a week ago Friday after a stockholders' meeting of The National Airlines, Incorporated. The meeting, held in the afternoon, had been remarkably serene. . . .*

Bedingfield slipped his reader into this one through the back door. He then steered the reader into the story with what could have been an old cliché about ninety-nine times out of a hundred. Basically, this transition had to be planned as part of the lead.

Sometimes the transition from the lead into the body of the story needs to reassure the reader. For example, faced with *The St. Petersburg Times*'s series about the crazy things the moon may do

---

* Copyright by *The New York Times.* Reprinted by permission.

to all of us, the reader might first assume that both the writer and the story had moon madness themselves. We all have a couple of common notions about the moon. One involves its romance-encouraging qualities, and the second takes us back to our childhood when we read about werewolves and other unearthly creatures that operated best in the moonlight.

When *The Times*'s Lowell Brandle examined the scientific appraisal of the moon's weird qualities, he had to make sure he hung onto his reader's respect as he moved from the lead into his story.

> Be careful today. The full moon is with us. Not that the werewolves or gremlins will get you, *nothing so old-fashioned as that.*
>
> *For strange reasons, which scientists can't yet explain, it appears that your chances of being arrested for some crime* will increase suddenly today.
>
> *Even more strange,* your chances of suffering serious bleeding—from a wound or from surgery—are suddenly magnified.
>
> *Blame it on the moon, but don't ask why.*
>
> *For thousands of years,* man has lived under the moon's soft light. . . .

With these transitions, Brandle took the reader from werewolves and gremlins to a scientific question mark, and finally into the background of the moon's effect upon human behavior.

Probably the transition from the lead to the body of the story is the most important one the reporter ever does. However, lesser transitions move the reader along inside the story.

Briefly, let's see how skillful writers use transitions to hold their readers on shifts that tend to lose them. The best-known techniques for moving from fact to fact are those involving the way sentences begin. In *The Christian Science Monitor,* L. Dana Gatlin shifted smoothly on a major depth piece discussing the question of whether football is a sport or an entertainment. Having introduced his reader to the football season and the Saturday gathering of the alums, he needed to put the whole thing into perspective with a series of relatively unrelated facts:

> *Make no mistake about it;* colleges, universities, are building bigger and better athletic plants, attracting athletes and generous alumni, all on the success of their football teams.
>
> *Despite the demand* for quality play, the romance of the fall Saturday still remains a vital part of the game's attraction. The man on his way up to old Seawash could stay home and see a far better game watching the pros—or even the collegiate game of the week on TV.

Nevertheless, he wants to see Seawash play State—with the bands and the cheerleaders and the conviviality of old friends reunited.

Most of all, he wants to see Seawash win, but to insure that result can be expensive—in money and sometimes in morality.

Not infrequently, it means pouring more money into the football coffer than into those of other sports in the school's physical set-up. Scholarships are set up, athletes recruited, post-season Bowl game bids talked about. . . .

Gatlin illustrates the smoothest use of the "meanwhile, back at the ranch" technique. In doing so, he carries his readers through a series of facts that interrupt the natural telling of his story, but which set up that natural outline for the rest of the piece.

The simple repetition of a name, a pronoun referring to the name, or a possessive pronoun may provide an easy vehicle for transition. However, it must be used skillfully, lest it make the story start reading like a record of court testimony. Note how *The Des Moines Register's* George Mills used it.

Four-year-old Marcia Bunge has taken her parents by the hand and has led them to wide horizons of love and understanding.

Happy little Marcia, a blue-eyed blonde, is retarded mentally. She was born with less ability than a normal child.

She probably will never be more than eight or nine years old mentally. She will have to have someone care for her all her life.

Her father, Victor Bunge, is high school superintendent here. The Bunges have two normal sons, eleven and nine.

Marcia's condition is known as "Mongolism." Having such a child is no reflection on the parents. Something happens to the child before birth that causes the abnormal development. Some authorities say Mongolism occurs. . . .

Sometimes time itself creates confusion that can be cleared up only by a good transition. A complicated depth story may have to take the reader back from today to a century ago and back again, and do it without losing the way. When Harry Wilensky of *The St. Louis Post-Dispatch* wrote about the modern city-county problem, he let the reader know this was something more than the usual approach. Look again at his lead, and then see how he kept the reader with him as he skimmed through the history of the problem in St. Louis County:

Cities, like people, make mistakes. A group of citizens is convinced that the biggest blunder in the history of St. Louis was committed when the city divorced St. Louis County in 1876 to free itself of a corrupt county political ring and the burden of supporting a poor rural area.

At first St. Louis was happy. . . .

[Now, Wilensky has his reader back in 1876.]

A plan to consolidate St. Louis and St. Louis County was offered *in 1926.* . . . A different approach was *tried in 1930.* . . .

[He has now moved to 1926 and 1930.]

In 1959, there was a proposal to establish. . . .

[Now he has brought the reader almost all the way back.]

Now another try is to be made. . . .

[And there you are, from 1961 back to 1876 and all the way back again without losing his reader, or getting his reader lost.]

Sometimes, the time involved is more compressed when a depth story is a roundup of a news story that has broken over several recent months. Here, the best answer may be a simple, forthright statement. In his story about the battle of the Ash Street ramp, *The Oregonian's* Don Holm had such a problem:

> Many of the newspapers or broadcast listeners followed the events that led up to the rhubarb of Wednesday, August 2, in city council, with various degrees of shoulder-shrugging. Few are aware of the full story behind the ramp or the real significance of the outcome.
>
> *The Ash Street ramp, or overpass, project started innocently enough two years ago.* . . .

With that simple sentence, Holm prepared his readers for a chronological roundup of a story that needed perspective.

Now look back once again to the cowboy hero chasing the rustlers off of the south pasture, while back at the ranch, the chief rustler is chasing the heroine. The problem here is to get the reader from place to place so that he can observe both of these interesting actions. Probably the reason the punch line—meanwhile, back at the ranch—is almost always good for a laugh is that an effort to be clever about this kind of a transition can most easily turn to corn. When you need to transport your reader from place to place, usually the best way is the most direct way. For example, the wire service use of a dateline—Washington, D.C. . . . New York . . . Paris . . . and so forth—may at some times become confusing. However, the reader is educated to allow the dateline to help guide him in his armchair survey of the world each morning and evening.

Within the story, this simple approach is probably also the best. Charles Hillinger of *The Los Angeles Times* had this place to place problem in a local story when he described a boom in the vast, growing, sprawling Los Angeles area:

> *North of Angeles National Forest and the San Gabriel Range* lies one-fourth of Los Angeles country—a triangular shaped high plain 943 square miles of virtually undeveloped flat land.
> One hundred times more people live in the county's *south half,* an area only twice that of the sparsely populated *northern plain.*
> Those who live or own land *on the other side of the mountains* are still waiting to be swept up in the boom. . . .
> The boom has yet to spill *over the hills,* although it has already spread *to all neighboring counties.*
> *South of the San Gabriels* within the county's limits live more than 6 million persons—a greater population than that of 43 of the 50 states.
> *To the north* in the county's portion of sprawling Antelope Valley live but 63,158. . . .

Mr. Hillinger had to carry his reader all over a county, over a mountain range, and into neighboring counties. He did it simply, with simple directions.

He could have said "meanwhile, back in southern Los Angeles, and so on . . ." and gotten a few laughs and a few sneers. Perhaps it is those sneers which have frightened newspaper writers away from one of their legitimate tools—the transition. But in the day of depth writing, it may be better to risk a few sneers and get the reader back to the ranch.

Case History of a Story

Student: Gerald Lamberson.

Idea: Urbanization of a rural area.

Guide Line: Nebraska's smallest county is suffering the biggest population explosion as farm and city meet.

Sources: Sociology, history, census reports, county officials, city and town officials, agricultural experts, school officials, Air Force officials, and both rural and urban residents.

Legwork: Personally interviewing most of his sources.

Organization: An outline based primarily on the guide line and the transitions he would have to make to cover all these facets that provided facts for his story. His lead and his ending were to complete a cycle.

Results: This story represented an experiment with weekly newspapers to see how they could handle a complicated depth story. The story was so well accepted by the editors in the section of the state around Sarpy County that it was used as an example by the editors when they participated in an editorial workshop called at their request at the University of Nebraska. The story represented a personal victory for its writer, who had been plagued throughout his college career with grammar problems. Outside of discussions in the idea and outlining stages with his instructor, the student produced the story entirely on his own. In this case, the first draft that reached the instructor was, with very minor editing, the draft run by the newspapers.

(Because this case history is designed to show student work with transitions, the entire story is not run. After the transitions have been illustrated, paragraphs dealing with the same subject have been eliminated. The transitions are italicized, and parenthetical remarks have been inserted to point up the technique involved.)

The Story:

Nine black and white Holstein cows graze quietly on an eastern Nebraska hillside near a big red barn. Just a mile north, hundreds of beef cattle are being fattened for market.

(From farm to suburb.)

But across the road from these two scenes is suburbia. Here hundreds of homes of many colors spread over the hillsides. *Here is where the population explosion begins.*

(From Nebraska to the national problem and back to Nebraska again.)

The cattle scene represents rural life. Suburbia depicts an urban movement. Near many metropolitan areas urban development has spread out and taken over much surrounding rural area. *Nebraska, traditionally the "Beef State" and known for its agriculture products, is one of the states experiencing such a movement.*

But the Nebraska scene is perhaps a little unique at present. Here the urban movement and population explosion has been largely concentrated in the smallest county—*Sarpy County.*

(Repetition of a noun carries the reader.)

Sarpy County has only 236 square miles of area. However, in population it ranks fourth in Nebraska with 34,346 people. The 1950 census listed only 15,693 population. . . .

Sarpy County was listed by census reports as an early population leader when Nebraska was first settled. But its position dipped to 59th in the 1920's. . . .

Just where is *Sarpy's growth?* Bellevue, the largest city, has jumped from 8,800 in 1960 to 10,169 in 1962. Papillion, the county seat, soared from 800 a few years ago to 2,800 today. LaVista is a new community, built between Omaha and Papillion since 1960, which has a population of about 2,000. Omaha proper is spreading into Sarpy County. Offutt Air Force Base is expanding its personnel.

(From the general to the specific.)

With such tremendous growth Sarpy County residents are being hemmed in by a movement they cannot escape, said assistant county agent Frank Morse. "The residents are almost helpless with nowhere to go," he added. "Omaha and its growing pains are to the north. The Missouri River serves as the eastern border with the Platte River bordering Sarpy on the south and west."

Farmers are not resenting the urban movement. Mrs. Milton Fricke, a Papillion housewife who lives on a farm only one mile from suburbia said that "farm folks are accepting the change. It is a part of a movement that we cannot stop. Therefore, we can only sit tight until the time we are moved off our places. . . ."

(From the farm to suburban living.)

. . . Changes have also been noted in 4-H where the emphasis of beef and crops has been switched to gardens and safety, he said.

But these changes to urban living are made to look attractive by descriptions in subdividers' own suburbanese. A sign near the entrance of LaVista Village says, "House of 9's on Easy Street in LaVista Village." As one enters, he can see. . . .

While traveling along Easy Street in LaVista one can notice husbands planting or working on their yards. . . .

(From suburban living to school problems.)

But even as city workers move to suburban areas, they bring population to a previous rural area. They bring children. And with children come the school problems that are plaguing Sarpy County communities.

First there is reorganization of the county which has almost been completed in Sarpy County, according to Papillion school superintendent Leslie George. . . .

(From current school problems to future ones.)

As Mr. George works to solve the present problems, he looks to the future enrollment and sees many more problems. The basic problem is finance. A still higher increase in the mill levy would be outrageous to the taxpayer, he said. The superintendent sees three solutions. . . .

(From town to town.)

Bellevue, too, has school problems, although they may be slightly different from Papillion's. Bellevue's superintendent Edwin Cramer said. . . .

(From schools to defense.)

Bellevue expansion has come via Offutt Air Force Base, which contributes about 45 percent of the population to the city and the area northwest toward Omaha, said Chamber of Commerce manager Harold Smock.

Many Bellevue residents work in Omaha which makes. . . .

(From now to the future.)

Sarpy County is growing. Where will it stop? Assistant agent Morse and others say the urban movement will extend southward until it hits the Platte River, leaving only a small area in the western part for rural life. Still other residents are predicting an urban complex between Omaha and Lincoln with Sarpy County becoming completely urbanized.

But as suburbia continues to develop in Sarpy County those nine black and white cows will probably leave their quiet pasture. In their place will be hundreds of new, vari-colored homes.

(This ending not only completed the cycle, but actually provided a transition into future stories about Sarpy County. Because it ended up in the gray area with many questions unanswered, the reader is conditioned to understand future stories.)

11

Gilt by Association

When twentieth-century journalism operated on the English language, removing one of the eight parts of speech, sterilization may not have been intended. But in too many cases that is what happened.

The operation took place some time after the turn of the century. Before then, American journalism was in its flowery period. It wasn't the flowers that became so obnoxious, it was the too highly scented perfume of the language of that day which drove the adjective out of the newspaperman's vocabulary. And not all that was flowery was bad. Read the following and then judge:

> The sun rose in an ominous setting of smoldering heat and a savage wind on July 26th, 1894. All day that gale from out of the south lashed at humans and vegetation. . . . The thermometer registered 104. The wind velocity . . . 40 miles. Thousands of acres of corn, dark, healthy, promising became a sacrifice to the insatiable appetite of the embattled elements. They still say, those who were here in July of 1894, that there was not a field of corn in the state which escaped without scars from the hot wind and merciless sun of a 24-hour period. It was entered upon the records as a total failure, a figurative term not wholly accurate, but near enough to describe Nebraska's experience that eventful year.

Not all the products of the flowery period were that good. The writer of that paragraph had felt the influence of William Allen White in the day of the giants of small-town American journalism. The writer was also unashamedly influenced by a fellow townsman, William Jennings Bryan, the silver-tongued orator. And the writer, the late James E. Lawrence, long-time editor of *The Lincoln* (Nebraska) *Star,* like Bryan exemplified a kind of writing and speech-making that has gone out of style.

Were Lawrence and Bryan wrong? By today's standards, they were old-fashioned. Yet, look again at that description by Lawrence of the drought of the 1890's—a drought that brought the Midwest to its knees and helped start the rise of Populism. You can't say it's bad, not if as a professional you recognize writing that comes from the heart. You can't deny that it paints a vivid picture. This kind of writing, or some modification of it, helps pump life into a story.

The problem, of course, is in the modification. Almost to the man the top professionals who have lent their writing brains to this book shied away from questions about description. They have learned their lessons well. Listen, while they talk:

Bob Wells of *The Milwaukee Journal*—"Ordinarily I don't use many adjectives. It is better to say a man weighs 243 pounds than to describe him as fat. If I do use an adjective, I make it a conservative one. I'd rather call a woman attractive (if she really is) than pretty, or beautiful, and I'd rather run her picture and skip the adjective entirely, letting the reader decide for himself."

Louis B. Fleming of *The Los Angeles Times*—"I prefer cautious descriptions rather than flamboyant, and I try never to use the style of balding John Jones or eager, quick Charlie Brown."

Ed Cony of *The Wall Street Journal*—". . . for instance, in the story there is a listing of equipment one American concern lost to Castro rebels. The story isn't content to say an American reports he lost a lot of diesel oil and some animals; instead we tell the reader the firm lost 31,640 gallons of diesel oil and nine mules. . . ."

Obviously, these men are cautious, but just as obviously they do use description. It appears, then, that there is description and there is description. One kind is bad, like too much sugar in the coffee. Another kind is good, like the right hint of garlic in the salad. The first kills the story. The second sharpens the flavor—the life—of the story. What is the difference?

To best find words to describe the difference, take one of my wife's words. She knows what it means. I know what it means. And our close friends know what it means. The word is *peensy.* To my wife it describes a person who is pinched in appearance, cheap in personality, and generally colorless in character. And now that it is no longer a family secret, it describes the kind of adjectives that do not belong in newspaper copy.

Peensy adjectives are, just as the word says, pinched, cheap, color-less words that don't tell the reader anything except that the writer isn't very good at description.

What adjectives fit the description? The kind we use in speech every day. They include *fat, thin, hot, cold, beautiful, ugly,* and so on *ad nauseam.* These are the kind of words we have thrown out of newspaper copy and justly so. They express writer opinion, they are excess verbiage, and worst of all, they do not say anything.

Can we describe without *peensy* adjectives? The question is rhetorical. We can, but should we? Does description have any place in what we have been calling the depth story?

Think again for a moment about what a depth story is supposed to do. Among other things, it is supposed to make the reader feel that he is either part of it or that he is part of the whole scene the story paints. One way to make him feel that this is his story is to take him by the hand and take him to the scene. In other words, with verbal pictures you let him look in as the event takes place before his mental eyes. If you are describing the action in a smoke-filled room, let him choke a bit on the acrid smoke. If you are describing the results of a broiling sun, let him also cook a bit.

Sometimes with word pictures you can take him to a scene that did not happen at all but represents an abstract thought. For example, later in this chapter we will look closely at a story written about the monotonous farm surplus problem. For such a story a writer could say the farm surplus problem is made up of many problems. Or he could say "it is like trying to diagnose a tennis elbow on an octopus." Nobody ever saw an octopus with a tennis elbow, nor could a picture describe it, but with words the reader can form an accurate mental image.

Now, we are beginning to get to the point. No one can deny that the right kind of description—not the *peensy* kind—lends color and life to the news story. And providing it is done with facts, it can be done legitimately. When it comes to observation, which results in description, the reporter's eyes are as good as anyone else's. It is not reporter opinion to describe accurately and with facts how a man looks. The facts are the way he looks; the description is the way the reporter uses those facts. Let's belabor the point. Throughout this book there has been no retreat from the proposition that depth reporting does not include the opinions of the reporter. However, his eyes are a perfectly legitimate part of his fact-gathering equipment. What he observes, he can describe. And what he describes can help hold his reader.

The *peensy,* generic adjectives do less than nothing when it comes to holding readers. In fact, they stilt our craft. If these were the only descriptive tools we had, then we should return entirely to the inverted pyramid and the sterile, almost dead story.

Happily, if we learn to describe with facts, our descriptive abilities are unlimited. There is a guide line to this approach; use facts that create a mental association with the reader's experiences.

For example, there is that much-talked-about subject, the weather. Scarcely a day passes when you do not describe the climatic conditions of the moment for someone. Your newspaper does it every day, sometimes several times a day.

Ignoring for the moment the newspaper's problems, let's simply talk some description. Suppose someone too lazy to look for himself or the prisoner of one of those miserable modern offices without windows asks, "What's the weather like?"

Outside, you know that it is one of those days when clouds cover the whole sky, the color of the clouds is gray, and there is a mist in the air that makes everything slightly damp. You could reply to the inquirer, "It is a misty, cloudy, gray day."

Your listener would probably understand that, but how might he react if you said:

"It is one of those cloud-covered days when the mist makes your clothes damp, but not quite wet."

There is a weather condition the listener can feel.

Now for another universally popular subject, the shapes of people's bodies. Our approach to this topic that should be interesting often illustrates our worst in description. For instance, there are women whose bodies lead us to say such idiotic things as "well endowed with Nature's benefits," "womanly mature," "full . . . ," and so forth. Of course, the reader gets the general idea from this sort of conversation, but what kind of an idea might he get from the following word picture?

"She was a brunette Miss America."

Admittedly, that description might paint one kind of a picture in the female mind and another in the male mind, but there can be little doubt that it paints a picture.

A less flattering picture, referring to the same general kind of female figure with a few more pounds, was used to describe some of Russia's women on the beach. The story referred to "bulging bikinis" that belied a reported food shortage.

Now let's take the woman not quite so well endowed. It would be easy to call her "thin" or "skinny," but how much better would it be to describe her figure as "boyish"?

Or take the thin man. We might also call him "skinny" or "thin as a beanpole" but the tragic scenes that writers painted for us after the capture of concentration camps in World War II gave us the description for the horribly thin man. Those writers wrote: "skeletons with skin."

For the overweight man, the word "fat" means almost nothing. For good description it obviously makes a difference where the fat is located. Sometimes the much-used word "barrel" does come close to fitting, but as Bob Wells points out, 243 pounds does a pretty good job, too.

There is no need to continue with these examples. In fact, to the delight of the writer who describes this way, there is no end of examples. Even the professionals who shy away from comments on description know this technique and use it.

Anthony B. Lewis of *The New York Times* described a characteristic when he referred to a troubling speech defect which bothered the subject of one of his stories. Lewis believes that the description of this characteristic brought the subject to life as a human being—and incidentally evoked sympathy for him, "I think, though he might disagree," Lewis adds.

Ed Cony of *The Wall Street Journal,* who likes to use facts instead of generalization, really describes with his facts. In a story about a very successful Hollywood agent Cony did not say that the man had a flashy sports car. Cony wrote, "the white Jaguar, Model XK-140, squeals to a halt at the main gate of Warner Brothers studio. . . ." Cony did not describe the man's office as "plush." He wrote about air conditioning and the beige carpet which contrasted harmoniously with the modern Danish furniture in a rich walnut. And to cinch the point he pointed out the original paintings by Matisse and Braque on the walls. Cony did not say the man ran up a huge phone bill. He wrote, "monthly phone bill—at least $200."

George Mills of *The Des Moines Register* used facts to describe a pitiful situation he found in an Iowa state institution for the mentally retarded. Mills discovered that a man had been kept in the institution for 59 years by mistake. The reporter did not say the subject had an above average IQ. He wrote,

> His IQ (intelligence quotient) is 120. That is above average for the entire population. An individual is regarded as fully normal if he has an IQ between 90 and 110.
> Many thousands of persons are getting along all right in everyday life in Iowa with IQ's in the 80's and even less. . . .

Mills does call this man a "gentle little man," but then he adds parenthetically (5′ 6″, 140 pounds).

Obviously, this is description. Perhaps, what we need is a new news definition of description. Good writers use it constantly, but when asked how they paint word pictures, they either say they do not or they are not very good at it. They are good at it—those who know how to use it—because their description flows easily into the story they are telling. It does not break in suddenly to say "now hold on while I describe this guy." Instead, with facts and phrases worked into the copy the reader gets a chance to build his mental picture of the subject.

We are not really so far from the age of flowery journalism as we may think. This is particularly true of our news stories which approach magazine article length and sometimes equal or exceed them in quality of writing. Perhaps what we now do, in really good writing, is describe the lily, but avoid the gilt. What we have done traditionally in journalism is ascribe to that lily gilt by association. Because we operated for the *peensy* adjective, we have too often forgotten to replace it with living, factual word pictures.

Case History of a Story

Student: David J. Malena.

Idea: To explain the farm surplus situation in the light of a new administration's approach to the problem.

134

Guide Line: Reduced to one county, instead of the entire Midwest, the farm surplus problems will make more sense to the reader.

Sources: History, political science, agricultural economics, census reports, Department of Agriculture publications, Department of Agriculture officials, county officials, county business men, county farmers, county representatives of state and federal farm programs.

Legwork: Reading of the research material and personal interviewing in Dodge County, Nebraska.

Organization: The whole story of farm surplus problems built around the history of farm surplus problems in one county. This required an outline, first of the major farm problems and then insertion into that outline of facts and figures from Dodge County, Nebraska.

Results: This story was published by both farm magazines and newspapers. In some cases, because of its length, it was run in installments by the newspapers. After publication, requests came for copies of it from papers in other parts of the country whose editors believed they could apply the technique to their own particular farm surplus problems.

(This story was particularly difficult to write because of the much used but often misunderstood vocabulary that has grown up around farm surplus problems. Furthermore, the readers are so used to hearing about farm surpluses in hundreds of millions and billions that they seem immune to such astronomical figures. Malena had to paint word pictures throughout his story to give his reader something to cling to. Since we are interested here in his use of description, examples have been excerpted from his story. Pertinent passages have been italicized and parenthetical remarks inserted where necessary.)

The Story:

Back in the 1940's, a farmer named Bob Beckwith decided the sandy bottomland soil on his farm in Dodge County needed a shot in the arm. The soil got it, and out of the incident grew a *million dollar headache for Dodge County.*

The needed boost, Beckwith figured, should come from some form of fertilizer. Finally in Omaha he found 2 tons of commercial fertilizer for which he had to pay nearly $100 a ton.

Fate took a hand when he applied the fertilizer. . . .

"The neighbors really took notice," Beckwith recalls, "and after that, more and more fertilizer was used around here."

That was the start of a march of technocracy that has resulted the country over, in one of America's greatest strengths—and one of its greatest problems. The only consolation for Dodge County is that its problem is shared by practically every county in the *giant green grain belt.* [Sometimes, even the *peensy* adjectives can form an effective alliteration.] *The headache, of course, is a thing called farm surpluses.*

The difference between the pains in Dodge County and the nation is only in degree. In Dodge County the *perennial headache throbs at the million-dollar rate. Nationally, it pounds away by the billion. Billion upon billion upon billion.* [Everyone has had a headache and the repetition of the word billion resembles its throb.]

How did this headache get started—what has caused it to grow —and is there a remedy? Many Americans believe and certainly hope there is a *long-range remedy, but meanwhile, as in all modern medication there have been painkillers.*

There was the Henry Wallace variety, the Ezra Benson variety, and now a new one compounded by Drs. John F. Kennedy, Orville Freeman, and a five-month-old Congress. The newest is admittedly only a painkiller. It carries in its title—The Emergency Feed Grain Program—the word "emergency," indicating that it only hopes to ease the throbbing until a more lasting cure can be found.

What about a more permanent remedy? . . .

(Familiar things help describe.)

Dodge County is approximately 22 miles square with a bit of land sticking out of its southeast corner like a thumb on a mitten. The fertile farming county is bounded by the Platte River on the south and the Elkhorn on the northeast. . . .

(Comparisons, even impossible ones, help paint mental pictures.)

Today Nebraska has a warehouse capacity of 437 million bushels. It would take a granary 20 feet wide, 15 feet high, and going around the world one and one-fifth times to hold all that grain. . . .

136

(A descriptive gimmick, such as the headache, can also be used as a transition.)

Dodge County had pains of a different kind when the county was just an infant. The youngster then was concerned with hunger and plagues. . . .

(A play on words sometimes amounts to description.)

The depression and drought of the 1930's arrived. Along with the *dust bowl* came another kind of *bowl—an alphabet soup bowl full of triplets and quadruplets of letters. WPA, PWA, AAA, CCC, FSIC, and SCS* became part of the language. *The steps of the Dodge County courthouse became the auction block for foreclosure sale after foreclosure sale.* Farmers killed little pigs by the thousands, and prices on livestock and grain hit rock bottom. The government came to the farmer's aid under the Roosevelt "New Deal." Price support became a by-word.

By the late 1930's rain began to fall again and one of the *symptoms that would lead to surplus could be heard rumbling over hill after hill.* Technology was on the march. Tractor wheels rolled over the fertile black soil of Dodge County. By 1940 there were 1,447 tractors compared to 570 in 1925. . . .

(Analogies help paint pictures.)

Now little *tin towns began to appear* at highway intersections, in the back yards of the county's existing towns, and in the middle of open fields. *The sole residents of these towns of tin* were corn and wheat. . . .

(Facts describe better than generic adjectives.)

The size of Johnson's farm is another symptom. His 440 *acres* and *three tractors* is a far cry from *the* 160 *acres* and a *mule or a horse* of the county's pioneers.

Johnson had 200 *acres of corn* last season, of which he sold 75 percent as seed.

"I remember when I raised 45 *bushels of seed corn per acre in* 1945. This year I had a 100-*bushel an acre yield,*" he added. . . .

(Malena could have said that Americans' eating habits had changed, thus increasing the surplus problem. Instead, he talked in terms that any housewife who has ever gone to a grocery store could understand.)

The second symptom turned up at the *dining table*. Americans were no longer satisfied with *bread, beans, and potatoes*. They wanted *meat, fruits, and vegetables*. Two Fremont grocers can tell that story to the *tune of the cash register*.

"*Fifty-pound sacks of flour have died; we almost don't carry them*," said V. A. Peterson.

The long-time store manager also added that his store carries 50 *percent less potatoes* than it did three years ago. . . .

(Malena's story illustrates the use of factual description that paints word pictures. In this case, the description did more than simply liven up the story. It took a complicated subject and made it more understandable.)

12

The Writer in His Habitat

There comes a time when you are the loneliest man in the world. There is nothing you can do about it. There is nothing anyone can do to help you. You are a professional reporter. You are a professional writer. You cannot, as do the boys who sit around and talk about it in the coffee shops, write only when you feel like writing. You are a pro. You make your living this way. You must write whether you feel like it or not. You must write whether you particularly like the story or not. Sometimes you are alone, but you don't feel lonely because the story beneath your fingertips turns out smoothly, a delight to you as you write it. But if you have been in this business as a student or a professional very long you know those times are the rare ones. The other times, the times you have to fight it, the times when no one can help you, are the usual ones—the lonely ones.

And you know that imagination, creativity, all the words that mean good writing, are part of the paradox of this demanding, emotional business of the master reporter.

Emotion—meaning, in this case, enthusiasm—is part of the best reporting, and no honest journalist can deny it. How can you possibly expect your reader to be emotional enough about your writing to choose you instead of the competition if you yourself cannot be emotional? Remember the "safe pilots" slogan? "There are no old, bold pilots." A paraphrase of it is true in our business. "There are no old, cold masters."

It does not matter that you probably write amid the noise of a crowded city room. You feel the thrill of good writing amid all that noise whether you show it or not. And you are lonely whether you show it or not.

Because now all the preparation is complete. Everyone who can help you has helped you as much as you can be helped. Your editor has assisted in the planning, you have researched, you have outlined. In essence, all that has been written in the preceding nine chapters involves preparation for this moment. All that preparation will be worthwhile if it now frees your mind and talent to concentrate on writing.

But, this is also the moment for an attack of writer's inertia. This is when you show you are a pro, because you know that all this talk about having to write to release what is inside of you is just that—talk. Writing is hard, demanding, lonely work. If you are like most good reporters this is the time when you will do almost anything to avoid getting started. You will have a bite to eat. A cup of coffee takes a bit of time. The typewriter may need a new ribbon. You may even clean the keys. An excuse, any excuse, to put off this moment.

Nothing that has been written to this point really tells you how to write. It only tells you what to do to get ready to write. Its sole purpose is to help prepare you for this moment when you can either start writing or sit there with a case of "write fright." Your guide line tells you where you are going. If your research is complete, it provides the fuel to get there. If your outline is good, you have the route. There is only one thing left to do—write.

It may help you, as it does many good writers when time is available, to assume that your first draft will have to be rewritten. Then you can write with comparative relaxation, knowing you'll get another crack at it. There was a day in the newsroom that is not yet over when the city editor could scream with outrage when he found a reporter writing the "first" draft of a hurry-up story. Traditionally in this business the first draft has been the last draft, but that day is passing.

Where quality is becoming more important than speed, that quality demands time to write well. Top professionals talked unashamedly in earlier chapters about first drafts, writing a chronology of the story, and rewriting a half a dozen times if necessary. This is part—an important part—of the birth of a depth story. So, now write.

Of course, as you write you are going to run into bumpy spots. That is what this chapter is about. Not to tell you how to write, but to offer some help when the going gets rough.

On many depth stories the first bump—the first apparently blank wall—will involve the statistics you may have collected during your massive research job. They are necessary to your story. No one will deny that. In them may lie the proof—the fact—that is the basis for your story. You cannot do without them, but as you write you make an alarming discovery. Suddenly you are writing with numbers instead of words. And if you have to write with numbers, something is wrong. Mathematicians the world over communicate with numbers. But your language is English—English words.

I know you may hate tables. I suspect you may hate other people's tables, not yours, because you know how important yours are to your story. But tables are the answer. If you have great bodies of statistical proof, they belong in well-edited, easily understood tables. They belong physically near your story so that you can refer to them.

Producing attractive tables—attractive is enough, nobody is going to make them beautiful—is the cooperative job of the editor and the reporter. Both must remember that their reader is lost if a table becomes complicated. If it is not complicated, if it is laid in properly with the story, then the reporter can and should refer to it as much as is necessary in the copy. And its comforting presence will keep him writing with words instead of numbers.

Unfortunately, though you should have been prepared for it, the next blank wall you hit may be the startling discovery that you don't have just one story. You believe suddenly that you have three or four or five. Your outline should have told you this, but outlines, thank goodness, are not infallible. As a matter of fact, this may be your first opportunity to tear up an outline and write another.

You may find that if the story is broken up into several parts with a subject for each part, the whole thing starts to fall together.

Good. Go ahead and write it that way if it will help. But keep in mind the experience of one of the men who has contributed to this book. He told you about writing a series over a several-month period, but it had never seemed right. Finally, he condensed the whole thing into a 1,500-word story that was right. It is entirely possible that he would never have produced the better short version had he not first written the long one.

You will find an honest difference among newsmen about series. Some say that a reader cannot be held for more than a column or two on one subject. They believe that long stories should be broken up and run in parts over several days.

Other newsmen cite readership figures which usually show a sharp drop in readership after the first or second installment of a series. This can sometimes be avoided by page-one play day after day. However, there is little doubt that most series lose readership proportionately with the number of days they run.

I side with those who are afraid they lose readers after the first installment. However, my reasons may not be the same as theirs.

First, it bothers me to talk about giving the reader a complete story when I may be giving it to him a little bit at a time. Second, I object to the competition's having a monopoly on holding the reader on any one subject for any length of time. Often you have heard someone say about a magazine article or a book, "I simply couldn't put it down." How many times have you heard anyone say that about a newspaper story? I know the answer to that, but I have a question:

"Why shouldn't they say it about a news story?"

If a depth story is really worth all the time and effort put into it —and I am sure it is—then it is worth the advantage of giving it to the reader the first day in one beautifully written and edited package.

Now, for the third blank wall. As you write you may have that queasy feeling that you are beginning to get dull. You could be wrong. You could be too close to the story. Writing is so much slower than reading that maybe the reader will not notice the dullness. But if you feel that haunting sense of dullness, you should heed it. At least, stop long enough to see if it also reads dully. If it does, do something about it. One thing you can do about it is to lean on your research. All the time you researched, whether it was through files, books, reports, or in personal interview, you should have been alert for anecdotes. And when you heard one, you should have put it down on a piece of paper, not simply saved it by memory to amuse the boys back at the office. They can be lifesavers—

those anecdotes—when you discover your story has grown dull. Earlier, anecdotes were discussed as transitions, leads, and endings. Don't be afraid to use them also to liven dull spots.

When I think of anecdotes, I also think of a bright young reporter who was sent to interview the president of a national Sunday school teachers' association. With due apologies to Sunday school teachers, I cannot think of many interviews with the potential for dullness as this one.

The bright young reporter was told appropriately, "For heaven's sake, try to find something that would interest someone besides the rest of the Sunday school teachers."

She returned from her interview smiling, but convinced of failure.

"Didn't you get something new?" she was asked.

"No," she said, "it was the same old stuff she has said before."

"Then," said the not-surprised city editor, "what are you smiling about?"

"It was what she said," replied the reporter. "She said, 'the trouble with teaching Sunday school is that teacher says sit still, and God says wiggle.'"

She put that quote in her lead and the story was picked up all over the country, even in cities where the Sunday school official had made the same old speech.

There is no need to keep pounding away at the importance of anecdotes. You enjoy a chuckle. Why shouldn't your reader, if it does not get in the way of the facts? Anecdote-collecting is insurance for the good reporter, not a hobby.

Other raw material collected by reporters can help those dull spots. That material, of course, is lively quotes. Good quotes, because they are said by people, can make a story live. But do you realize that quotes can also kill a story?

It is easy for a writer to say to himself as he starts to use quoted material, "Now, for a moment, I am off the hook. I am not writing; this guy is talking. How he talks is his own business."

But when you leave a source on his own in your story, you have abdicated from control. You cannot afford to do it. Quoted material can be as deadly as the dullest writing. You should judge it just as critically as you judge your own writing. If the quote is verbose, complicated, or confusing, don't use it. If you know what the source meant (and you must) then paraphrase it so the reader can understand also. There is nothing sacred about the way a source says something. What is sacred is what he says. If you quote him directly, you must leave his words alone. If you paraphrase him, you must leave his idea alone, but you can express it in a way that the reader can understand. That is your obligation toward quotes.

Punctuation, too, can help you make quotes more valuable. There is one technique which the beginner normally overdoes or misuses. That is the technique of breaking the long quote with attribution. The beginner invariably does it too often and makes the break in the wrong place. For example, look at this quote:

"The world either must learn to live peacefully with the atom or it will die by it."

It could be broken like this:

"The world either must learn to live peacefully with the atom," he said, "or it will die by it."

That break by the attribution, "he said," may even have helped that quote. It placed additional emphasis on the last six dramatic words. Now look at what it could have done.

"The world either must learn," he said, "to live peacefully with the atom or it will die by it."

In that case, the break by the attribution also broke the thought of the quote. That, of course, is the clue. If you break a quote, break it logically where a speaker might pause, or where the mind reading it might like to pause. Do not break it just for the sake of breaking it.

Quote marks along with quotes are sometimes abused. There is a tendency to overuse quote marks. Some of it involves an effort to be fair, and some of it is pure snobbishness. Let's take the last kind first. Probably because they have been told too often that they are writing for a sixth- or eighth-grade audience, too many writers are very conscious of their own vocabularies. Sometimes they use a word which they doubt their sixth- or eighth-grade audience would understand. Nevertheless, they know it would be the best word for that particular spot. So they use it but very carefully enclose it in quotation marks. In essence, those quote marks say, "I know this word. It is the right word, but you, you uneducated boob, probably don't know it."

Why do that? If it is the right word and you doubt that your reader understands it, then use it, but define it. Don't throw it in his face all wrapped up in snobbish quotation marks.

The reverse sometimes happens, too. From the idiom of the language, from the colloquialisms, from the slang, you pick a word that is just right for a particular situation. But this time you are a little self-conscious about using it. So, you throw some quote marks around it and what do they say? "This is not a word I normally use. I know better, but you'll understand it. And it happens to fit here."

Again, if the word fits, if it is the word to use, if you feel it is the best word for the situation, then it is part of your vocabulary and don't denounce it with a set of supercilious quote marks.

There is another use of quote marks that is too often superfluous. It involves the use of partial quotation marks. Often in paraphrasing, you may use only a phrase from the original direct quote. Normally, you are tempted by ethics and a sense of fairness to put quotation marks around that phrase. Simple honesty is involved if that phrase expresses opinion. If it does, it is both ethical and sometimes effective to use the quote marks. If, however, the phrase is simply a coincidence between the original quotation and your paraphrase then don't confuse the reader with the extra quotation marks. That quotation about living with the atom is an example. You might paraphrase it like this:

If the world does not learn to live peacefully with the atom, then mankind will die by it.

Your paraphrase and the original quotation coincide in two phrases: "to live peacefully" and "will die by it." Assuming that the reader understands clearly that you are giving the opinion of the speaker there is no need to put quote marks around the first phrase—"to live peacefully." However, the second phrase—"will die by it"—has a sense of opinion. Quote marks seem legitimate here and they add a dramatic touch.

Finally, quotations mean only as much as their perspective. That is not as confusing as it sounds. Take the quote we have been using as an example. It is a good one. It gives a momentous message to the world. But the world has a way of not getting very excited about momentous messages unless it knows more about their source. If you put a quote like this into its environment, you also put the reader into that environment. He can then properly judge the importance of the quotation. Suppose the following information had accompanied that quote:

"This is where I can put the atom into its perspective," said Dr. William Smith.

He glanced around the living room of his comfortable, 30-year-old home. His wife, Jeane, brought their year-old daughter, Bonnie, for a goodnight kiss from daddy. The Nobel-prize-winning physicist ruffled Bonnie's black hair and affectionately patted her on the bottom. The Smiths' three other children watched television in the next room.

"My wife and I like big families," Dr. Smith chuckled. "Obviously, we think the world can live with the split atom."

He puffed at his after-dinner cigar for a moment. As he blew away the smoke he smiled again.

"Yes," he said, "here with my family I can put the atom into the perspective it must assume. Here I know that the world will either learn to live peacefully with the atom, or it will die by it. And I know that man and the civilization he knows must not cower before the atom."

It took more space that way, but it was also many times more effective.

The verb tense you use can also slow you down. The beginning reporter is told, "Use active, not passive verbs." The advice is good. It is a little difficult to follow, but it is good. In the first place, not very many people really understand the difference between an active and a passive verb. They know, for instance, that the being verbs—am, is, are—are passive. Beyond that, they find it a bit difficult to tell the difference. That is because it is difficult.

The writer with experience may find that he gets more to the point when he worries about the tense of verbs. How many times, when writing, have you found that you have worked yourself into a perfect tense? If you want an example, look at that last sentence.

Perfect tenses have a way of automatically slowing down your story. They add one and sometimes two more words to the verb and seem to remove the reader one step further away from the action. That does not mean you should never use perfect tenses. Basically, you are in the business of using good English. If a situation calls for the perfect tense, then use it. However, avoid getting into perfect tense and staying there. That may be the very thing that is ringing those alarm bells in your mind, telling you, "This story is slowing down; it is getting dull." When that happens and you notice you have been using the perfect tenses, particularly past perfect, it may help if you work your way as quickly as possible out of the perfect tense. Perhaps an example will help:

> Lt. John Jones crouched low in his shallow foxhole. He could hear his men in the darkness all around him. Some groaned. Others were silent with the silence of the dead. A few, like himself, were uninjured. [Now, comes a necessary switch into a perfect tense.] But Jones, who *had been* in the front lines for only five minutes, knew that if he didn't act in the next five minutes, the entire platoon would be wiped out.
>
> The time was September 23, 1944. The place was a French vineyard. Jones *had been* sent up to Company D as a replacement. He *had been* told he would not have to assume command at once but would have a chance to observe battle conditions. [Note how the past perfect tense already is beginning to strain.]
>
> To Jones, it seemed as if the orders sending him up to the front *had been* made in another world. As he *had dug* deeper into the muddy hillside, he *had remembered* the general's exact words.
>
> "Jones," General Hugh Smith *had said,* "I want to know what is happening up there on Hill B. When you go up there, find out for me."
>
> Jones *had grinned* at the general. "Yes, sir," the young officer *had said,* "this is what I have been waiting for."
>
> [It is time to get out of the perfect tense.] The young lieutenant *stepped* from the door of the general's headquarters into a waiting Jeep and *drove* northward. . . .

It is, admittedly, a little thing. Perfect tense was perfectly grammatical in this case, but it slowed the story and made it read roughly. The sooner the writer got out of it, the better off were both he and his reader.

Earlier, there was a suggestion that you try present tense to give life and directness to your story. Don't be afraid to do it. You will find that simple present tense and simple past tense frequently help you move your story along when more complicated tenses tend to slow it.

There also have been some suggestions about the person in which you write. It is possible that newspaper writing has divorced itself too much from the first and second persons—*I* and *you.* Try them. See if they are effective in getting directly to the reader or in making the reader feel he is part of the story.

However, while journalism has divorced itself from this personal approach, it still uses too often those great, generic, first-person pronouns that mean gloriously "all of us." You know the kind I mean: The chairman said *we* all have to get *our* shoulders behind *our* Community Chest drive or *we* will fail. In direct quotes, those words are fine, even if they don't mean very much. But outside of quote marks there is little excuse for them. Who is "we"? What is "ours"? "We" may be the people who contribute to the Community Chest drive in Zanesville, Ohio. If so, say so. Facts are better than adjectives, and they also are better than glorious generic pronouns.

In keeping with the philosophy of this book, none of what has been said in this chapter has involved taking you by the hand and telling you how to write. That is still a lonely mental process between you and your story and you and your reader. All that has been discussed amounts only to suggestions for help over the bumpy spots. There is one more proposition you should consider.

It is something many of us learned by accident. Have you ever lost a page out of a long complicated story? And, having lost it, made the embarrassing discovery that you not only didn't need it, but the story read better without it? If that hasn't happened to you . . . next time a story slows down on you . . . next time a paragraph or a sentence or a phrase or a word bothers you . . . next time you try to work it over and save it, but it just doesn't seem to write right . . . when that happens, try doing without it. What you leave out of a story sometimes helps it immensely.

13

Of Men and Boys

Journalists in the newsroom and in *academia* have a good time fighting over the worth of journalism schools. This release of professional pontification is probably healthy for both groups since there are ulcers outside the newsroom as well as in it. However, the running to-be-or-not-to-be battle over journalism schools doesn't settle very much in the way of the major problem in the business today.

We can spend another decade or two alternately tearing down and defending journalism schools. During that ten years another generation of sharp young people who should be in the newsroom will have roamed into other businesses.

There are also those who claim these bright youngsters roam into journalism. That theory—I call it the "roam-in reporter" myth—is one of the weakest alibis of a business whose personnel work can most kindly be described as eccentric. This myth goes something like this:

"The best newspapermen are not particularly trained in their business. Usually they are graduates of liberal arts, business, teachers college, engineering, law, and what have you. They're bright kids, you understand. They just don't quite fit in the field they trained for. In fact, they just stumble around for a while without knowing just what they want to do. Finally, they fall into journalism—to fill an empty stomach, often as not—and from then on they climb to the top."

In a day when American newspapers are called upon to make

sense of a steadily more complicated world, this myth approaches the absurd. If a man without training decides that he has the ability to practice medicine, we call him a quack and send him to jail. The same is true in a dozen other professions, but in journalism we have been plagued with a myth that has produced a few top-notch newsmen, and given city editors ulcers over the thousands who were just fumbling their way into and out of the business.

Run an ad in your local daily newspaper advertising for a reporter. No matter where that ad runs, you will be amazed at what it produces. They'll pour in on you—complete with trench coats—from the plumber's shop, the TV repair business, the school teachers' ranks, and from the unemployment bureau. They'll have just one thing in common:

"I always thought it would be kind of fun being a newspaper reporter, and lots of people think I have talent."

This may be stretching it a bit, but not too much. Far too many American editors hire their help, using the myth of the "roam-in reporter." Take the editor who hired a very bright-appearing, well-groomed young man, despite the protestations of his city editor. When the city editor returned from lunch to find the young man sitting in the newsroom at a desk, he stormed into the editor's office.

"Did you hire that guy?" he demanded.

"Yes, I did," the editor replied.

"But," the city editor almost screamed, "he can't even type."

"I know," replied the editor, "but he has such a fine personality."

Of course, the roam-in-reporter myth has, like most myths, some basis in fact. There are some magnificent newsmen who got into the business this way. Some of them, Pulitzer-prize winners, Neiman Fellows, are quoted in this book. But for every one of these success stories, only the nation's city editors know how many failures there are. The city editors caught them as they roamed into the newsroom. The city editors tried, in the midst of the newsroom rat race, to train them. Then, nine times out of ten, the city editors sent them roaming back to the plumber's shop, the TV repair business, the school teachers' ranks, and the unemployment bureau.

However, it must be true that you can make a reporter out of a man in six months on a newspaper. Heaven knows, it has been said often enough. It must be equally true that a copyreader of sorts can be built from raw material in the same length of time.

It is probably just as true that a trainee in a doctor's office can learn to recognize measles and how to jam a thermometer into the patient's mouth. He might even learn how to read the thermometer in six months. But it would scare you to death if he got within ten feet of your appendix.

Some newspapers do have very good on-the-job training programs. Many of them, however, are giving further training to journalism graduates. Editors in other newsrooms, where six months are supposed to produce newsmen, are beginning to wonder. They know they can in six months produce from, say, a strictly liberal arts graduate, a hack. With few exceptions he is good enough to get by, but not good enough to be good.

Now, don't loose upon me the wrath of all the liberal arts graduates among the nation's best newsmen. Liberal arts must play a major role in journalism education, providing it provides a truly liberal education. In fact, the next section of this book is devoted to liberal education.

However, it is time the nation's editors shove back their chairs and do a little thinking about those twin truisms—the roam-in reporter and the six-month wonder. Having thought, they must decide what kind of reporters are really needed to write in depth. Then, they must decide where they are going to get them.

First, what does it take to report in depth?

It takes brains, imagination, creativity, intellectual discipline, liberal education, ability to write, professional know-how, and a love of the business.

Where are we going to find all of that?

I would like to reply, "In the schools of journalism." I must reply, "In *some* schools of journalism."

We have had quite enough school of journalism products who are only graduates in criticism of the business. Educated criticism should lead to improvement of the profession. But, too frequently, these bachelors of criticism have spent so much time learning to defame their business that they have not had time enough to learn the business itself.

We also have had quite enough of the journalism professors who shudder and look for a hiding place when they hear the word, "technique." Their word for it is "trade school," and they would like to make journalism into a social science.

I know of journalism professors who at social functions call themselves social scientists "to avoid embarrassing" their other university colleagues. I sometimes wonder if these men would also like to make social sciences out of medicine, dentistry, law, and architecture. I suppose an architect could be a social scientist. He frequently is interested in better living standards, slum clearance, and aesthetics. But I also hope he knows how to design a support beam for my ceiling so that the roof won't fall in.

Obviously, for depth reporting we need men and women who can use both the techniques of the profession and broad liberal arts educations. They could be acquired one at at time—the liberal arts in college and the techniques later in the Utopian newsroom that is also a professional school.

However, in the right schools of journalism future newsmen can get both at the same time. Is that better? Think for a moment about that architectural student. Put him in an engineering class on structural supports. If he knows that later he is going to use that information on support beams, is he going to be more or less interested?

Now substitute that architectural student for a journalism student in a class on political science, history, economics, or any one of a dozen background areas. If the nation's thinking editors could be wielding the whip in those liberal arts classrooms they would be demanding that their future newsmen be the best students in the place. They would be pointing out that no other students would put the information to better use.

But the nation's thinking editors cannot be in those classrooms. They can only hope that their liberal arts graduates will remember enough so that it will be of use when they do get around to learning to write.

There is something better than blind hope. There is the kind of journalism school that teaches the techniques—yes, the techniques —in such a way that journalism students know they have to be the sharpest youngsters in the liberal arts classrooms.

Individually, neither the liberal arts nor the techniques mean much. You can learn about political science, but it does not do you, the journalist, much good if you can't apply it to local governmental problems, and do it in understandable, readable English. You can sharpen your writing, but it doesn't do much good in the newspaper business if you don't have any facts to write about.

What does all this have to do with depth reporting?

Everything.

What kind of students can do this demanding and important job?

They have to know enough about history to go to the right places to ask their questions. They have to know enough about political science to ask the right questions. They have to know enough about English to make it work for them. They have to know enough about writing to be the equivalent of the average two-year veteran in the average newsroom. And they have to have enough imagination— creativity, if you like—to be able to see a half-dozen ways to attack an assignment, not just one. There are a lot of blind alleys on the trail of a good story.

How do you find out all this? You give the students a chance to find out for themselves. It quickly separates the men from the boys.

Earlier you read a delightful piece by the AP's word-master, Saul Pett. He had a nasty suggestion:

> Want to separate the men from the boys? Give a man a good feature assignment and then take away all his alibis in advance. Tell him he has all the time he needs. Tell him if the first two interviews don't do it, he can go back again. Tell him all we want is the best story he can do.

How often can that be done in the newsroom? Not very often, if at all—for the beginner. But it can be done in the right schools of journalism. A student can be told:

"You have all the time you need. You can think about and talk about your story idea as long as it takes to get just the right approach. You have all the resources of a university within walking distance. If you have to travel or telephone long distance, there may even be money for that. And when you write, you can rewrite six times, if necessary, until both of us are satisfied. All you have to do is produce a depth story that the newspapers will be anxious to run."

There it is. And Pett is right. It's a nasty thing to do. To the student it may mean investing 100 hours in one story. To the instructor it may mean investing outside of class an average of three to four hours for every student. But it gets results.

Introduction

The research for this section started when one too many students asked, "What book can I read to help with this depth story?"

The question, of course, was a healthy sign. The student had discovered why he had been told a journalist needs a broad, liberal education. He had discovered that the origins of most depth stories lie somewhere in the knowledge accumulated by one or more academic disciplines. Already the discovery had sent him scurrying back for help from a political science, history, or economics professor under whom he had taken classwork. The shocked, but pleased, professors were helpful, but the student soon ran out of professors. He had not and could not have taken classwork in all of the 15 or 20 basic areas into which his depth stories sent him. He soon realized that he needed something to fill in the holes—something to give him a starting point in the many areas in which he had not taken formal instruction.

He knew there was no substitute for the proven combination of a good teacher and good textbooks. But lacking those, he needed a book or possibly several books. He did not expect the book or books to replace 12 hours of classwork. He just wanted to start by learning enough to ask intelligent questions. That, when you think about it, is not too bad an educational goal for any journalist.

After a parade of these requests that would have warmed a librarian's heart, I became embarrassed. I had very quickly run out of answers. Someone had to find out if there were books, understand-

153

able to the liberal arts student, in more than a dozen basic academic areas. In this case, the someone was me (see Bergen Evans on English usage) and Mrs. Emily E. Trickey, my research assistant.

After we started the search professional journalists heard about it and asked for copies of the result. Their questions also added another facet to our quest. We were now also looking for ready, factual reference materials from these academic areas. This proved a worthwhile expansion. Among other things, I made an embarrassing discovery. I could have saved my former publishers great anguish over expense accounts had I only known what was available in nearby libraries. And that was beyond the factual inaccuracies I could have avoided.

This section is the result of our search. We do not claim it is complete. But we do believe it is a starting point to fill in holes in this vague thing called a broad, liberal education. We do believe it is a refresher for those long enough out of the classroom to be hazy about the basics they learned there. We believe it provides any number of launching platforms for educated questions—the only kind that get depth answers.

14

Quest for a Nibliography

A typographical error in one of the first drafts of this section produced the word *nibliography*. We could not, had we tried, have coined a more perfect word.

Out of all the books in all the academic disciplines we can hope only to give you an enticing nibble. We hope, of course, the nibble will lead to an 18-course Chinese meal. It started with our quest for a *nibliography*. We sought the proof to an almost sanctified theory on the education of a journalist:

"What journalism needs is more expert reporters with sound, well-rounded, liberal educations."

That is the very logical conclusion that inevitably approaches the problem of getting better young reporters into the business and keeping them there. This reasoning takes place everywhere from a journalism faculty meeting to coffee at the city desk to a cocktail at the American Society of Newspaper Editors convention. The proposition goes something like this:

Ideally, we should have an expert reporter who is also an expert in a given area.

We should have these experts for every major news area on our newspapers.

Unfortunately, except for a few metropolitan papers, none of us can afford that many reporters, let alone that many experts.

Therefore, what we need is more expert reporters with sound, well-rounded, liberal educations.

Having made the circuit in the favorite journalism personnel proposition, the thoughtful newspaper executive and journalism teacher have only one other question they must answer:

"How do you know you are getting a reporter with that sound, well-rounded, liberal education?"

The good executive or the good teacher can usually tell whether he is getting a man with the potential of a good reporter. The right kind of journalism education coupled with practical experience during college years should provide ample evidence. Normally, if a student has had the opportunity to produce under professional guidance, a qualified observer should be able to tell a great deal about that student before he graduates. There should be evidence of desire, willingness to work, alertness, and the ability to dig. Also, if that student has had the opportunity to develop his writing skill under professional guidance, there should be at least hints of evidence about his writing ability.

Now, consider the second half of the proposition—that sound, well-rounded, liberal education. How do you judge that? In the case of the fresh graduate, do you examine his transcript of grades, assess the quality of the institution from which he graduated, and then try to guess if this student was a grade-grabber or a learner, or both? And how about the man already in the newsroom? Do you give him tests over the vast expanse included in liberal education?

Obviously, the joker in our search for the liberally educated journalist involves assessing something that cannot be accurately assessed. Maybe we should go at it in another way.

What is a liberal education supposed to do for a reporter?

Rather simply, it should provide him with an educated nose for news, which amounts to a platform from which he can spot the significance of a story, ask intelligent questions of the real experts, and then research, organize, and write his story. That's all a liberal education needs to do for a reporter, but that is one whale of a lot.

The books recommended in this section could not begin to replace a formal liberal education or a lifetime of reading. This section is not designed to do so. However, it is patterned after the idea that a liberal education should:

1. Provide a launching platform for educated questions.
2. Provide a starting point for research leading to a depth story.

These two points formed the base from which we launched our search for a practical academic aid for the newsman. Normally, you are only expected to be interested in the results of research, not the process with which it was performed. This time, however, you need to follow along on the search. You must do this in order to judge the results. If someone suggests that you read a book, you have a right to know why. So come now on a treasure hunt in *academia*.

First, we confess that this bibliography probably violates every rule ever designed for one. Librarians were among the many who advised us. We may have repaid that kindness by bending and breaking professionally proven rules for annotation. If we have, we are sorry. This reading list has a special purpose for special people. Our effort was to make it fulfill that purpose no matter what rules were violated or what sensibilities offended.

We set about our work with only one initial proposition—that you cannot recommend a book without knowing its content. Consequently every book had to be carefully examined.

Of course, we had to choose the areas from which we wanted books. That widely accepted newsroom proposition that ends with the need for a sound, round, liberal education dictated the areas in advance. We had to choose academic disciplines that provided general background. We had to avoid areas that led quickly to specialization. Agree or not, we settled upon the following areas:

Geography, geology, chemistry, physics (the physical sciences), the biological sciences, psychology, anthropology, history, sociology, political science (and law), economics (and agriculture), mathematics, the fine arts, philosophy (and religion), and English.

Actually, both religion and agriculture are used in this reading list as examples of specialization. Books on law relate only to finding the law. The remainder were considered basic background areas.

Having chosen the areas, we had to apply a strict discipline to ourselves. We had to remember for a period of months that if we were experts, we were experts in only one area—journalism. We did not pretend that we could initially pick out the proper books.

For that initial choice we went to the experts in each area and asked them for help. However, we carefully defined what we were after:

1. The readers of this list are not uneducated. In making recommendations, the experts were to assume that these people have good minds, intellectual curiosity, and usually a good education.

2. However, they were to assume also that these people lacked technical training to any great degree in any of these areas.

3. The books recommended had to have the respect of the area, or academic discipline, they reflected.

4. If possible, though not absolutely necessary, the books should be readable. This point represented a compromise in case the best information in a given area might not be well written. Happily, this was only rarely the case.

5. Finally, the book had to be understood by us, the annotators, who were forced to set ourselves up as the average in education.

When the experts understood these ground rules, they were asked for the following kinds of information:

1. Any good representative encyclopedia, dictionary, and glossary in their field.

2. Any good introduction to their field.

3. Any good interpretation of their field.

4. The classics which might form the backbone of their discipline.

5. Anything else, providing they understood the audience, they would recommend.

One limitation was imposed both upon the annotators and the experts. That was a limitation in the number of books recommended. There was no specific number over which we could not go. There was simply the rule of thumb that too many books would destroy the whole effort.

Once the experts had made their recommendations, we took over. Every book was thoroughly examined. Some immediately fit the need. Others immediately did not and were discarded. A few were added. These usually were books that for a special journalistic reason seemed good. For example, a few were added simply because they represented good writing, a thing we thought we could judge.

Our apologies for taking you through this list of rules. Honesty compelled us to make sure you understood how these recommendations were made. Quite frankly, the need for this honesty became apparent as we examined some bibliographies obviously prepared

by persons unacquainted with either the subjects of the book or
the needs of the reader to whom the bibliography was directed.
Perhaps we were naive, but we were shocked to discover reading
lists including books which had not even been seen by those doing
the recommending. This discovery of what we considered an intellectual dishonesty led us to let you in on our approach to this
bibliography.

Of course, a series of rules does not solve all the problems. Just
as no teacher or editor can anticipate all a reporter's problems in
writing a depth story, no one can anticipate all of them in doing
any kind of a thoughtful job. We discovered very early that this
quest, like a story, needed an over-all guide line. It was not hard
to find. Journalism deals in mankind. It may deal in many things
that are not immediately human, but always they are associated
with humans. We simply decided that every area would be examined as it dealt with mankind. We were interested in the world that
surrounded man. We were interested in his examination of himself. We were interested in the products of his mind. We were interested in the way he talked and the way he wrote.

We found in many areas well-written books aimed not at the
specialist in the field but at someone else. Usually, that someone
else was close enough to the journalist to make the book readable
and understandable.

For example, in this day when automatic computers loom to
many persons as awesome, mystical electronic monsters, we were
guided to a book written for businessmen. Normally, the literature
on computers is designed for scientists and engineers. This book,
written for businessmen, is carefully defined, well written, and easily
understood by the journalist.

We found also that good writers in some fields had written well
the story of how their area tied in with others. One such author
wrote about mathematics and Western culture. His book carries
the reader, via mathematics, of course, into such places as painting,
sculpture, religion, and others. These are not places one normally
associates with mathematics, yet, in this book, the association becomes normal.

In one respect, we served as prosecutor, judge, and jury. Any
book that obscured the meaning of the content by poor writing was
summarily discarded. Happily, we exercised this mental axe much

less frequently than we had anticipated. We found, instead, many instances of beautifully written material, and, frankly, some of this would have been included as an example of good writing on a complicated subject if for no other reason.

In some cases, you will find that we have included books by historical names. There are certain people about whom every liberally educated person must know. And one very good way to become acquainted is through that famous person's writings.

Men and what they do and think make up the world—at least the world of the journalist. So there needed to be an exposure to the great puzzles that exist about man himself. There needed to be an awareness, for instance, that evolution of man and the study of it has not dimmed, but has accelerated many times since World War II. Is it important to the journalist? Listen to Julian Huxley:

> Furthermore, I have attempted to present a point of view: It is always based on facts, but is in many respects a particular and personal one. I hold strongly that without some kind of knowledge of evolution one cannot hope to arrive at a true picture of human destiny.

The study of man involves men and their lives. Every good reporter knows that one of the best ways to tell a story is to tell it through a human experience. For that reason, biographies were frequently chosen.

You also will find recommended several collections of readings, or anthologies. Here, we trod carefully. We knew that too many anthologies appear to be the easy way to publication—via the pastepot. Maybe they are simply the result of a professor's fulfilling the publication requirements of his college. Maybe they are the result of an organization's executive secretary fulfilling the demand that "there should be a collection of readings published in our area."

This kind of anthology, unless it is well done, deserves the only legitimate kind of censorship—the refusal of a good mind to waste time.

We also found any number of books that are not included here, but should have been page one news stories. We are often too quick in the newspaper business to relegate all new books to the book review section. Sometimes a new book should be the source of a hot news story, not the subject of a review.

Often an author spends years developing research on a subject of public importance. Often the results, published as a book, are timely, significant, and new. Those elements add up to a news story today, not a review in the book section of next Sunday's paper.

Then, of course, there was the choice of the encyclopedia, the dictionary, the atlas, or the glossary. Here we let our minds be the slide rule. Of the respected encyclopedic volumes suggested to us, we chose those which seemed to best fit the journalist's needs. Sometimes we recommended only one of several excellent reference works. In such cases the recommendation simply serves as an example of what is available to the fact-hungry journalist in a given field. In fact, much of this reading list is an example, a starting point. To have listed every one of the acceptable encyclopedias for each specialized area would have destroyed by volume alone the whole idea for the bibliography.

You might like to know how encyclopedias were approached. We make no claim to having read our way through a 20-volume set or even a 1,500-page single reference. But we did examine them from the newsman's viewpoint.

Lest we be guilty of the surface approach for a depth bibliography we asked for and sought examples of books that bridge all the areas and point out problems beneath the surface of an age that reaches for the stars. We were delighted with one by C. P. Snow. Here is a quote from our annotation of that little volume:

> His access to the top figures of both worlds gives authority to his contention that there exists a serious and ever-widening gap in the understanding between the two.

Snow, of course, was worried about the widening gap between the scientific and the literary worlds.

At first glance, some of the areas included in this bibliography would seem to be highly specialized, just what the annotators said they were not going to do. But normally these specialized areas represent examples of what the journalist himself can do if he has need for highly specialized background. In other cases the title of the area alone does not tell the depth story of its general worth to liberal education.

Such is the case of the bibliography for religion. Although this bibliography includes very specialized encyclopedic information, that is not its primary purpose. Religion has the unique distinction of being one of the most thoroughly covered and most neglected

areas of American journalism. Here, surface is the rule almost
without exception. Here, where man puzzles over the great question
marks of his being, the newspaper usually tells about his traditional,
routine observance of worship in church. One of the writers annotated in the religion section phrases it this way:

> Not only is this an area in which many people are partially informed,
> but it is one to which these same people are seriously committed.

For this reason religion in this bibliography not only includes
Biblical reference materials but tries to cover the depth area that
is the philosophy of religion.

Perhaps most difficult of all was the examination of English.
This is literature. This is semantics. This is criticism. This is lin-
guistics. And this is usage or grammar—the tool, the everyday tool
—of the journalist. What does the journalist want to know about
English? More to the point, what should he know about English?
My feelings on this subject should by now be painfully clear. The
journalist, if he wants to be a good writer, had darned well better
be having a serious love affair with the English language. Thus,
English in this bibliography is an examination of usage.

As you go through this bibliography you will immediately miss
some old friends—some factual stand-bys. That is because most of
them will be found in the last chapter of the section on general
reference materials of all kinds.

This bibliography is not an afterthought to a chapter or to a
book. It has been given its own section of this book because of its
importance.

It also has its own index in the back of the book. This index is
designed to guide you through the bibliography. With it you can
pick and choose as your needs dictate. It is organized by title,
author, and subject. It is also thoroughly cross-indexed.

Bibliographical rules have been bent and broken, annotations
have been lengthened, eyes have been strained, and tempers short-
ened to produce something that can be part of a journalist's liberal
education.

The men who helped us were top professionals. They were aware
of the need for a liberal arts education, and they were sincere in
their efforts to help us in our search. But we were forced to conclude that it is much easier to say that journalists need a broad

liberal education than it is for them to get it. All this spurred us on in our quest for the beginnings of a journalist's liberal arts bibliography.

The idea was to provide something valuable, sensible, thoughtful, and if possible, interesting. Its success, like the success of a news story, depends upon you, the reader.

15

Man and Matter

In a very general way, this chapter deals with the physical makeup and the physical laws of the earth and the universe in which man lives. Like most arbitrary divisions, this one does not quite fit.

Obviously, geography is not purely a physical science, such as physics and chemistry. Geography is a very broad science, embracing parts of many disciplines. For this very reason, it leads off this bibliography, but is otherwise illogically placed with chemistry and physics—the nearly pure physical sciences.

Despite the specialization of the individual sciences, there are basic references and readings that reach across several. You will find those at the end of this chapter. Since they relate to both the physical and biological sciences, they can serve as a bridge between the two. This chapter is organized as follows:

Geography
Geology
Chemistry
Physics
General references and readings on man and matter

The World Around You

Geography—some say this is the almost forgotten title of a dying academic discipline. They believe it to be the victim of specialization. For the sake of future journalists, let's hope not.

In the age of specialization it has been said that the avid reader of geography can appear to be thoroughly educated but have no knowledge in depth. Those who say this are obviously lukewarm to geography as a discipline. Certainly geographers who have made the subject a memory course have not contributed greatly to its intellectual prestige. But geographers and geographies can logically weave man and the world together in a way very helpful to the journalist seeking a broad education. A journalist often must start with a broad geographic point of view. When an assignment pinpoints a part of that broad viewpoint, the reporter usually learns in depth as he researches. This is a very proper intellectual use of a broad academic discipline.

And we would make two points to those who complain about geography as a "quick way to an apparent education."

First, some of the high school courses that have gobbled up or replaced geography are even broader.

Second, no teacher or writer can have endless control over the use a student or a reader makes of the subject. There are people who read the intellectually respected *Saturday Review* but never read a book. *The Saturday Review*'s editors can do little about these people who read their magazine so that they may sound well read without reading.

The share of the blame geographers must assume for the atrophy of their discipline probably cannot be determined short of the hereafter. However, no one can blame them for the use to which their art is put by mental sloths.

Do you want the history of the climate of your region? Do you want a concise paragraph on the economy of a nation in the news? Do you want to check the basic facts about a county seat in another state? Do you need a map, a gazetteer, an encyclopedia of nations?

Geography has these answers and many more. It has answers in concise, digested form. For the journalist this can be a perfect starting point. He may have to go to economics for details. He may have to go to geology or meteorology for the complete background. But he can start with a few accurate, basic facts in geography.

Geography may also be an end in itself. The literature of the discipline is crammed with facts. In some cases the facts are almost raw. There may be no interpretation, no perspective. In other cases the facts, interpretation, and perspective are woven together in a regional geography. In any case, the facts assembled by geography can be a journalistic gold mine.

You can start, for example, with a glossary of geographic terms. No one is going to suggest that you sit down and read a glossary. But if you need definitions before you venture into more specialized disciplines, you may very well find it in this glossary.

Within geography you will find other glossaries: meteorology, for example. How many days a week does a newspaper have to interpret weather terminology to its readers?

You will also find the working partners of the map world—the gazetteers and the atlases. Most newsrooms have atlases; few have gazetteers. The combination is nearly perfect. What the map cannot show, the good gazetteer can tell.

For regional accuracy and detail, aeronautical charts produced by the U.S. Air Force are recommended.

For a geographic digest of the whole world, you will find an encyclopedia of nations. There also are examples of regional geographies.

Finally, there are samples of specialization within geography itself. In this case, the examples are of political geographies.

The reasons geography has in part disappeared from the high school, and in some cases the college classroom, are tied in with the nature of geography, the nature of growing specialization, and the nature of evolving educational theory. In recent years in the post-Sputnik era, geographers and their art have risen a bit in academic esteem. There have been those bold enough to suggest its return to the high school curriculum.

As you sample this journalist's bibliography of geography, you can make your own judgments.

A Glossary of Geography

Stamp, L. Dudley, *A Glossary of Geographical Terms*. New York: John Wiley and Sons, Inc., 1961. Because geographers believed they needed a glossary, this volume was produced. The words it includes cover the vast fields that the term, geography, itself covers.

The journalist may find this glossary an excellent starting point before he ventures into other academic disciplines.

A Glossary of Meteorology

Huschke, Ralph E., ed., *Glossary of Meteorology*. Boston: American Meteorological Society, 1959. This book can serve as a major weapon in the unending battle teaming the newsmen and weathermen against hard to understand technical words. While the glossary is prepared with sufficient detail for the working specialist and understandable to the undergraduate of a technical college, it is also a handbook for the layman.

Examination of this book will quickly tell the journalist that he, too, can understand much of it. Weather has become part of his daily working life.

A couple of the ground rules for preparation of this glossary helped the newsman:

1. Mathematics could not be used as a substitute for words.
2. The first sentence or two must stand alone as a definition.

Many words from sister sciences also can be found here. Among the other sciences are hydrology, oceanography, geomagnetism, and astrophysics. The newsman who used to smile unknowingly at such obviously technical areas today only glances at the wire report and hopes the writer knew a little about the language of his subject.

Gazetteers

Seltzer, Leon E., ed., *The Columbia Lippincott Gazetteer of the World,* and supplement. New York: Columbia University Press, by arrangement with J. B. Lippincott Company, 1952. This book is an alphabetical listing of geographic places and things.

The detail is almost unbelievable to the nongeographer. Each listing includes certain basic facts. A town, for instance, is listed with census, historical facts, industry, and sometimes more. Such a gazetteer works perfectly with a good atlas. What the map cannot show, the gazetteer can tell.

Gazetteers of the Office of Geography, U.S. Department of Interior, Washington, D.C. Official Standard Names, country by country, as approved by the United States Board on Geographic Names.

This book is probably the most complete list of names available. Each entry includes coded information on location of places. These paperback books are available from the Government Printing Office.

Atlases

Williams, Joseph E., ed., *The Prentice-Hall World Atlas*. Englewood Cliffs, N.J.: Prentice-Hall, Inc., 1958. This is a beautifully reproduced atlas, well organized, thoroughly indexed, and easily understood.

The first section portrays the systematic geography of the world; the second, world economic maps; and the third, physical maps of the continents with separate maps of their geographic regions.

Maps, properly used, give better physical perspective than words or pictures. Newsmen will not only find these maps informative but should study them as examples of excellent perspective by cartography.

Espenshade, Edward B., Jr., ed., *Goode's World Atlas*, 11th ed. Chicago: Rand McNally & Co., 1960. There are 168 pages of maps showing everything from the usual "relief" maps to such things as physiography, surface, ocean and air transport, languages and religion, population, agriculture, types of farming, temperatures and annual rainfall, mineral deposits and vegetation.

There is an extensive pronouncing index, as well as a glossary of foreign geographical terms and a world comparison table giving area of principal islands, principal lakes, oceans, seas and their areas, principal mountains and their heights, and principal rivers and their lengths.

Regional Maps

World Aeronautical Charts, The Aeronautical Chart Service of the U.S. Air Force. At relatively low cost, these maps can be obtained for almost any part of the world.

For a few dollars, any newsroom can equip itself with these highly detailed maps. They show towns, roads, railroads, rivers, elevations, and almost any other information possible on a map.

An Encyclopedia

Cohen, Benjamin A., editor-in-chief, *The Worldmark Encyclopedia of Nations*. New York: Worldmark Press, Inc., Harper & Row, Publishers, 1960. Give or take a nation or two, as world changes play havoc with the map business, this volume is a digested guide to all nations.

It includes geography, history, politics, and social and economic status. The first section takes up nation by nation in alphabetical order. The information includes national symbols (flags and so on), physical description, climate, animal and plant life, language, religion, history, and biographical data on famous national figures.

The second section deals with international bodies, the United Nations, other international groupings, and such other international agreements as tariffs. For the amount of information in this volume, the journalist will find its 456 pages relatively few.

A Man-Oriented Geography

Hoyt, Joseph Bixby, *Man and the Earth*. Englewood Cliffs, N.J.: Prentice-Hall, Inc., 1962. This is a textbook with a wealth of information about man's environment and man as the modifier of his environment.

This book illustrates well the all-inclusive scope of geography. It starts with man, shifts to the physical aspects of the world, and returns again to man and his part in the physical world. The physical chapters include climate, water resources, vegetable and animal life, soil, and mineral resources. News, of course, is made when man takes a hand in modifying all of these basic elements of environment.

This well-illustrated, well-indexed book is of special value to the journalist because of its emphasis on man, whose activities are the daily newsroom fare.

Some Regional Geographies of America

Wright, Alfred J., *United States and Canada, A Regional Geography*, 2nd ed. New York: Appleton-Century-Crofts, Inc., 1956. This is an economic geography of "that portion of North America occupied almost wholly by English-speaking people."

Well illustrated with maps and photographs, it is divided into geographic sections with brief economic background, products, dominant economic forces of each area, and tables. It provides a good, quick over-all survey of geographic areas of the U.S. and Canada and the types of land and what they produce. There are bibliographical references at the ends of the various sections.

White, C. Langdon, and Edwin J. Foscue, *Regional Geography of Anglo-America,* 3rd ed. Englewood Cliffs, N.J.: Prentice-Hall, Inc., 1963. This is a widely used textbook that can serve the journalist as background reading, and, to a degree, as a reference. Awareness of the geographic regions which shaped the development of life on this continent gives a new mental dimension to North America. This book deals heavily in that dimension. It also places emphasis on the end of the frontier and the need for beginnings of conservation.

This is an example of the textbooks on this subject. The well-planned volumes, such as this one, provide a three-dimensional platform upon which the journalist can build information.

Regional Geographies of the World

The foregoing regional geographies of North America illustrate the handling of the world's regions by geographers. There are a number of excellent volumes dealing with various regions of the world. In some academic disciplines, such as history, the very volume of publications makes it difficult to locate books dealing with a large area of the world. This is true in a number of disciplines, so it is sometimes necessary to cross discipline lines to get a starting point. For example, both anthropology and geography have good regional works that can help you get started in such areas as history, economics, and political science. The following titles are by no means the only titles, but they do illustrate some of what is available in world regional geographies:

James, Preston, E., *Latin America,* 3rd ed. New York: The Odyssey Press, Inc., 1959.

Hoffman, George W., ed., *A Geography of Europe Including Asiatic USSR,* 2nd ed. New York: The Ronald Press Company, 1961.

Ginsberg, Norton S., ed., *The Pattern of Asia.* Englewood Cliffs, N.J.: Prentice-Hall, Inc., 1958.

Fitzgerald, Walter, *Africa,* 9th ed. New York: E. P. Dutton & Co., Inc., 1961.

Samples of Specialized Geographies

East, W. Gordon, and A. E. Moodie, eds., *The Changing World.* London: George G. Harrap & Co., Ltd., 1956. Some twenty ex-

perts from five countries have contributed to this lengthy (1,024
pages) discussion of political geography.

After an introductory chapter by the editors on world background, the book is divided into chapters devoted to one political-
geographic segment, such as Scandinavia and Finland, the Medi-
terranean, and so on. As might be expected, a rather large section
is devoted to the USSR.

As in the case of the Alexander book, which is annotated below, many changes have taken place since this volume was
printed. But the many clear and explicit maps and tables, as
well as the very readable text, make this an excellent choice for
the journalist.

Alexander, Lewis M., *World Political Patterns.* Chicago: Rand
McNally & Co., 1957. An over-all look at the political units
throughout the world, this book on political geography has 101
maps and is indexed mainly by geographic name rather than by
political terms or phrases.

The author states that his main concerns are given to the nature of the political control in a given region, the effects of such
control on nonpolitical aspects of the region, and the pressures
which exist for change in the type and areal extent of this
control. This whole book is an attempt at analyzing the world
political pattern.

There have been many changes in political control of regions
in the few short years since this book was published. Still, it is
most useful to the journalist as a background into some of the
how's and why's of changing political domination in many of
the restless land areas of the world.

Geology—Physical Geography in Depth

It need not concern the journalist that there may be some academic disagreement about the proper relationship of geology and
geography. If you glanced through the catalogs of various universities, you would find them listed variously as individual departments, in the same department, and perhaps as areas within a department called earth sciences.

The difference probably depends upon what is taught within the
various classes. If geography in a given university has become pri-

marily economic, then geology alone may deal with the makeup of
the earth. However, this again need not upset the journalist looking for answers from this bibliography.

The books selected under geography are relatively all-inclusive.
You will indeed find some geology there. However, to make sure
that geology as a study of the earth itself is clearly included, we
have added four purely geologic references.

Indeed, as you will find, geology itself cannot simply be classified
as a science—at least as far as the journalist is concerned. Frequently the findings of geology are the basis for international politics and economics. You need but be reminded of the occasions in
recent history when oil fields became the pawns in an international
game of chess. And, of course, oil is not the only result of geological
study that can literally change the face of the earth this science
makes its laboratory.

The following books are listed more or less in the order of their
difficulty. For example, you will find it easier to study the history
of the earth if you have a foundation in principles of geology. Also
note that almost any one of these books could serve as a reference
for the multiplicity of geology-based stories that make headlines
every day.

Principles of Geology

Gilluly, James, A. C. Waters, and A. O. Woodford, *Principles of
Geology*, 2nd ed. San Francisco: W. H. Freeman and Company,
1959. This is a respected textbook that can also serve as a reference.

For the nongeologist this book may be more understandable
than one that does more classifying and categorizing. Its authors
try to teach basics of this science by leading the reader through
the reasoning that led to discoveries. They did not forget the
political and economic influence of this science. Often these must
be the journalist's prime concern with geology.

Emmons, William H., George A. Thiel, Clinton R. Stauffer, and
Ira S. Allison, *Geology—Principles and Processes*, 4th ed. New
York: McGraw-Hill Book Company, Inc., 1955. This is a textbook
designed for both the geology student and the liberal arts student.

This well-illustrated book is recommended in this bibliography
primarily because its authors recognized the need of liberal arts

students. When such a book gains the respect of the science it represents, the journalist should also know about it.

Historical Geologies

Moore, Raymond Cecil, *Introduction to Historical Geology,* 2nd ed. New York: McGraw-Hill Book Company, Inc., 1958. This is an introductory book that assumes no previous acquaintance with the subject.

The assumption of no technical know-how and an enlightened use of specialized vocabulary make this a good book for the nongeologist. Much of the technical jargon is included on illustrations, but does not slow down the text.

Kummel, Bernhard, *History of the Earth—An Introduction to Historical Geology.* San Francisco: W. H. Freeman and Company, 1961. This is a well-organized, advanced book.

Its author presupposes background in principles of geology. The nongeologist reader will appreciate a rather lengthy introduction to the subject.

Given some background in geology, the journalist will find that this highly detailed textbook also makes a good reference.

The Smell of It

On college campuses there is always one department that literally stinks—and is proud of it.

It could be the odor that chases journalists away from chemistry, but it is not. Chemistry is not normally the easiest way to fulfill the science requirement of an arts and sciences curriculum. It requires prerequisites, such as mathematics, which journalists also traditionally do not take. And most chemistry departments, beyond their introductory course—and sometimes even including the introductory courses—are patterned for the major. These people will eat, drink, sleep, and even smell chemistry for their four years. The work they take is much too specialized for the journalist who is seeking a liberal education.

And who's to say this is not as it should be? A liberal education cannot be something made up of 14 majors.

This does not mean that the journalist need not know something about chemistry. It is possible that chemistry departments could help to a degree. They offer courses for students whose major may require some chemistry. For example, agriculture students and home economics students frequently are required to take a certain amount of chemistry. Although it would be a bearcat to teach, a course aimed specifically at the liberal arts student who takes no more formal training in chemistry would be of great value. Beyond that the newsman would need to acquire two valuable tools:

First, he would have a basis from which he could ask questions about a vast branch of the physical sciences.

Second, he would know enough about publications in the field to go to the right dictionary or encyclopedia to check facts and to get definitions.

Does the newsman need even this much knowledge about such a highly specialized field? The day's news report answers that with a resounding question mark. It asks, What is fluoridation? What is water pollution? What is smog? It asks these and many more.

This bibliography is designed to help answer those questions and to supply some basic reading that may help in lieu of a chemistry course for the liberal arts students.

Several dictionaries and encyclopedias are recommended because they can be most easily understood by the nonchemist but still retain the respect of the profession. There is a dictionary written for the chemist but edited with the possible use by the nonchemist in mind. There is an encyclopedia containing the work of some 500 chemists. Another is edited not only for chemists but for those in allied fields. A very practical chemical formulary would help the journalist understand formulas used in all fields of industry.

Finally, a beginning chemistry textbook is recommended. One of several written for the first year of college chemistry, it presupposes no earlier training.

Dictionary

Thorpe, Jocelyn Field, and M. A. Whiteley, *Thorpe's Dictionary of Applied Chemistry*. London: Longmans, Green and Co., 1937. This is an extensive dictionary (11 volumes) of chemistry written for the chemist, but edited for possible use by nonchemists.

The last volume, which includes a general index and glossary, is a helpful guide to the journalist.

While many of the terms are necessarily highly technical, so are the terms that greet the thoughtful journalist examining the raw results of research in the age of technocracy. It may encourage the journalist to turn to these volumes for help if he knows that the editors "have done their best to ensure that special articles are written in a manner which will be understood by the ordinarily cultured reader."

Though the definitions of that phrase might vary, they would have difficulty not including the journalist.

Encyclopedia

Clark, George L., editor-in-chief, Gessner G. Hawley, managing editor, and William A. Hamor, advisory editor, *The Encyclopedia of Chemistry*. New York: Reinhold Publishing Corp., 1957; supplement, 1958. In one volume and a supplement, this encyclopedia brings together accurate, understandable information from more than 500 scientists. It includes not only the technical terms of chemistry, but the everyday ones that result from the science of chemistry. For example, within 20 pages it includes such topics as: "Fission, Nuclear," "Fixing Agents (Dyeing)," "Flameproofing Agents," "Fluidization," and "Fluorine."

The editors wanted to produce something of use to anyone with "a bowing acquaintance with chemistry." If so, most journalists who look carefully at the foregoing example—starting with "fission" and ending with "fluorine"—will realize they must have the "bowing acquaintance."

Try this word-association game with a touch of news sense:

fission, nuclear—bombs, power, submarine, space travel . . .
fixing agents (dyeing)—Pure Food and Drug Act, textiles, cooking, hair style . . .
flameproofing agents—fire hazards, fire safety, home construction, space re-entry . . .
fluidization—gasoline cracking, oil industry, conservation . . .
fluorine—tooth decay, dentistry, compulsory medication, socialized medicine, politics, religion. . . .

There's a game played at most news desks almost every day. Do you have the answers?

Kirk, Raymond E., and Donald F. Othmer, eds., *Encyclopedia of Chemical Technology*. New York: The Interscience Encyclopedia, Inc., 1947. The editors of this 15-volume work have organized it as a specialized encyclopedia. It is neither a dictionary nor a handbook. Their intent was to cover the entire field of chemical technology for the specialized audience of professional chemists and chemical engineers needing to be acquainted with methods employed outside their own particular area.

The editors put it this way:

> The subject matter covered is descriptive of technologically important materials, methods, and phenomena. It is not primarily theoretical and mathematical except insofar as . . . necessary to bring out well-established principles and to give a background that will enable the user to understand and apply the information given.

This encyclopedia gives some brief bibliographies as selected further reading, and is illustrated with diagrams, flow sheets and a few photographs. Formulae and equations are given where pertinent. Names and naming procedures are handled with special care. The articles on each subject or topic were written by a variety of men, each a recognized authority in his special field.

These volumes apply specifically and only to chemistry, unlike Van Nostrand's *Scientific Encyclopedia* which covers science generally and less technically and more briefly.

Formulary

Bennett, H., editor-in-chief, *The Chemical Formulary*. New York: D. Van Nostrand Co., Inc., 1933; rev. ed., 1958. The subtitle is "A Condensed Collection of Valuable, Timely, Practical Formulae for Making Thousands of Products in All Fields of Industry." In nine volumes (with cumulative index) the *Formulary* gives ingredients and proportions for making a long list of items from alcoholic liquors through waterproofing compositions.

Introductory Text

Nebergall, William H., Frederic C. Schmidt, and Henry F. Holtzclaw, *General Chemistry*, (rev. ed.) Boston: D. C. Heath & Company, 1962. This is a beginning chemistry textbook that does not presuppose earlier introduction to the subject, yet is written for the first year of college chemistry.

This book serves as an example of the kind of beginning vol-

umes that are available for the journalist who is insufficiently
specialized in science but wants to learn basic information.

An Involuntary Image

If the world succeeds in blowing itself up, physics probably will
be blamed. If the world avoids blowing itself up, physics will be
said to have succeeded in spite of itself. In either event, journalism
represents physics' only hope for a fair hearing. And it will be a
tough assignment for the journalist, especially if he does not understand the subject.

It is not public relations, in the usual sense, that physics needs.
This science has enjoyed an image that would make a public relations man's heart thump happily ever since our first controlled
nuclear reaction at Stagg Field, University of Chicago, December 2,
1942. Since that dawning of the nuclear age, the physicists themselves have had difficulty following their mushrooming public
esteem. The physicists, particularly those associated with nuclear
work (and who among laymen knows the difference?) have become
a group set apart.

They often discover that they have become pundits on almost
everything from elementary education to national politics. Many
physicists were gun shy of publicity about their own work long
before Stagg Field. They feared misinterpretation resulting in in-
accuracy. Then, Enrico Fermi and friends made Stagg Field famous
for something other than being an intercollegiate stadium with no
intercollegiate sports. Since then the men of physics know that their
comments on politics are just as likely, if not more so, to make page
one as their comments on science.

Some have retreated further into their cloak of "no comment"
and have restricted their public statements to international scientific forums, where reporters are lost souls. A few—too few—have
tried to exorcise the ghosts the public believes haunt the house of
physics. It may be awe. It may be envy. It could be fear. But it most
certainly is misunderstanding.

Both the physicists and the newspapermen would be better off if
they teamed up to help the public. To begin with, most physicists

would appreciate it if the public realized that physics had been around for some time before Stagg Field. Furthermore, there are a good many kinds of physicists besides the nuclear variety. For example, there are many times more physicists than astronauts working on man's race to the stars.

However, because both the space and nuclear programs are embroiled in international politics, so are the physicists. Often a physicist may comment on something strictly within his discipline, yet, because he, like everyone else, cannot escape his environment, his statement is also political. As such, it is legitimate news copy that the journalist is obligated to write for his reader. Furthermore, each reader is also a part of this dynamic, sometimes frightening, usually confusing, environment of scientific break-through. And every reader has every right to know how he fits into it.

Newspapers and other printed media not only must do this job, but are the only ones who can. Television covers magnificently the major physical break-throughs of science. Millions can watch an astronaut take off on a space flight. They can see the landing. They can, eventually, see what the astronaut sees. And, they can see that astronaut given a hero's welcome upon his return to earth. But all of this is only what they can see.

They cannot see the science behind the flight. They cannot see the blending of scientific and political implications. When the television show is over they rush to their newspapers. Do they find the depth to the surface news they have witnessed? Not often enough. The fault lies only partly with the newspapers. Newsmen, perhaps better than anyone else, can understand the political implications of space flight. But their stories are not complete without the scientific implications. It is here that scientists have been misinterpreted and have subsequently become shy of their responsibility to the public. But help must come from these scientists, in this case, the physicists.

A few of them have tried, despite an affliction of many of their colleagues which causes them to curl a lip over the word, "popularization." Of course, newsmen cannot escape their responsibility for the fear and the sneer of scientists about popularization. Too often newsmen have undersold their reader as they have used one or both of the following judgments on scientific stories:

"He wouldn't understand 95 percent of this, so I'll just give him the five percent he will understand."

Or in the case of a statement dealing with both physics and politics:

"He wouldn't understand the scientific gobbledegook, so I'll just give him this hot political stuff."

In either case, both the physicist and the newspaperman come off second best, to say nothing of the poor reader. It is a two-way street. As a C. P. Snow book, to which you will be referred later, puts it, "it is an ever-widening gap between two worlds." And the reader is being steadily lost in the middle. Mr. Snow didn't say that—we did.

What television can do to narrow the gap is limited by the number of hours in the day, the economics of telecasting, and the point beyond which simple visual presentation cannot go. No thoughtful newsman denies that television is effective in presenting the breaking news event and part of the background. However, excepting all this, newsmen in both television and on newspapers realize that they can go only so far in explaining certain things visually. For example, something as complicated and, at times, abstract as the blending of physics and world power sooner or later cannot be explained with pictures. The explanation must be spoken or written. It then breaks down to a choice for the reader. Can he follow the story better if it is spoken to him? Or, can he understand it better if he reads it? In the first case, an interruption may be fatal. In the second, it is only annoying.

Obviously, much of the depth of scientific stories must come from the printed media. Television couldn't afford to do it all, even if it were able. Magazines can do it once a month or once a week on a fairly broad basis. Their editors must adroitly allow for the time that lapses between the news break and the date the magazine is slipped into the mail box. Sunday newspapers, such as *The New York Times's* Sunday edition and the innovating *National Observer*, can, in their newspaper format, reduce this time lag. But daily newspapers, geared to depth, can add perspective very soon after the event. And they can do it locally.

If the gap between science and the general public is to be narrowed, much of it must be done by the newspapers. But they cannot do it alone. Many newsmen are a bit weary of the scientist who is willing to use the press for educational and political pronouncements, but is reluctant to use it to enlighten the public about his own discipline.

We do not mean to be picking on physics. We found many physicists deeply concerned and anxious to help. But the physicist, like any person in the news, must bear more than his share of responsibility and notoriety. His discipline provides the near-perfect example in our search for the journalist's bibliography to science. It is newsworthy, and it will be for a long time. It is involved in the international power struggle, and it will be for a long time. It is complicated, and it will be—to the layman, at least—probably forever.

Now, what has been done for the journalist who would read to better background himself in physics?

You will find following this introduction a number of books which can help the journalist understand some basics of physics. Actually, physics also is largely involved in the more general annotations you will find at the end of this chapter.

As you approach the bibliography for physics, keep in mind, if you miss some old friends, that there also is a general bibliography following the one for physics.

"Popular" Introductions

Gamov, George, and John M. Cleveland, *Physics: Foundations and Frontiers.* Englewood Cliffs, N.J.: Prentice-Hall, Inc., 1960. This is an introduction to physics that can apply both to future physics majors and to the liberal arts student.

Its authors have held the need for advanced mathematics to a minimum. They assume high school algebra, do not use calculus, and include the limited amount of trigonometry needed in the text.

Gamov had already succeeded in making the physical sciences interesting in his respected book, *Matter, Earth, and Sky,* before teaming with Cleveland in this volume. In fact, this book includes portions of the first book. The result is a blending of the appeal of the first book into a "sound and harmonious synthesis of classical and modern physics."

This kind of introductory textbook does help fill the physics void in liberal arts. Its application by the journalist is obvious.

Holton, Gerald, *Introduction to Concepts and Theories in Physical Science*. Cambridge: Addison-Wesley Press, Inc., 1952. Because this book was written for several audiences, it can help the journalist.

It is, as the title indicates, an introduction to the whole area of the physical sciences. As such it is directed primarily to the students who do not intend to become chemists or physicists.

Thus it can serve the journalist as a basis in the physical sciences and as a rather general reference. It lacks the detail of larger volumes and series that are recommended elsewhere in this bibliography, but it could serve well as a handbook.

From a Problem, A Series

Science Study Series. Garden City, N.Y.: Anchor Books, Doubleday & Company, Inc. Designed for high school science, useful in some college-level work, this series is an open door up an easy incline for the layman.

In 1956 a group of physicists, teachers, journalists, and others met at the Massachusetts Institute of Technology. The meeting resulted in the formation of Educational Services Incorporated, which holds the copyrights on this series.

The object of the series was to provide the writing of distinguished authors on the "most stirring and fundamental topics of physics." The results include such titles and authors as:

The Universe at Large, Herman Bondi
The Restless Atom, Alfred Romer
The Nature of Violent Storms, Louis J. Battan
How Old Is the Earth? Patrick M. Hurley
The Watershed (*A Biography of Johannes Kepler*), Arthur Koestler.

The worth of some of the titles in this series is obvious in the title itself. They apply directly to practical news problems. Others provide general background. However, all are relatively short and well written by respected authors.

A Famous Name

Einstein, Albert, and Leopold Infeld, *The Evolution of Physics*. New York: Simon and Schuster, Inc., 1961. Here is the story of the evolution of ideas in physical science from the earliest thoughts to the complicated ones of today.

First published in 1938, this edition represents the 19th printing. Because of the rapid advance in science since 1938 and the death of Einstein, its co-author, Infeld, has added an introduction. In it he cites a number of advances that outdate the original manuscript. However, most of the book has held up solidly for more than two decades.

Even if this were not written for a reader with a "complete lack of any concrete knowledge of physics and mathematics," no journalist should ignore it or some other work of Einstein. It would seem almost uncouth for the modern newsman not to have exposed himself to one of the greatest minds ever to have graced the earth.

Happily, Einstein and his fellow researcher did write for the layman. Yet, they admitted that this would not be quite like reading a novel. They worried about the reader, but they realized that he would have to read carefully, understanding one page before he could understand the next.

Perhaps the authors were overly pessimistic. Perhaps this can be excused in the man who gave birth to the theory of relativity. But in this book he and Infeld have told the exciting story of man's efforts to understand the world and universe around him.

Bridges Between the Sciences

A number of the highly recommended books on science bridge specialization. They include information that is applicable both to the physical sciences and the biological sciences. They form a bridge between these two which explains our placement of them here. It also explains a relatively short list for physics because that discipline plays a major role in the following general references:

Scientific American Books. Copyright by Scientific American, Inc. Published in New York: Simon and Schuster, Inc.

The magazine, *Scientific American,* is considered by many to be "the most authoritative and liveliest in its field." When a scientist ponders recommending it to a layman, he frequently pauses and says, "You will understand most of this, and it's well written."

His pause may be accounted for by the scientist's natural concern that the layman may not be able to fathom scientific writing by scientifically respected sources. His decision to recommend the magazine probably is based on his awareness that one objective of the publication is to produce articles that will keep the scientist up-to-date in areas other than his own. And any number of scientists helping with this bibliography said, "We don't understand each other any better than you understand us."

Scientific writing is a spot in which the much overused word, communication, does fit. For here communication from scientist to scientist and from scientist to layman often does break down. The brilliant, almost inspired, editing of *Scientific American* provides communication between a roster of contributors *The New York Times* says "reads like a *Who's Who* of contemporary science."

When the editors of the magazine put their talents to selecting and re-editing articles on a given subject for a series of books, they achieved another communications goal, if, indeed, they had not already. They cleared the lines between the scientist and the layman.

While the conscientious layman reads, he may forget one nagging concern that bothers the thoughtful person who seeks knowledge in an area so complex that it can produce momentary mental hysteria. That nagging doubt is whether he can safely enjoy readable scientific writing without fear that popularization has bent accuracy all out of whack.

In this series the layman can breeze along through "chapter articles" just as readable as those in a newspaper or popular magazine.

For the journalist there are two treasures here. One is information—authoritative and understandable. The second is a lesson in scientific writing that *reads*. And for the newspaper writer-editor team there is a bonus. Here are articles, conceived by authorities in science and midwifed by experts in editing. And the offspring is a success in print.

You should be acquainted with some of the titles in this series without fearing deception by their simplicity. They include:

The New Astronomy, The Physics and Chemistry of Life, Twentieth Century Bestiary, Atomic Power, Automatic Control,

184

Plant Life, The Planet Earth, New Chemistry, The Universe, and *Lives in Science.*

Asimov, Isaac, *The Intelligent Man's Guide to Science.* New York: Basic Books, Inc., 1960. Volume I—*The Physical Sciences*—starts with "What Is Science" and gives a brief historical sketch of the beginnings and derivations of Greek philosophy and science.

After this summary, the volume is divided into chapters on the universe, the earth, the atmosphere, the elements, the particles, the waves, the machine, and ends Volume I with the reactor.

This section is not at all technically written, but gives a very good basis for further reading on points that may be in your particular area of journalistic research or interest. The important scientists and their discoveries are woven in, with all pertinent dates and details. The volume reads more like an interesting story than a treatise on the over-all field of the physical sciences.

Volume II—*The Biological Sciences*—begins with the molecule, its structure, the men who made important discoveries about its substance, and its breakdown, and considers here both organic and inorganic matter. The succeeding chapters take up the proteins, the cell, the micro-organisms, the body, the species, the mind, and concludes with a special appendix, "Mathematics in Science."

At the end of Volume II is a chapter-keyed bibliography, selected by author Asimov, and highly recommended by him as further reading in the particular division to which the books are pertinent.

Van Nostrand's Scientific Encyclopedia, 3rd ed. Princeton, N.J.: D. Van Nostrand Co., Inc., 1958. This is one large (1,839 pages) volume of alphabetically arranged scientific terms in fields ranging from aeronautics, astronomy, and botany through radio and TV to statistics and zoology.

The definitions are given as briefly as possible, covering as little as one word to as much as several pages, depending upon the complexity and applied uses of the subject.

This is a good place for the journalist to get a quick, concise definition in layman's terms.

McGraw-Hill Encyclopedia of Science and Technology. New York: McGraw-Hill Book Company, Inc., 1960. This is a 15-volume encyclopedia (Vol. 15 is the index volume) divided by subject matter.

There is one general article surveying the field with a number of separate articles, alphabetically arranged, covering main subdivisions and more specific aspects. There are nearly 50,000 cross-references to guide you from the general to the specific, and even further into specialization on one single facet of a subject. Most of the articles begin with a definition, state the scope and coverage, and then progress into the scientific and technological aspects. After this general opening, the articles go on to increasingly difficult and detailed discussion. By this arrangement, a reader can stay with the article only as far as his needs require.

For a journalist with a specific need for further information on a subject, most of the longer articles have their own bibliographies on the subject under discussion.

Snow, C. P., *The Two Cultures and The Scientific Revolution.* New York: Cambridge University Press, 1959. Author Snow is, in his own words, "by training a scientist, by vocation a writer." His access to the top figures of both worlds gives authority to his contention that there exists a serious and ever-widening gap in the understanding between the two. He outlines the problem now existing between the "two cultures" and goes on to explore the impact such a growing divergence, coupled with the scientific revolution, will have on our civilization.

This brief book (only 58 pages) should be of great interest to the journalist who may, in the course of one day's work, be called upon to write about some segment of either, or both, of these "cultures."

16

Man and Man

This chapter deals with man's studies of himself, his past, and possibly his future.

The links from area to area go something like this:

The biological sciences—a term being steadily more accepted as applicable to all the various branches, such as zoology, botany, and so on, that deal with the examination of living things.

Psychology—the examination by man of his own mental and emotional reactions.

Anthropology—the examination of man's past through the use of artifacts and archeology.

History—the examination of man's past by his deeds and written records.

Political Science—the examination of man and his governing organizations.

Sociology—the examination of man as a member of a group.

Economics—the examination of man's ways of making a living and most particularly his use of its results.

Agriculture—an examination of one of man's ways of making a living, and in this case, an example of specialization for the reporter.

From Frog to Man

There is nothing wrong with an amoeba. There is nothing wrong with algae. For that matter, there's nothing wrong with earthworms or frogs. But newspapers are seldom written for or about amoebas,

186

algae, earthworms, or frogs. Newspapers are written for and about people.

That may be one of the lowest forms of making a point, but it sometimes appears in the education of a journalist that the point is forgotten. There is nothing wrong with the examination of one-celled life and the carving up of earthworms in beginning science courses. There is nothing wrong with journalism students taking these courses. In fact, there is everything right about it.

However, somewhere between the frog and higher forms of life the journalism student and his instructors too often seem to lose track of their objective—learning about man.

So that we did not lose track, this bibliography for the biological sciences is totally oriented toward man. We hope that the books suggested may bridge the wide gap between classroom frogs and the study of man.

Think for a moment. Why do you want to know about man? You are not a doctor. Your interest is not basically in how his body is put together. Then what are you interested in?

There is a good chance that you want the biological sciences to tell you about where man came from and where he is going. If that is what you want, you expect help on the answers to some of the basic issues of today, yesterday, and tomorrow. What issues?

—The origin of life is one. Today, as men look to the stars, they wonder more than ever about how life, and more specifically, man, got started on this earth. Religion is involved. Theory is involved. And basic disagreement between scientists is involved.

—Heredity is another. Heredity in the twentieth century is much more than some experiments with pea plants in the nineteenth century. Today it is Hiroshima, Nagasaki, birth control, and a future overshadowed by nuclear warfare.

—Science and politics is a vital subject in the atomic age. Other than simply knowing that certain Russian scientists have proposed a theory on heredity that appalls scientists of the free world, what do you know about mixing science and politics?

There are many books on these subjects. Those in this bibliography may give you a start.

One of them deals in the human implications of the biological sciences. If you need a refresher or even a basic understanding of the sciences and human beings, this book will provide it. It is a

188

reference and it is a bridge from the classroom frog to the man you write about.

For a basic understanding of the principles of human genetics, read Curt Stern's book.

Then you should be ready to take on what many biological scientists consider a classic. It is *The Origin of Life on the Earth* by A. I. Oparin. The writer is a Russian. While his theories meet with some disagreement from American scientists, they take him seriously. You should know something about him.

Julian Huxley's *Evolution in Action* will help bring to focus this business of human evolution and genetics and the technological world of today.

Then you will be ready for something like Garrett Hardin's book which pinpoints the importance of research in evolution in the atomic age.

Now, you may want to return to Huxley for his discussion of the East versus the West on the subject of heredity. You will learn about the disagreement itself. Possibly even more important, you will find that it is an action study of the ethics of science mixed with politics.

Finally, you will find we have listed a book by P. B. Medawar entitled *The Uniqueness of the Individual.* Here is an example of the scientific approach to such puzzlers as "an unsolved problem of biology (aging)."

Understand, as you approach these books, they are simply examples of what you can find for yourself. But they were chosen because they deal with man, and they deal with man and the issues of now. Now is news. Without some basic background in the biological sciences, are you sure you can recognize it? Are you sure you can handle it if someone else recognizes it for you?

Bibliography

Hardin, Garrett, *Biology: Its Human Implications,* 2nd ed. San Francisco: W. H. Freeman and Company, 1952. Whether a book can serve both laymen and specialists often depends upon the author's objective. In this case, the objective was twofold:

1. To answer this question: "What should a student learn in a college course in biology if he will never again be exposed to formal instruction in the subject?"

2. To fulfill this goal: ". . . an early emphasis of the humane aspects of science helps to prepare the professional student for one of the obligations that he must later assume, namely, that of interpreting science to the lay public."

With such objectives, this introduction to biology with its emphasis on human implications can provide the very launching platform a journalist may need for his questions. It is the kind of a book the journalism student or professional should take time to read and remember as a reference.

Stern, Curt, *Principles of Human Genetics,* 2nd ed. San Francisco: W. H. Freeman and Company, 1960. Because this textbook was written for students from several academic areas, it also serves well the journalist who must have some backgrounding in almost everything. It describes well-established principles of human genetics, some of which have been accepted for decades. It also includes results of recent studies taking place in and resulting from the nuclear age.

The journalist will find that the first ten chapters are written for "all students," thus providing a basic background. The remaining chapters are designed for specific areas of study. They include such topics as: "The Genetic Hazards of Radiation," "Heredity and Environment," and "Genetic Aspects of Race Mixture."

May the author forgive us for lifting these subjects from context, but they help illustrate that the subject of human genetics is daily newspaper copy.

Oparin, A. I., *The Origin of Life on the Earth,* 3rd ed., translated from the Russian by Ann Synge. New York: Academic Press, Inc., 1957. Many scientists consider this a classic on one of the subjects that has long puzzled mankind since the beginning of mankind.

It involves faith and science, and has been the subject of famous news stories. It is not a dead question today, but one that constantly shows up on the news desk.

All scientists, who consider this book an important part of their literature, do not agree with all the author's views. But this should not be strange ground for the journalist used to dealing in disagreement. The good newsman knows he need not fear disagreement if he tells the whole story. To write intelligently on the origin of life, he needs to be acquainted with Oparin.

Huxley, Julian, *Evolution in Action*. New York: Harper & Row, Publishers, 1953. A little book in size (182 pages), this is an informative discussion of evolution from which side issues have been stripped away.

Its author traces the story of evolution quickly through such subjects as: "The Process of Evolution," "How Natural Selection Works," "Biological Improvement," "The Development of Mental Activity," "The Path of Biological Progress," and "The Human Phase."

This book is also interpretive. The author puts it this way:

> Furthermore, I have attempted to present a point of view: It is always based on facts, but is in many respects a particular and personal one. I hold strongly that without some kind of knowledge of evolution one cannot hope to arrive at a true picture of human destiny.

The journalist may agree or disagree with Mr. Huxley. But no journalist can deny that human destiny is his business.

Hardin, Garrett, *Nature and Man's Fate*. New York: Holt, Rinehart & Winston, Inc., 1959. "Believe what you will of evolution in the past: but you had jolly well better believe it will take place in the future if you hope to make political decisions that will give your descendants a reasonable chance to exist."

With that statement in the prologue of his book this author pinpoints the importance of research in evolution in the atomic age. His major objective is to bring the reader up to date on the "latest thought in evolutionary theory, so that the reader can see its implications for the future." But to do this, Hardin also reviews the past.

This is a well-written book that could be of value not only to science writers, but others dealing in sociology, politics, welfare —the stuff of which daily news is made.

Huxley, Julian, *Heredity: East and West*. New York: Henry Schuman, Inc., 1949. Subtitled *Lysenko and World Science,* this is essentially the fervid protest of a scientist against mixing politics and science.

Specifically, it outlines and documents the case of Russian scientist Lysenko and his contention that acquired characteristics can be inherited. Huxley sets forth the scientific problem, the ideological issue involved, and the deep concern of Western scientists that tailoring scientific theory to conform to the party line will inexorably spread to more and more of the sciences.

Medawar, P. B., *The Uniqueness of the Individual.* New York: Basic Books, Inc., 1957. For many readers the phrase, "evolution of man," transports them back at once to the era of Darwin. The author of this book is concerned because many people do not realize that research into man's evolution is more active today than ever.

To make his point, he has assembled a series of his own essays and lectures on such pertinent contemporary subjects as: "Old Age and Natural Death," "An Unsolved Problem of Biology (Aging)," "The Imperfections of Man," and "The Uniqueness of the Individual."

In the Age of the Atom, men do seem to be more concerned about their own evolution. Here is a relatively modern collection of facts and thoughts on a fascinating subject.

This last book in the biological sciences bibliography has been placed here because it so well illustrates the answer to the journalist's need in biological science.

Milne, Lorus J., and Margery J. Milne, *The Biotic World and Man,* 2nd ed. Englewood Cliffs, N.J.: Prentice-Hall, Inc., 1958. For the reasons this book is recommended, read the author's words:

On biology oriented to man—

Initially, no doubt because students are animals and not plants, discussion of topics related closely and obviously to man and mammals has a far stronger appeal to most beginners. . . .

On terminology and detail—

To save space for emphasis on biological principles and values of biological study to mankind, we have dispensed with much cherished terminology and detail. Facts are easy to memorize, to look up, and to forget. Principles require for their understanding both factual background and a higher category of mental activity. Understanding becomes a kind of adhesive web to which present and future facts can cling. . . .

On glossaries—

As in the previous edition, in lieu of a glossary, each technical term is indexed. We believe that a term or its definition has little importance on its own. It is but the hook on which to hang all future information on the topic. No one gains an understanding of baseball as an exciting game from nine, two-line definitions of the playing positions and a diagram of the field. No one gains an understanding of a community of plants and animals, or of the cooperating cells composing each one, or of the company of molecules in living substance, from brief definitions of the component parts. For this reason we encourage the student to develop instead a general understanding of each word.

If for no other reason, and there are other reasons, the journalist who is tired of the namby-pamby approach to definitions should look at this book to see how they are handled. For too long a time journalists have either not used the right word, for fear it would not be understood, or have tried to sneak the definition into the copy so that the reader scarcely knows it is there. The authors of this book have learned how to use the right word and then define it.

Heirs to the Newsroom

Often enough to have committed the journalistic sin of redundancy, the word *creative* has been tossed at you in this book. It has been used in every way except as a beatitude—Blessed are the creative, for they shall inherit the newsroom.

It is easy enough to say that journalism needs creative people. It is even easier to agree. But can anyone tell how to find them or develop them—or even to recognize them, for that matter? If anyone can help, it is the psychologists. Their business is man and his mental reactions to his environment. In the case of creativity, psychologists have tried to find the qualities of which it is made. They have tried to develop tests to help locate those qualities.

"Fine," you say, "so they can tell us if we have a creative guy in the newsroom. We can tell that by looking at his work."

Of course, you can; providing he has been properly trained and disciplined professionally; providing he has been properly educated so that his creativity will have facts to feed upon; providing you have him in the right job to best use his creativity; providing. . . .

"Oh," you say, "those are simply the chances we must take."

Must we? Is there a possibility that we can take some of the chance out of it? Is there a chance that we can discover a tendency toward creativity much earlier?

If there is such a chance, then it may be found in psychology. For example, in recent years the public and the newspapers have begun to realize that conventional classroom brilliance may not be coupled with creativity. It is possible for a student to make top grades in most subjects, but to fall far short in a class that places a premium on imagination and/or creativity. This realization gave some of us the jitters. In a system based on grades, how many creative people have we missed?

Our jitters were a bit late. What we were just realizing, of course, was not a recent break-through. Psychology had just progressed far enough in its study of creativity to make a few tentative suggestions. Unfortunately, we reacted just as we always do to the tentative findings of any science. Lacking complete information, we cheered, "Good boys!" And then we added anxiously, "Now let's hurry to test all of those little stinkers before we miss some more creative types."

The psychologists replied that it was not quite that simple, and, anyhow, they had been studying this matter for a long time before most of us realized it. They were ready, they said, to help us out, but not with a simple true-or-false test.

We probably said something about "those cautious head-shrinkers," but we had learned a lesson about the social science of psychology. It, like the physical and biological sciences, could not often give us pure black or pure white answers. After we thought for a bit, we realized that where man's mind is involved, we don't really expect simple "yes" or "no" answers. We can only expect educated help. And, come to think of it, that is a great deal more than we have had without psychology's help.

Psychology, like the so-called purer sciences, can be and has been misunderstood. The psychologists talk about abnormal psychology, and we smile knowingly. "They mean the oddballs," we say. "You know, the nuts." Psychology talks about intelligence quotients, and we say, "They mean the IQ boys. You know, the brains."

The psychologists were reluctant to be as positive about intelligence quotient (IQ) as were most of us. "Come on," we said. "If my kid is smart, he is smart. Don't keep it a secret. Tell me all about my little genius." But the psychologist warned us that there was more to it than that, and he appeared to hedge in his answers.

But we just wanted the magic number to "the kid's IQ." We

forgot about the caution. Later, when we began to hear about creativity tests that did not necessarily correlate with IQ tests, we growled, "So, now you tell us."

This illustrates the rather obvious gap between the general public and psychology. The newspapers also have a job here, and it can be done properly only in depth. We deal almost daily with stories based in psychology, and now and then, we realize it.

We know, for example, who lays the basis for psychological warfare. We also know who was called in, along with the psychiatrists, when the phrase "brainwashed" chilled us during and after the Korean Conflict. We know vaguely who is behind at least part of the testing our children receive in school. But we in the newspaper business need to know a good deal more, and quite frankly, the psychologists and their publications could be more helpful. At first glance, many of the books in the field appear to be written in a mixture of English and psychological double-talk made up just to confuse us. However, if the physical and biological sciences can have their own language, we can hardly complain if some of the social sciences have theirs.

But we can direct a common complaint to all of them. It is perfectly all right if their brand of science requires a special vocabulary. Even so, if they want to be understood—if they do not want to be misunderstood—they need to provide something for the rest of us that they respect and that we can understand.

In this bibliography of psychology we felt we needed to offer some frank words of caution and some unorthodox suggestions for reading. First, the caution. Do the highly orthodox thing. Take a good introductory course and/or read some good introductory literature. Just as you would in physics or mathematics, you are going to need some background, basic vocabulary, and basic definitions.

Then, you can proceed into what, quite frankly, are the more interesting aspects of psychology. Even with a little background, you may at times think you are reading an almost strange tongue. For example, you could find this was your reaction when you read in the fascinating subject of personality, as psychologists use that word. If you run into trouble, glance through the table of contents for a subject that particularly interests you. Turn to it and read it. Afterwards, come back to the subject that all but lost you. You may find that it begins to make more sense. We suggest that once having gained some background, you use this entire bibliography in that way. You will find that it is generally divided into accepted psychological divisions.

An Introduction

Murphy, Gardner, *An Introduction to Psychology*. New York: Harper & Row, Publishers, 1951. This book, or one like it, can be the basis for more advanced reading in psychology.

We chose this one as an example because we felt it might make the same author's "classic" on personality easier reading.

At any rate, as was indicated in the introduction to this bibliography of psychology, the more advanced and more interesting readings of the field are more worthwhile if you have the benefit of an introduction.

Personality

Murphy, Gardner, *Personality—A Biosocial Approach to Origins and Structure*. New York: Harper & Row, Publishers, 1947. This is considered by many psychologists to be one of the classics of the field.

This book may not be for the beginner, but parts of it will be fascinating for anyone who is curious about his mind and his mental reactions. Actually, much of it comes easier if you have first read Murphy's or someone else's introducton to psychology.

While the author might be scandalized, you may get more from this book if you read the introductory chapters and skip into areas that interest you. Having read a chapter to which you were attracted by the title, you then will find yourself sampling others.

Look at some of these chapter headings to see if they spark interest:

"The World of Symbols," "The World of Values," "The Perceiver," "Imagination and Thought," "Creativeness," and "Compensation for Inferiority."

While much of this seems highly technical, at least in language, it is not too hard to read. It does not exactly glue your eyes to the page and your seat to the chair. But give Murphy a fair trial. He has something to say, and ends up saying it quite well.

Hall, Calvin S., and Gardner Lindzey, *Theories of Personality*. New York: John Wiley & Sons, Inc., 1957. A collection and examination of the major personality theories.

For psychology students this book could serve as a starting point. Examination of one psychologist and his theory could lead to detailed examination in other sources. For the journalist this book could serve the same function. When time allows or an assignment brings pressure, this can provide the background for an excursion into a specific area.

Here you will find digests of Freud's psychoanalytic theory; Jung's analytic theory, the social psychological theories of Adler, Fromm, Horney, and Sullivan; Murray's personology theory; and others.

One note of caution. The approach of this book is not simple. You will do better to attack it after a more general introduction has been absorbed.

Abnormal Psychology

White, Robert W., *The Abnormal Personality*, 2nd ed. New York: The Ronald Press Company, 1956. This is an easily read, easily understood book on the abnormal personality.

After a quick historical roundup of the origins of abnormal psychology, the reader is then given several case histories of disordered personalities. References are made to them throughout the remainder of the book.

For a book on a complex and at many times "cloudy" subject, the author writes in remarkably clear, uncomplicated English. The many specialized terms of psychology and psychological disorders are defined simply without throwing up a smoke screen of technical jargon.

Psychological Measurement

Nunnally, Jum C., Jr., *Tests and Measurements, Assessments and Prediction*. New York: McGraw-Hill Book Company, Inc., 1959. Have you ever taken an IQ test? Do you know what a true random sampling is? What is a Stanford-Binet? How would you go about making a multivariate prediction? Do you know the difference between mode, median, and mean? Did you know that the simple biographical data obtained on a personnel application can be used to predict your success as a salesman?

This fact-packed volume on terms, tests, how they are made, given, and evaluated, probably gives much more specific information than a journalist will ever need. In this test-happy world of ours it might be just as well to have some idea of the complex factors that go into the seemingly simple process of testing. From kindergarten (and perhaps before) to your last job, the average American of today takes a variety of tests—from IQ to classroom work to personnel testing.

Developmental Psychology

Munn, Norman L., *The Evolution and Growth of Human Behavior.* Cambridge, Mass.: The Riverside Press, 1955. This is an introductory textbook to the field of evolution and growth of human behavior. Munn's book of 1938, *Psychological Development,* has been expanded and revised to include much new material in this area of genetic psychology.

The first third or so of the book lays some background by explanation and interpretation of experiments with lower orders of life in their responses to varied stimuli and test situations.

The remaining two-thirds of the book is devoted to the developmental characteristics of man, from prenatal days through senescence. Differing theories of the growth and development of the human personality are set forth with statements about their general acceptance or rejection.

This is a lucid exposition of many aspects of human behavior and gives as much detail in so large a field as is possible to include in one volume.

There is a bibliography at the end of each chapter so that a journalist would have no difficulty in digging further into any area in which he needed more specifically detailed information.

Social Psychology

Lindzey, Gardner, ed., *Handbook of Social Psychology.* Cambridge, Mass.: Addison-Wesley Publishing Company, Inc., 1954. This is a graduate-level work in two volumes made up of contributions by a relatively large number of social psychologists.

Because of its level, its would-be reader needs introductory background before proceeding. Actually, these volumes are also designed for use by the practicing psychologist. However, the industrious journalist can gain information on such news topics as "leadership," "mass phenomena," "prejudice and ethnic relations," and the "psychology of voting."

Even on such topics as these, do not expect this material to be easy. But you may expect it to be interesting—if you are really interested.

Hare, Paul A., and Edgar F. Borgatta and Robert F. Bales, eds., *Small Groups: Studies in Social Interaction.* New York: Alfred A. Knopf, Inc., 1955. This is a detailed examination of a relatively new field of psychology.

However, at least part of the discussion will strike a familiar chord for the reader. He need only substitute for the phrase "small group" such words as "seminar," "group discussion," "group problem solving," "executive board," and, yes, "committee." In this light, the study of small groups makes vital sense to the newsman who spends much time dealing with and about small groups.

Of course, the psychologist's study of small groups means much more than a study of the committee approach. This branch of psychology seeks, by studying small groups, to better understand the behavior of large groups. This, too, often parallels the newsman's interest.

From Clay to the Stars

Mankind in the space age is not unlike the crowd which assembles to watch a fire in the upper floors of a tall building. Some day an enterprising news photographer will get the truly human picture of such a fire. He will ride up on the ladder or the fireman's boom and shoot back at the upturned faces. This fire's-eye view will, of course, produce a picture of people all looking up.

At times, as man races for the stars, it would seem that all humanity is, at least mentally, looking skyward. That should please those primary teachers who must constantly preach to their little

charges: "Look up. Don't always look at your feet. Look where you
are going."

The advice makes a good deal of sense. Yet one wonders, if it does
not also lead to some stumbles. Certainly in the world of research,
while some sciences look to the stratosphere, others must continue
to look at man's feet of clay. Anthropology—dirt anthropology—
must, of course, continue to look downward and backward. That, so
far as the journalist is concerned, is the major job of anthropology.
It is the job of helping man chart his future by better understanding his past. This also would seem to be the job of history, and it is.
However, it is easy to become confused about the differences and
boundaries of history, anthropology, and archeology. Actually, there
are no clear-cut lines. Perhaps an oversimplified arrangement of the
three would go something like this:

Archeology studies the civilizations of the past through the discovery and examination of artifacts, physical evidence of these civilizations. In a sense, the dirt anthropologists, which is what they
often call themselves, do much the same thing. However, anthropology more generally is a study of man's races, cultures, civilizations, customs, and myths. At least some of this study may be based
on the findings of archeologists. Both sciences contribute to history,
sociology, psychology, political science, and possibly other academic
disciplines. Obviously, there is much overlapping. The sooner the
student gets over the idea that he can neatly partition these disciplines into their little pigeon-holes, the sooner he will be able to
start understanding them.

The working newsman and the observant journalism student can
easily recall instances in which anthropology and archeology either
made news or were a part of it. It may have been the race to save
artifacts of an Indian village before the site was covered by the
water of a new power dam. It may have been a discovery that
rocked the world, such as the Dead Sea Scrolls. Or it may have been
something quite different, such as the denouncement by anthropologists of a racial myth founded upon bigotry.

The tendency is to remember the Dead Sea Scrolls, which brought
a religious furor, but to forget that anthropology also deals in such
touching modern problems as racial prejudice. Hence, the newsman
who would get the most from anthropology would consider it a
background to history, a link with the past, and an over-all exami-

nation of man and his customs. While it might at first seem that anthropology does not belong in a bibliography as strictly confined to general background areas as this one is, second thought quickly erases that doubt. The newsman is interested in everything, particularly interested in everything that has to do with man—his primary subject and his reader. Any academic discipline which devotes itself to the study of man must be part of the journalist's background.

Introduction to Anthropology

Kluckhohn, Clyde, *Mirror for Man*. New York, Toronto: Whittlesey House, a division of the McGraw-Hill Book Company, Inc., 1949. This book is basically an explanation of the anthropologist to the layman. It explains the anthropologists' use of archeological finds as well as the examination of race and languages. We see the anthropologist at work and watch as he looks at the United States and the world.

    This is less of a reference and more of a basic background volume in so far as the journalist is concerned. A relatively short book (313 pages), in a few hours it can provide a launching platform for questions.

Kroeber, A. L., *Anthropology*. New York: Harcourt, Brace & World, Inc., 1948. This is a large single volume that could have many uses, but for the journalist its basic value would be as a reference. A detailed table of contents, 856 pages of well-organized text, and 38 pages of index easily put it in this category for the non-anthropologist.

Archeology—How It's Done

Clark, Grahame, *Archeology and Society: Reconstructing the Prehistoric Past*. Cambridge, Mass.: Harvard University Press, 1957. This volume gives a brief definition of what the prehistoric past means to the archeologist and the historian.

    This book, almost a how-to-do-it book, describes in some detail the many ways in which finds are made. It discusses the archeologist's approach to problems presented by different sites, and, to a degree, ties the archeologist's work in the past to the stream of history.

This might be of interest to the journalist who must become enough specialized to understand why archeologists need to exercise their science before civilization destroys the evidence.

An Encyclopedia of Archeology

Cottrell, Leonard, *The Concise Encyclopedia of Archaeology*. New York: Hawthorn Books, Inc., 1960. This a reference, a reader, and a handbook for the "intelligent amateur."

Its editor recognizes the narrowing gap between the professional archeologist and the general reader. He also recognizes that archeological findings and interpretations are being reported more frequently in newspapers and magazines.

With this recognition, he has guided the production of a one-volume encyclopedia that can help the newsman. Should the newsman care?

He should if he is interested in the following fascinating notion: We might know more about where man is going if we know more about where he has been.

This book is well illustrated. It is organized alphabetically, but the editor has supplied a classified grouping to help locate information on single broad subjects.

Equally valuable is the editor's introduction entitled "What is archeology?" The journalist who realizes that he must look not only at man's race to the stars, but also at his starts and stops of the past, needs to know the answer to that question.

Anthropology and Culture

Linton, Ralph, *The Tree of Culture*. New York: Alfred A. Knopf, Inc., 1955. This is an almost encyclopedic tracing of the history of man's culture.

It can serve as a reference or a guide through the history of man on the shirttails of his cultural development. History and political science help to understand this aspect of man, but they leave an incomplete picture to be filled in by anthropology. The journalist may very well need to read this well-organized book— or one like it—to become a man well rounded enough to write about man.

202

A Sample of Specialized Anthropology

Driver, Harold E., *Indians of North America*. Chicago: The University of Chicago Press, 1961. This is a comprehensive examination of the American Indian culture from the Arctic to Panama. It was designed as an anthropology text, an introduction to the study of American Indians, and a basic reference.

This book is cited because it exemplifies the kind of specialized or regional information available from the field of anthropolgy. There are, of course, many other publications.

Samples of Regional Anthropology

SOUTH AMERICA. Steward, Julian Haynes, and Louis C. Faron. *Native Peoples of South America*. New York: McGraw-Hill Book Company, Inc., 1959.

AFRICA. Kimble, George Herbert Tinley, *Tropical Africa* (two volumes). New York: Twentieth Century Fund, 1960.

OCEANIA. Oliver, Douglas Llewellyn, *The Pacific Islands*. Cambridge, Mass.: Harvard University Press, 1951.

INDIA. Chicago University College, *Introduction to the Civilization of India*. Chicago: Syllabus Division, University of Chicago Press, 1957.

EUROPE. Coon, Carleton Stevens, *The Races of Europe*. New York: The Macmillan Company, 1939.

NEAR EAST. Childe, Vere Gordon, *New Light on the Most Ancient East*, 4th ed. London: Routledge & Kegan Paul, Ltd., 1952.

Perspective from the Past

How long has it been since you have read some history?
Was it yesterday's newspaper?

Professional historians might not agree that yesterday's newspaper is history, but 20 years from now yesterday's newspaper will have become a part of their raw material. Before you conjure up a mental picture of a historian leafing carefully through yellowing and brittle pages of yesterday's newspaper 20 years hence, put yourself in the place of that historian. If you are going to write in depth, you are going to have to become part historian, too.

Scarcely a news day goes by that history has not played a conscious or unconscious part of it. Try writing about the emerging nations of Africa without the perspective of history. Try writing about a national presidential nominating convention without the help of history. For that matter, try writing about a bond issue for a new city hall without giving the reader some history.

Ideally, almost every story written in the newspaper would be better if the reporter knew the history of his subject. Far too often it is not intentional distortion or sloppy writing that is at fault when a story loses perspective. Usually, it is because the writer simply did not know and understand what came before the story. When that happens a story that fulfills all the criteria of accurate quotes, accurate facts, and even completeness on the surface can end up saying the opposite of the truth.

Perhaps it is because journalism students and newsmen work unconsciously with history all the time that they neglect it. Doubt not that it is neglected. There are not enough journalism students who have taken more than the basic required courses in history. There are not enough students and professionals who read history as an avid avocation. Maybe that is because it is not an avocation. It is a working tool of the profession of journalism.

Some professional historians might not like to hear their discipline called a working tool. For them it is a lifetime study and evaluation of the activities of mankind. For them, this often is enough. For the journalist, it is not. The journalist must learn to live with and use history.

Fine, you say, what do you want me to do, go back and read my American history textbook? Then, do you want me to go to the history section of the library and start reading until I have read it all?

The answer is "No." Practically, if you went to the history section of the library and started reading you might conceivably finish up in time to start drawing Social Security. There is perhaps no other field as thoroughly written as history. It is the nature of the beast.

There are historians of all kinds. Their fields of interest stretch from the minute examination of one group of immigrants who settled in one tiny town to the whole world. The publications of history run literally into the hundreds of thousands. Ask a librarian which is his most difficult area for ordering books and keeping up to date. Almost without exception, or even a pause, he replies, "History."

So, don't expect anybody to take your hand and lead you to a brief list of books that will give you a liberal education in the area of history. Instead, you need to learn why history is valuable, what history and its methods can do for you, and how you can make it part of your background.

The nature of history and its countless recorders and interpreters of facts turned this search for a bibliography into at least a temporary nightmare. Honest and respected historians shook their heads and started making long lists when they were asked to produce a representative and respected bibliography. Then before their list was complete, they realized they must refer us to another colleague and another and another, each with a specialized knowledge. It did not take very long to realize that history could not be approached this way.

The answer, of course, was to come out from behind those stacks of history books and get to the point:

What does the journalist need from history, and how can he acquire a liberal education in it?

The answer to the second half of the question comes first. To have a liberal education in history—a mental platform of knowledge —there is no way out for the journalist but to read. If he is a student, he needs courses in history that are only a start to a lifetime of reading. If he is a professional, he needs only a starting point and then the same lifetime of reading.

Obviously, the problem is the starting point. This bibliography is designed, in part, to give it to him. In an area so bountifully supplied with written records, we would be naive and inaccurate to suggest that our titles are the only ones. In this area, perhaps more than in any other, the titles are examples, suggestions—at least something for lack of nothing in the midst of so much.

We found a tiny volume that is the key book in a series of little books entitled, *Teach Yourself History*. Don't laugh. The whole philosophy of this series should make sense to the newsman. Through the lives of historically famous persons this series attempts to give insight into historical events.

The series itself was not what caught our eye. It was the key book, entitled *The Use of History.* There, in 247 pages, in a small format, is as neat a pitch for why you or any other educated person should know history as you would care to find.

We make no apologies for recommending only it. We simply say that while others may have done it, and probably have, we found it done by an Englishman named A. L. Rowse. Whether you read the rest of the series or not is also up to you. The various volumes are listed for your judgment.

The reporter who really writes in depth also has a special lesson to learn from history. He may discover, to his surprise, that the historical method of research actually fits his own needs. Perhaps at no point in the production of a depth story is a student or beginning professional more at sea than when he must approach the seemingly impossible job of research.

Since historians, too, must deal in ferreting out and organizing the facts, they have done some of the groundwork for depth reporting. Among the books on this subject is one by Louis Gottschalk. His *Understanding History—A Primer of Historical Method* was designed to teach embryo historians. However, it is also written for the general reader who needs to find standards for judging historical writing. You will find this book in the bibliography to help you to understand history and possibly to adopt some of its research methods.

You might need these methods because there is one level at which this highly published field of history is most often lacking. That is the very level where you must do your most important work—the local level. No bibliography can help you through the problem of locating local history. Instead, we can only offer general suggestions about what is available and how to go about finding it.

How would you find out about local history?

First, there is the possibility that your community may have celebrated a historical birthday. Such birthdays are very popular, for various reasons. You may find that your own newspaper produced the most complete historical account of your town's first 100 years. And if you talked to the men who wrote and edited that history, you would find that they had acquired a large bulk of their information from the files of their own newspaper. Beyond that, they would have used whatever was available—and often that is not very much.

Check for local histories that might have been produced during

WPA days. Some simply amount to the selection and typing of news stories on local events. Others were published as guide books to a community or to a state.

Among the most reliable sources for local and state history are the state historical societies. In many states, the society is subsidized by state funds and has a well-staffed historical museum. The better of these museums include files in both microfilm and volumes of the state's major newspapers. They have collections of papers left by officials and other important state figures. Often professional historians and archeologists are part of the staff. Many even produce their own historical quarterly, which does some of your work for you. Newspapers are usually on the mailing lists for such quarterlies. If not, they should be.

Beyond the state level, you will find that historians are organized by regions of several states. These groups, too, often produce historical quarterlies. Since many of the contributors to such quarterlies are professionals you will find their work carefully footnoted—a technique which helps the journalist be sure of the source.

These are the obvious places to acquire local history. But sometimes you have to use historical method, amass the raw materials, and produce your own history. This is plain hard work, and you had better realize that when you start. It will carry you to the county courthouse, the city hall, and to many other places where public records eventually become historical raw material. The growth of a city, for example, is recorded statistically in such places as the water department, the electrical company, the tax assessor's office, and even the office that records building permits. Usually, you collect many times the information you can use, but this is the way of history—and also the way of good journalism.

At this point it might seem quite logical for you to ask, "Why do this? Of what real use is a city's history?"

In the first place, every newspaper should have written and published such a history—whether it sells ads or not.

Think for a moment, and if you have bought our premise that the doings of men are the business of journalism, you will find the reason. A city is like a person. At first glance, or at first word, a person is sour, a person is friendly, a person is liberal, a person is conservative. So are cities. To understand why a city may be conservative you need to examine its history. No reporter can really

write intelligently about his city if he does not understand how it
got the way it is.

This little lecture on local history may seem far afield from the
problems of the liberally educated reporter. It is not. It is simply
part of the liberal education a newsman must acquire when he
makes his living reporting the activities of the people who make up
his city. It also helps make a point yet unmade about liberal education. Liberal education for the reporter starts somewhere, but it
never ends. Perhaps this is why we wonder if a freshly graduated
journalist truly has a liberal education. At best, all he can have is a
basis from which he may start his liberal education. Perhaps liberal
arts colleges fail if they do not provide a basis in use and method
for the lifetime it takes to study history.

History must be part of the journalist's liberal education. He
must read and read and read. We can only help him get started.

You should know what historical encyclopedic information is
available to check the facts, to refresh your memory, or to add facts.
You will find recommended several encyclopedic approaches to history. These are only several of many. For example, you will find
one on American history, another on world history. You will find
references in which you can check names and dates. The professional historian will quickly point out to you that this is not all of
history. But he, too, knows the importance of factual accuracy as
he interprets and he, too, leans on encyclopedic collections of facts
as an accurate background for historical perspective.

We do not apologize for failing in this area to provide as clear-
cut a route to a basis in history as we have to a basis in some other
disciplines. If you cannot understand why, go to a library and find
the history section. Stand there among the stacks and you will know
there is only one answer. You have a lot of reading ahead of you.

Use of History

Rowse, A. L., *The Use of History*. New York: The Macmillan Company, 1948. This, the key book in a series, makes an eloquent
case for the practical use of history. For the journalist who deals
in depth the argument may not come as a surprise, but this can
do a good deal of fortifying.

This little book (247 pages in pocket format) tries to put history into its perspective academically and practically by applying,

with examples, the value of such men as historically oriented national leaders.

Since its author believes that history is best approached through the biographies of great men, the series introduced by this book is oriented around the lives of men. The journalist, who knows that people make his stories live, could hardly argue with this approach. He probably would be delighted to discover that the series includes such titles as: *Lorenzo De' Medici and Renaissance Italy, Louis XIV and the Greatness of France, Oliver Cromwell and the Puritan Revolution, Thomas Jefferson and American Democracy, Whitgift and the English Church, Agricola and Roman Britain,* and *Alexander The Great and the Hellenistic Empire.*

These are only samples of the nearly forty titles in this series.

There are many books, such as these, which weave history around the lives of men. While there may be something wrong about getting sugar-coated education, there is nothing wrong with enjoying yourself while you learn history.

Method

Gottschalk, Louis, *Understanding History—A Primer of Historical Method.* New York: Alfred A. Knopf, Inc., 1950. This book would seem to be written only for embryo professional historians. Primarily, that is its audience and the training of its members the purpose. But beneath that purpose are two treasures for the journalist:

1. Its author has kept in mind the general reader who needs "to acquire standards of judging historical writing."

2. Its elemental discussion of historical procedure can help the researching reporter. There are interesting parallels between historical method and journalistic research.

Encyclopedias

Morris, Richard B., *Encyclopedia of American History.* New York: Harper & Row, Publishers, 1953. Here, in one volume, is a basic reference to American history. Its user can find his subject by date, subject (index), or possibly by topic if it involves a broad area of American history. To make this possible the volume is divided into three sections, plus an index.

The first section is a chronology by date. The second is a topical coverage that also is chronological. For example:

The American Economy
   Agriculture
   Commerce and the Tariff
   Industry
   National Public Finance
   Banking and Capital Markets
   Business Cycles and Price Trends
   Labor, Slavery, and Social Reform.

Where the date or general topic will not help, the detailed index probably will.

The third section is a biographical account of 300 notable Americans.

Langer, William L., ed., *An Encyclopedia of World History.* Boston: Houghton Mifflin Company, 1940. This is a revised and modernized version of Ploetz's *Epitome,* translated from the German and first published in the United States in 1883.

This encyclopedia is a chronologically arranged record of ancient, medieval, and modern history, ranging from the prehistoric period through World War II. The encyclopedia is further divided by geographical areas under the time periods set forth. It also has many genealogical tables of various dynasties and houses, as well as maps of empires and countries as they have changed through the ages.

An Example

Morison, Eliot Samuel, and Henry Steele Commager, *The Growth of the American Republic,* 4th ed. New York: Oxford University Press, Inc., 1950.

This is a thorough, smoothly written history. While it concentrates on the white man's life in the United States, the early pages carry the Indians' ancestors over the Bering Straits. This edition brings the story of the Republic down through post-World War II years.

There is almost no limit to which additional detail can increase the mass of a volume or volumes of American history. This two-volume set illustrates the middle ground between some one-volume, highly digested textbooks and the multivolumes of the encyclopedic approach.

It would serve the newsman well to become acquainted with some of the more complete histories of the United States.

The Political Animal

"I spent $250 in phone calls for one story today," a Midwestern editor bragged. The city editor was proud of himself. His boss, the editor of the medium-size daily, was also proud.

"Our city desk called every city our size in the country today," said the boss as he admired the city edition. "Now we've put an end to all those questions about whether we pay more for our street paving than other cities. It cost us $250, but it was worth it."

Both newsmen had reason to be proud. They had done a complete job on a local story that, primarily because of lack of facts, had kept their city stirred up for weeks. The motives of this editor and his city editor were admirable. But their economics were poor.

The street-paving figures that had cost $250 in phone calls and nobody-knew-how-many-reporter hours could have been had free not five minutes from their office. In a university library within ten blocks of the newspaper were even more complete street-paving figures than those they had wrung out of sources by telephone over the entire country.

No good newsman is going to complain because a couple of his colleagues went all out to do a complete job on an important local story. If the American newspaper is going to continue to be the main source of information for the fact-hungry reader, it will have to go all out even more often than it now does.

But in this strenuous search for the complete story, we can't forget two factors:

1. We can't deplete the newsroom budget on every all-out effort. (If we can save money on telephone calls, it's better off in salaries for good men.)

2. We can't afford to take any chances with accuracy. (The telephone is frequently about the third-best fact-gathering tool in this department.)

These points apply to all news stories, but are particularly pertinent on the governmental or political writer's beat in the maze of modern government. Often this reporter builds his best story from a base that is almost completely statistical.

I know. I was that Midwestern city editor responsible for that $250 telephone search for street-paving statistics. Unhappily, that was not a lone example. It simply best illustrates lousy newsroom economics.

The questions that have caused harassed city editors to push their staffs to the limit are as endless as the topics of the changing days' news. Look over the questions that follow. Are they academic examples or are they the stuff from which much good governmental reporting is made?

How do our city governmental pay scales compare with the rest in the country?

How does our street-lighting program compare?

Has this proposed amendment to the city charter been tried elsewhere?

How does our police protection rank with other cities our size?

Does the "buddy" system work—one fireman and one policeman in each patrol car?

Should there be one or two officers in each patrol car? Who has tried the system we do not use?

Is the organizational change being recommended by the local League of Women Voters part of a trend in city government over the country?

Are our state department heads really underpaid?

Without going through Blue Books from almost every state, can I check election statistics for the whole country?

What is the voting record of not only our state but the surrounding states for the last eight years?

How do I trace the law in this story about a district court judge's upsetting a local police case?

How do I locate the right federal official in the complicated structure of national government to ask this question about our state highways?

Who in the vast federal government is responsible for this area in the school lunch program?

This list of questions which every veteran governmental reporter has run through his mind at one time or another could be unending. The point is that much of the basic background for the answers could be found in the results of work by political scientists.

Furthermore, if you are not worried about the time and money it might take to trace down this kind of background by telephone, you should be worried about the accuracy of your results. The veteran newsman who has tackled such governmental problems by phone also knows that Mr. Alexander Graham Bell's invention is only third best for gathering many types of information. It isn't Mr. Bell's fault, but it is true that telephone calls, particularly those dealing with specific details, can't help but be less accurate than direct contact with the information. And, as far as governmental reporting is concerned, no academic area can provide so much direct contact with information as can political science.

There are all kinds of political scientists. Some of them practice practical politics in government itself. Others lecture in classrooms and do research in universities. Still others spend full time in political research as the employees or directors of various kinds of governmental and political institutes.

The kinds of information that come from all these sources are as varied as the sources themselves. There are books which discuss generally accepted theory and practice of government. There are other books that are simply bound volumes of periodical collections. There are loose-leaf collections of information brought up to date weekly. There are pamphlets, periodicals, and other less sizeable published materials. There are institutes for every level of government and almost every state working year around on specific governmental problems that make news daily somewhere in the country.

All this just keeps proving that Aristotle was right. "Man is a political animal," he said. He could have added that a reporter is a man who must keep on the trail of the political animal. And there are times when the reporter could use help.

Happily for the newsman, the political scientists themselves have made overtures that have resulted in the beginnings, at least, of a marriage between political science and journalism. The American Political Science Association has sponsored contests and held expense-paid seminars for top governmental reporters. The Association also has sponsored congressional fellowships and included many journalists as participants. The newsmen who have participated in these programs know very well that political science can do much as a practical background tool. Many of the rest of the nation's governmental reporters may need to find it out.

Let's get more specific.

Have you bothered to check the university campuses in your state

to see if they have governmental research institutes? You will find
there is one in almost every state, and in some cases, more. Frequently, they are tackling the practical problems that come up
almost every week in your city council meeting, or at least every
time your legislature meets. Usually these institutes not only have
files and publications that are available to the press but they encourage newsmen to use them.

Since the 1930's, almost every legislature in America has realized
the need for research before and after legislation. The result has
been the growth of the legislative council in the nation's state-
houses. Of course, this council makes news when it submits its
major reports a few months before each legislative session. Unfortunately, too many statehouse reporters wait for the council to
make news instead of using it as the year-around source for background materials that may lead to important legislative changes.

At the national level, there are a number of institutes dealing
in specific fields. Some of these are supported by organizations of
public officials. For instance, there are organizations for almost every
one of the major municipal officials. There are police chiefs' associations, city managers' associations, treasurers' associations, and so
on throughout the municipal table of organization.

Among the very best sources for background information are
the publications and studies of such groups. For example, the
International City Managers Association produces an annual called
The Municipal Yearbook. Do you want to find out how your street-
building expenditures compare with the rest of the country? Check
this source. And the happy thing about this type of information is
that the publications frequently are available right in your own
city hall.

There are a number of similar organizations, and frequently,
one phone call directed to the right home office can result in complete and accurate statistics dealing with your news problem.

Some institutes are financed by various charitable foundations.
These usually are involved with relatively short-term research into
government. Others, such as the National Election Institute in
Washington, D.C., exist on an almost permanent basis. This particular institute is the one that could provide you with detailed,
accurate, well-organized statistics on the elections in every state of

the union. If you are writing a political backgrounder that would be more complete if you knew the election results of the states surrounding yours, the volumes produced by the Election Institute would save a search through a dozen state Blue Books.

The publications from the Election Institute, by the way, illustrate again the desire of political scientists to team up with the newsman. The foreword of these volumes cites the needs of journalists as a specific reason for publication.

If for no other reason—and there are many others—perhaps the nation's newsmen should look to political science and its studies for the answers to some $250 questions. More specifically, the newsmen can look to the discipline's books and other publications for some of those answers.

Political Science Terms and Research

Riker, William H., *The Study of Local Politics*. New York: Random House, 1959. This is a guide for field research at local political levels.

It would be useful as an aid to journalism students and professionals when public opinion sampling becomes part of political coverage. It is short and concise, with additional bibliography on most steps in this type of newspaper research.

Theimer, Walter, *An Encyclopedia of Modern World Politics*. New York: Holt, Rinehart & Winston, Inc., 1950. This is an alphabetical survey of political terms, systems, trends, and problems.

It gives political sketches of most countries, their constitutions, parties, tendencies, and problems. There are some brief biographies, but its author calls it not a *"Who's Who* in politics," but a "what's what in politics."

This is a political handbook that provides for the journalist a reliable starting point on everything from Aristotle to gerrymandering.

Zadrozny, John T., *Dictionary of Social Science*. Washington, D.C.: Public Affairs Press, 1959. This dictionary gives definitions of specialized terms used over a broad span of social sciences.

It is valuable to the journalist using professional writing and research for reference material, and especially helpful in translating professional terms into more commonly used language.

Municipal Facts, Theory, and Practice

Chatters, Carl H., and Albert M. Hillhouse, *Local Government Debt Administration*. Englewood Cliffs, N.J.: Prentice-Hall, Inc., 1939. This is a manual for planning, selling, and administering local bonds, complete with examples, glossary, and bibliography.

It might be particularly valuable as over-all background for all city bond stories.

International City Managers Association, *The Municipal Yearbook*. Chicago: International City Managers Association. This is a basic handbook of municipal statistics and trends. It covers census, personnel, finance, activities with trends, and has a directory of city officials as well as a bibliography.

The Municipal Yearbook is a journalistic must for authoritative, comparative, easy to find, up-to-date facts on city government.

Note: There are any number of special associations for governmental officials. The International City Managers Association is cited as an example because of the thoroughness with which it covers its particular field of municipal government. It is a professional society of city managers and municipal administrators. It conducts management information services. It sponsors the Institute for Training in Municipal Administration. Its publications include: (1) *Public Management,* monthly; (2) *City Managers' Newsletter,* semi-monthly; and (3) *The Municipal Yearbook.* It also publishes the *City Managers Professional Series* dealing with techniques for handling municipal problems and for training programs for municipal departments.

Other associations for governmental officials can be located through library reference or simply by asking officeholders with whom reporters deal at every level of government.

Moody's Investors Service, *Moody's Public Utility Manual.* New York. This publication lists public utility enterprises, both American and foreign, with details of history, background, mergers and acquisitions, subsidiaries, business, construction programs, principal plants, and properties. There are data relating to rates, franchises, and contracts.

The Public Utility Manual gives names and titles of officers and directors along with the general counsel, auditors, date of annual meeting, and the latest number of stockholders and employees. It also gives bond ratings ranging from Aaa to C. Financial reports are given for larger companies, covering the past seven years.

The blue paper insert is the statistical and historical survey. And it includes a discussion of activities of the federal government in the electric power industry along with factual data covering various federal power projects.

The journalist will find that there is a great variety of information published by Moody's. Some of this information is cited elsewhere in this bibliographical section. However, for today's city hall reporter, who deals almost daily in stories about municipal debt and public utility bonds, this particular Moody's publication requires special note.

Reed, Thomas Harrison, *Municipal Management.* New York and London: McGraw-Hill Book Company, Inc., 1941. The author gives both theory and examples of city organization in total and by units. The functions, procedure, and working relationship of units or departments are discussed. The over-all viewpoint is based on the practical working of American municipalities. Courts and elections were omitted because of their nonlocal character.

This is journalistically valuable as an over-all look at municipal administration. Some of the specifics are outdated, but it is still practical for most U.S. municipalities.

Smith, Ray, editor-in-chief, *Municipal Corporations.* Chicago: Callaghan & Co., 1951. This is the third edition of these twenty volumes. The index volume divides references by section from "Abandoned Legislation" through "Zoological Societies." There is also a yearly cumulative pocket supplement for each volume.

Although legal research is detailed at the end of this political science bibliography, this particular reference is so specialized in municipal problems that it is mentioned here.

State Facts, Theory, and Practice

Council of State Governments, *The Book of the States.* Chicago: Council of State Governments, biennially. Here is an authoritative source of information on state structures, working methods, financing, and functional activities. It covers executive, legislative, and judicial branches with their intergovernmental relations and with the major areas of public service performed by them.

Following publication in even-numbered years, one supplement is issued early and another in the middle of the following odd-numbered year. Each book emphasizes the events of the two years preceding publication.

Council of State Governments, *Reorganizing State Governments.* Chicago: Council of State Governments, 1950. An examination of current trends of state organization, it is based on the work of state agencies established to study over-all operations.

It is valuable to the journalist because consolidation of studies shows the trends in almost every state bureau or department. Tables provide a quick means of comparison between your state and the rest.

Note: The Council of State Governments performs much the same function for state administrative officials as does the International City Managers Association for municipal officials. For this reason it has also been chosen as a special example in this bibliography. At the municipal level there are many organizations and institutes besides the ICMA. And there are many organizations and institutes dealing with state problems besides the Council of State Governments.

However, the Council is one of the best known and most all-encompassing. Organized in 1925, its headquarters are at 1313 East 60th Street, Chicago. It provides staff services for such conferences as the Governors' Conference, the Conference of Chief Justices, National Association of Attorneys General, and others of a similar nature.

Key, V. O., Jr., *American State Politics: An Introduction.* New York: Alfred A. Knopf, Inc., 1956. Examples, both statistical and descriptive, give the reader a general foundation in politics at the state level. Historical trends are discussed and the author gives his estimates of the reasons for changes. Since Southern politics are handled in a separate volume, there is very little concerning them in this book.

It should be useful to the journalist to have the major issues and problems common to many states consolidated in one reference volume.

Key, V. O., Jr., *Southern Politics.* New York: Alfred A. Knopf, Inc., 1949. The complexity and peculiarities of Southern politics are

218

set forth along with a broad outline of the structure and character. This particular volume supplements *American State Politics* by the same author.

This is valuable to the journalist as a comparative and factually informative book, and particularly for newsmen outside the South during a historical period when the South is constantly newsworthy.

MacDonald, Austin F., *American State Government and Administration*, 5th ed. New York: Thomas Y. Crowell Company, 1955. This is a comprehensive examination of the history, workings, and administration of state government.

Encyclopedic in coverage, almost popularly written, this volume describes almost every aspect of state government. Its appeal to reporters is enhanced by the inclusion of the pros and cons on many continuing state governmental issues.

State Blue Books are published through the offices of the secretary of state or the legislative council of most states. They usually contain election statistics, organization, budget information, biographical sketches of state officials, and frequently some state history. The supply is normally limited, so newspapers need to make sure they are on the mailing lists.

Just as government overlaps at all levels, so does its bibliography. For example, county government is almost entirely state government at a local level. Thus, much information which applies to state government is a projection of county government. To a lesser degree there is overlap between the state and federal levels. For example, national election statistics are simply collections of state election statistics. You will find that some state information may be included in the federal bibliography that follows.

Federal Facts, Theory, and Practice

Barker, Ernest, *Reflections on Government*. New York: Oxford University Press, Inc., 1942. This is a widely respected basic reference on philosophy, theory, and practice of government.

This is journalistically valuable as a background reference on almost ageless governmental philosophies. This type of reference, considered a basic background for the student of government, can be equally valuable to the reporter of government.

Brogan, D. W., *Politics and Law in the United States.* New York: Cambridge University Press, 1941. This is an examination of the extraordinary part written law plays in U.S. government and politics. This tiny book (127 pages) was written to help British readers understand this aspect of U.S. government.

It could be helpful to the journalist as a review or starting point since it is a mixture of legality, constitutional and otherwise, with a Briton's interpretation.

Reading this brief book is for the American journalist like reading an American's examination of the Magna Carta or parliamentary elections would be for a British newsman. While there would be disagreement with interpretation, the fresh viewpoint would help one understand oneself. There are several other books about American government and politics by this Briton.

Mallory, Walter H., ed., *Political Handbook of the World.* New York: Harper & Row, Publishers, 1961. Subtitled "Parliaments, Parties and Press," it is exactly what it says. It lists the heads of governments, type of cabinet (progressive, coalition, and so on), cabinet members, résumé of recent political events (for some), or political events since 1945 (for others), party programs and leaders, and gives the major newspapers, their circulation, political affiliation, and their top executives. All data are compiled by the Council on Foreign Relations and are revised and republished at regular intervals.

Peaslee, Amos J., and Martinus Nijhoff, *Constitutions of Nations,* 3rd ed. The Hague, Netherlands: Nijhoff, 1956. The texts, summaries, annotations, bibliographies, and comparative tables of the world's nations are given in three volumes.

This could be a basic reference for news writing involving constitutions and comparisons.

Public Affairs Information Service. New York: Public Affairs Information Service, Inc., 1961. This is a weekly listing of books, pamphlets, periodical articles, government documents, and other useful library material in the field of economics and public affairs. Cumulation of weekly editions is published five times yearly. The fifth cumulative issue is the annual bound volume superceding all others for the year.

This is a valuable journalistic aid as an up-to-the-week guide to the latest statistical summaries and other factual findings in all areas of government from municipal units to international affairs.

Congressional Quarterly. Washington, D.C.: Congressional Quarterly, Inc. This is a combination of an almanac, weekly reports, and a quarterly index covering such things as membership, congressional committees, how the congressmen voted, and digests of what Congress did.

It is published as a basic reference work and to assist journalists with congressional coverage.

Ranney, John C., and Gwendolen M. Carter, *The Major Foreign Powers.* New York: Harcourt, Brace & World, Inc., 1949. An examination of the people, politics, and government of Great Britain, France, the Soviet Union, and China.

It is journalistically helpful for comparison of these foreign governments with each other and with the United States.

Scammon, Richard M., ed., *America Votes.* Pittsburgh: University of Pittsburgh Press, 1959. These are election statistics handbooks compiled and edited by Richard M. Scammon of the Government Affairs Institute.

Designed in part for journalists, these volumes are an authoritative source for factual information on the raw material of political life. For voting records it is almost like having a Blue Book for every state.

Statistical Abstract of the United States. Washington, D.C.: U.S. Bureau of the Census, annually. This book is a voluminous compilation of statistics, primarily national; a basic reference for all kinds of statistics; and a guide to additional available statistics. While most of the data are national, it does give some regional and state breakdowns.

This is a basic national fact manual for newspapers. Its primary value is as a source of statistics for comparison with local statistics.

United States Government Organization Manual. Washington, D.C.: Federal Register Division, National Archives and Records Service, General Services Administration, annually. This manual contains descriptions of agencies in legislative, judicial, executive branches; includes brief description of quasiofficial agencies, selected international organizations, charts of more complex agencies, governmental publications, and ancillary material; and contains names of many high federal officeholders and executives.

The journalist will find this valuable as a guide to complex federal structure, responsibilities, names of agencies, officeholders, and addresses.

Whitaker's Almanack. London: J. Whitaker & Sons, Ltd., annually. The index lists more than 20,000 references in government, finance, population, commerce, and general statistics of various nations of the world. Although oriented toward the citizen of Great Britain or the Commonwealth, the American journalist seeking some odd or obscure fact, as well as general information, might well find it here.

White, William S., *Citadel—The Story of the U.S. Senate.* New York: Harper & Row, Publishers, 1955. *Citadel* combines history, tradition, political maneuvering, and senatorial personalities in an interpretive look at our highest legislative body.

It should be interesting to the journalist as an attempt to convey the distinctive flavor of "the most exclusive club in the world."

Wilding, Norman, and Philip Laundy, *An Encyclopedia of Parliament.* London: Cassell & Co., Ltd., 1958. This book covers history, procedure, ceremonial, administrative and political offices, and parliamentary institutions throughout the British Commonwealth. It has an extensive parliamentary bibliography. The history is divided by reign under the name of the sovereign.

This could be journalistically valuable where American perspective is needed for many stories constantly reminding readers of the close ties with the British Empire.

There are many organizations that can be helpful to the reporter. The following is an example of one of these.

The American Political Science Association—Organization of American Political Scientists. Headquarters at 1726 Massachusetts Avenue, N.W., Washington 6, D.C. It maintains addresses of its members, information on their research, and communication with foundations sponsoring research; serves as a focal point for research organization; and publishes quarterly *The American Political Science Review.* The quarterly includes professional articles in all areas of political science, book reviews, bibliography, and professional notes. This organization has sponsored some of the most effective efforts to link journalism and political science.

Finding the Law

While some of the references already cited may deal with aspects of the law itself, it was necessary to establish an entirely separate section for this vast and important area of bibliography.

The legal profession, probably more than any other, must depend upon its publications for guidance. Almost every law problem involves some library research. While the journalist must rely upon legal experts to help in even slightly complicated legal stories, he often needs to do some of his own research.

This section makes no effort to suggest that most, if any, journalists should try to learn to do complicated legal research. Their job of telling it so their reader can understand it is large enough in itself.

What has been provided here is simply a series of guides in finding the law in the vast library of legal literature.

Current Index to Legal Publications, published weekly by the University of Washington Law Library, gives article, author, and where to find it. The Index is divided by titles, such as Administrative Law, Banks and Banking, Constitutional Law, and so on.

Index to Legal Periodicals, Dorothea A. Flaherty, exec. ed. New York: American Association of Law Libraries, H. W. Wilson Co. Published every four years in hardback accumulation, this contains indexes of periodicals, subjects, authors, and book reviews, as well as a table of cases and a list of subject headings.

Hicks, Frederick C., *Materials and Methods of Legal Research,* 3rd rev. ed. Rochester, N.Y.: The Lawyers Co-operative Publishing Co., 1942. Designed as an aid to law students and lawyers in legal research, this book contains the definition and history of laws, their legal development, their application, and other legal growth, such as legal precedent based on judicial decisions; explanation of bibliographical history; and bibliographical listings.

For journalists, certain chapters should be part of education. Other materials can serve as a guide to research into legal stories.

Price, Miles O., and Harry Bitner, *Effective Legal Research*. Englewood Cliffs, N.J.: Prentice-Hall, Inc., 1953. Written by lawyer-librarians to help law students and lawyers answer the question, "How to find the law," many published resources of this profession, which relies upon its literature perhaps more than any other, are organized and categorized.

Some chapters the journalist should read for his education; others can help him answer at most "how to find the law" and at least "where to start asking questions."

Roalfe, William R., general editor, *How to Find the Law*, 5th ed. St. Paul, Minn.: West Publishing Co., 1957. Prepared as a textbook for law students, it serves as an introduction to the legal materials available, offers some bibliographical information, and gives guidance for legal assignments.

Its chief value to journalists is as a means of understanding the availability and use of legal publications, some definitions, and location of law. It, like others mentioned in this section, helps answer the question of how to find the law. Newsmen using it should first read the introduction.

The availability of legal publications will often depend upon the size of the community in which the reporter works. He may have to depend upon the law library of an attorney in his town. This usually will contain at least the basic books plus special publications on the law of his particular state. There will be digests, additions, corrections, and indexes.

The reporter who works in a county seat will find some type of law library in the county courthouse.

State capitol buildings contain large law libraries.

Universities and colleges with law schools contain excellent law libraries. Often schools, in cooperation with the bar associations, publish valuable law reviews.

Finally, there will be some legal literature in almost every public library.

In addition, the local, state, and national bar associations are important sources. The bar association is often a legal part of a state's judicial system. As such, the society actions often are a part of governmental news. Frequently their committees examine legal problems that are as newsworthy as any governmental coverage.

The Social Animal

As a reporter, could you use demography? Would the words "power," "class," or "leadership" mean anything to you?

If you are a reporter with some knowledge of sociology, all of those words mean that you have extra background on some of the major news stories of our time. If you doubt it, try these words on your sense of news: "population explosion," "birth control," and "mortality rate." They ring some news bells, don't they? Each of them is a subject for study by a branch of sociology. That branch is called demography which involves the study of human populations.

Now add some other words to the word "power." Try these: "the power behind the city council," "the international power struggle," "the power of public opinion." These are a few of the ways sociology looks at power.

As for that word, "class," have you heard any of the following opinions lately?

"To achieve equality, we have made the middle class universal."

"Democracy does not abolish the class system, it only ignores it."

"The power of the Democratic party is centered upon the working class."

"The power of the Republican party is centered upon the wealthy class."

Yes, you have heard quotes like that recently. In fact, the only use you have heard of the word "class" when it was not the subject of sociological interest was probably when it referred to the appearance of a sophisticated young lady.

The word "leadership" is almost too obvious. How recently have you heard someone calling for community, city, county, state, national, or party leadership? Once again you were hearing about a subject often scrutinized by sociologists.

If all this seems to indicate that sociology covers a fairly broad area, it is because it does. Sociology deals with man—your reader —as a member of a group. You will find very few people unable to meet that qualification. Sociology deals with as vast a group as the whole human race, and as small a group as the family. Sociology deals in the very theoretical and the very practical.

You might say that it is pure theory when a sociologist says, "Let me study samples of the vocabulary of your community's leaders. I will tell you whether that community is progressing or standing still. For example, I want to know how often they use the word, 'if.' " (Don't be too sure that that was entirely theory.)

You can, however, recognize the extremely practical approach when sociologists tackle small town problems. Everywhere in America small towns struggle for a broader economic base, for more industry, for more stable industry, for more community cooperation, and, in some cases, for simple existence. All over the country this struggle, its symptoms or its results, trickle into the newsroom. And all over the country sociologists are taking on the problem. Check your own university. You may find the story about a different kind of community fight—a fight for survival.

For example, should you check at the University of Nebraska you would find a bureau of community service. It was established in 1948 by sociology professor Otto G. Hoiberg. The bureau has helped hundreds of communities do everything from start industries to build swimming pools. Hoiberg's book on the experience, *Exploring the Small Community,* was published in 1955 by the University of Nebraska Press. It was designed for community reading, and the newsman of the Midwest is certainly a member of that community.

Hoiberg's book is easily read because of the audience to which it is directed. However, if you wish to have a thorough background in sociology, you will also have to read books for sociologists by sociologists. You will find here, as you will in psychology, that the sociologists have their own language.

We do not mean to seem unduly resentful of these specialized vocabularies. It may be that we expected them in the physical and biological sciences but not in the social sciences. We have not hesitated to point out communications problems in the physical sciences. We cannot ignore them in the social sciences.

In sociology, as in psychology, you should get an introduction to the specialized vocabulary before proceeding into the more advanced and more interesting reading. It will be worth the bother.

You will find much of value written about the overwhelming—almost unanimous—numbers of mankind who are irrevocably members of a social group.

An Introduction

Broom, Leonard E., and Philip Selznick, *Sociology,* 2nd ed. New York: Harper & Row, Publishers, 1958. This is a thorough introduction to sociology. A detailed table of contents, good organization, and attractive format make it a reference as well.

For the journalist, this respected volume can supply background and give working knowledge of the discipline. That knowledge can be applied practically to such newsworthy items as segregation, population problems, and family life.

About Leadership

Bell, Wendell, Richard J. Hill, and Charles L. Wright, *Public Leadership.* San Francisco: Chandler Publishing Company, 1961. Newspapermen, among others, seek, demand, praise, and denounce *leadership*. Reporters look for and analyze the *leadership* in every legislative body. Political writers examine the public *leadership* of parties and speculate on the behind-the-scenes *leadership*.

In all of this activity, one word stands out in mental italics—*leadership*. Sometimes an aura seems to highlight the word. Sometimes its backdrop is sinister. But most often it is surrounded by a haze that makes the word itself almost unidentifiable. When anyone tries to burn away some of the haze, the press should pay attention.

This particular volume is a review of much of the study about public leadership. Its authors base their work on five general questions:

1. How many people are involved in the various types of public leadership roles?
2. What are the social characteristics, social and educational backgrounds, and career patterns of these people?
3. What are the general population's attitudes toward and images of public leaders?
4. What motives are involved in original participation, continuing participation, and nonparticipation in public leadership roles?

5. What educational experiences might be attractive and beneficial to persons either currently or potentially in positions of public leadership?

The answers to these questions are vital background to any number of news stories.

About Class

Kahl, Joseph A., *The American Class Structure.* New York: Holt, Rinehart & Winston, Inc., 1957. This is an examination of classes as they exist in the United States. Occupation, income, politics, and race are a few of the areas involved.

Although this book was written as a classroom text, other audiences were not forgotten. Among them are the journalists to whom the writer says specifically, you "find social class to be basic to the American life" you seek to understand.

Perhaps here in this specialized area of sociology, the journalist may find the most easily understood reasons for knowledge of sociology. While some other subjects of sociology may offer more in the way of facts, the newsman spends his life seeking additional background also. The fascinating subject of class provides not only good reading but much long-term background.

About Power

Schermerhorn, Richard A., *Society and Power.* New York: Random House, 1961. In this book the sociologist considers a field normally thought to be that of the political scientist. The subject—power —is part of news stories, from a small community meeting to an international meeting at the "summit." The journalist, who often covers these power struggles, is also considered by some to be the tool of power. He would do well to get help on the subject from both political science and sociology.

Demography (Population)

Wrong, Dennis H., *Population.* New York: Random House, 1956. This is an introduction to demography, the study of human populations.

There is a specialized field of social science that deals initially in pure numerical data. Interpretation comes later. An introduction to demography serves as a basis for questions about such common news words as "population explosion," "birth control," and "mortality rate."

Social Psychology

Newcomb, Theodore M., *Social Psychology*. New York: a Holt-Bryden Book, Holt, Rinehart & Winston, Inc., 1950. In this book and in this area sociology and psychology meet.

Does an individual act as an individual or does he act and react as a member of a group? In a sense, this question is answered by the very existence of social psychology as a recognized area of study.

This book can serve the journalist as an introduction to social psychology, where sociology and psychology team up. It may also give him some insight into news stories. The journalist, who must write, meet his deadline, and hope the reader understands, would be interested in the prepublication criticism of this book. Students used the manuscript as a text and indicated passages that bothered them. These were rewritten before the book was published.

Those Little Numerical Lies

Huff, Darrell, *How To Lie With Statistics*. New York: W. W. Norton & Company, Inc., 1954. This is a short (142 pages), popularly written treatise with many comic illustrations on how to sharpen your perception on the deception of statistics. While this book does a good deal of spoofing about the use of numbers, it has a serious purpose in an age when everyone tries to prove everything with statistics. Read it, laugh with it, and be warned by it.

The Worldly Philosophy

In a world suffering from *economic digititis,* the reporter suffers most of all. He must turn economic digititis into pocketbook economics, and the gap between the two is exceedingly wide.

What is economic digititis? Literally, it is inflammation of economic numbers. Figuratively, it is a term we made up to describe the indescribably complicated high finance of today's big business and governmental economics.

How does the journalist protect himself against economic digititis? The prescription is simple. The cure takes a bit longer.

First, of course, comes inoculation by acquiring background in economics. For the student this may take place in required course work. But if it is too late and the classroom is far behind, self-medication must be practiced by the professional journalist. After the inoculation, both the student and the professional must maintain immunity by reading and thinking and understanding.

The effectiveness of the cure can be easily determined by the patient. He simply applies his liberal education in economics to his particular case of economic digititis. It should reduce the swelling to easily digestible pocketbook economics. If the swelling remains, he needs more treatment.

Now, more about that treatment. For the student, it starts with introductory—often required—courses. Though these offerings may suffer the blight of all beginning, everything-for-everyone courses, they can provide a base in economic theory. Yet, it will be the rare introductory course that also bridges the gap between economic digititis and easily understood pocketbook economics. Other classwork can bridge that gap.

There are excellent advanced courses on such subjects as government finance. The journalism student who takes them must remind himself constantly that he, perhaps more than any other person in that classroom, is acquiring a working tool. He is trying to learn enough about economics so that he can explain to a reader how a complicated financial system affects the bulge of his own wallet.

Unfortunately, the student journalist in search of a liberal education can major in only one or two of the 15 or 20 areas he really needs tucked away in his brain. Thus, the economics major or economics graduate student is a rarity in the newsroom.

Perhaps this is just as well. The nation's most successful business newspaper, which is edited for anyone interested in making a living, seldom hires the highly specialized economist. Instead, *The Wall Street Journal* looks for intelligent reporters who can understand and write. They then may acquire a liberal education in economics as they work.

230

This bibliography is designed to help find that liberal education. It is the kind of an education that makes a reporter tell his reader about the interest on a huge government loan in terms of the reader's own mortgage on his house. It is the kind of education that makes the farmer's wife understand parity in terms of her chicken-and-egg money. It is the kind of education that makes the grocer understand a multimillion dollar business merger in terms of the price tag and label on a can of corn. As you seek your liberal education in economics, keep in mind that can of corn, the chicken-and-egg money, and your own home mortgage. When you lose sight of them, you open yourself up to an attack of economic digititis.

With the can of corn, the chicken-and-egg money, and your own mortgage in mind, take a look at the following bibliography. Pick and choose as your degree of economic digititis dictates.

You will find dictionaries to help you with the jargon of economics. A directory of labor organizations is cited as an example of the kinds of materials available in raw form to economists. You will not find some items such as the *U.S. Statistical Abstract,* which you might normally expect here. Though it is a prime source for economists, it is also used in many other fields (see Political Science) and so has been included later in the general bibliography. You will find basic economics texts used in introductory courses to develop the basic theories of economics. You will find a markedly human book, *The Worldly Philosophers,* from which we, quite humanly, stole the title for this chapter.

Anthologies may acquaint you with the diverse areas and diverse opinions in this broad field. An example of a specialized economic study, of which there are multitudes, will be found in a book on the national economy and national defense. The conservative and liberal viewpoints of the American economy are represented. So are such contemporary problems as the emerging nations. And finally, for a little thought, and a little agreement or disagreement as it pleases you, there is *The Affluent Society* by John Kenneth Galbraith.

At the end of the general economics annotations you will find a very specialized one. It is included because there is at least one economic field in every section of the country which requires a full-time reporter. If you publish a paper in Duluth, Minnesota, shipping, the docks, and allied industry make up a full-time specialized beat. If you write in Oklahoma City or Tulsa or Dallas there are specialized beats in the oil industry. In Florida, tourism may require a specialist.

For the one specialized bibliography in this entire bibliographical section, we have chosen agriculture because of its effect on almost every part of the country. Its inclusion violates the early rules we established for the annotations. We were interested not in specialization, but liberalization. Nonetheless, you need to know just how specialized you can get if necessary.

Because this bibliography of agriculture violates our own rules, we did not do its annotation. Instead, because in such an area you need a specialist, an agricultural librarian assembled the list.

Now, as it pleases you, skip through this bibliography, finding what you need for your own case of economic digititis.

Dictionaries

Sloan, Harold S., and Arnold J. Zurcher, *A Dictionary of Economics,* 3rd ed. New York: Barnes & Noble, Inc., 1953. There are more than 2,800 terms in this 345-page dictionary. There are two appendices. The first consists of specimen financial sheets analyzed in terms as defined in the dictionary; the second gives names of national monetary units. The definitions are concise, but clear, and very well cross-referenced for further explanation.

Horton, Byrne J., with Julien Ripley, Jr., and M. B. Schnapper, *Dictionary of Modern Economics.* Washington, D.C.: Public Affairs Press, 1948. This 365-page dictionary, although several years older than Sloan and Zurcher's, contains many references not found in theirs, and vice versa. The two are good complements on many terms, each giving information not contained in the other.

A Sample Dictionary

Directory of Labor Organizations, Western Hemisphere, U.S. Department of Labor, Bureau of International Labor Affairs. Washington, D.C.: U.S. Government Printing Office, 1960. This is a listing of names, addresses, membership, and officers of labor unions in the Western hemisphere. It also gives a brief description of the country, that is, how its economy is based, population, and division of labor force into agricultural, industrial, and commerce and banking.

This is an example of the types of directories that are available to the journalist.

Samples of Basic Textbooks

Harriss, C. Lowell, *The American Economy*. Homewood, Ill.: Richard D. Irwin, Inc., 1953. This is a basic text on the American economy. Description and analysis provide facts and interpretation.

The inclusion of significant elements of the contemporary American economy provide examples as well as statistics and theory.

For the journalist this book can provide a rather detailed backgrounding of the American economy. While it is a textbook, designed for the classroom, it is well enough organized and indexed to serve also as a reference.

McConnell, Campbell R., *Elementary Economics*. New York: McGraw-Hill Book Company, Inc., 1960. This is a thorough (759 pages) introduction to the principles of economics.

The journalist can find this book so complete that he uses it as a reference. However, it is so well keyed to modern American economics that it may also serve as good reading in its entirety.

The field of economics is especially well defined. The discussion of the Soviet economy and the "challenges it poses for the 'free world'" is especially interesting to the journalist who deals almost daily with this subject. The same is true of the approach to economic growth and the role of government.

History by Biography

Heilbroner, Robert L., *The Worldly Philosophers*. New York: Simon and Schuster, Inc., 1953. This is a beautifully, wittily written book on "the lives, times and ideas of the great economic thinkers."

The author begins with the very first economist, the appropriately named Adam Smith, and carries the reader through succeeding economic eras up to the modern day.

For any journalist who has thought of economics as dull, dry statistics and theory, this volume will come as a delightful surprise. All the basic economic theories are here, stripped of the confusing professional jargon and presented simply and clearly in a highly readable style—a good job of readable depth reporting.

History by Anthology

Harris, Seymour E., ed., *American Economic History*. New York: McGraw-Hill Book Company, Inc., 1961. This book contains the work of 20 scholars of economics. It not only includes economic history by subject, but is written, as the editor points out, by economists with a wide diversity of philosophies.

It gives the journalist a basic economic reference to such subjects as money, fiscal policy, population and immigration, pattern of employment, unions, and agriculture. It also provides an easy acquaintanceship with 20 widely known economists.

Opinion by Anthology

Problems of United States Economic Development, published by Committee for Economic Development, 711 Fifth Avenue, New York 22, New York, 1958. This is a selection of 48 papers, of approximately 2,000 words each, on the question: "What is the most important economic problem to be faced by the U.S. in the next twenty years?"

The fields covered are (1) international relations, (2) relations between wealthy and poor countries, (3) economic stability, (4) uses of economic growth, (5) philosophy of free institutions, (6) problems resulting from economic growth, (7) congestion of urban problems, (8) problems resulting from changes in size and composition of growth population, and (9) national security.

The problems posed, and the tentative solutions put forward, are as varied as the men (and women) who wrote the articles. The authors include economists, professors, journalists, industrialists, and statesmen.

It is valuable as a cross section of diverse statements and solutions of economic problems in the U.S.

This book is one of a series of many volumes by the CED on all phases of economic development.

A Sample of Specialization

Lincoln, George A., *Economics of National Security*, rev. ed. Englewood Cliffs, N.J.: Prentice-Hall, Inc., 1954. This book's subtitle, *Managing America's Resources for Defense,* helps explain the viewpoint of the author and his associates in the Social Sciences Department of the United States Military Academy. Organization helps guide the reader in search of specifics. The sections include:

I. History and description.
II. Resources which produce military power.
III. Finance and stabilization under emergency conditions.
IV. International aspects and effect of these aspects on U.S. way of life.

In an era when scarcely a day passes when the question of defense is not linked with the nation's economy, this volume can become a handbook for newsmen. While there is personal opinion that can help interpret, there also is much outright factual material on a subject frequently fraught with opinion—and highly emotional opinion at that.

In the numerous books related to economics there are many as specialized as this one. Would it be asking too much to ask a reporter to read one before starting on a special economics assignment?

A Conservative Viewpoint

Wallich, Henry C., *The Cost of Freedom.* New York: Harper & Row, Publishers, 1960. This is a straightforward, well-written exposition of the "conservative's" approach to present-day economic problems.

Elsewhere in this economics bibliography is the "liberal" approach as set forth by Hansen. Wallich was at one time a student of Hansen's, but his thinking has developed in an entirely different direction. It would be profitable for the journalist, no matter what his own private feelings on the U.S. economy, to read these two books at the same time. Both provide a banquet for serious thought and both throw a great deal of light on various areas of the U.S. economy, its present problems, and some projected paths for the future.

A Liberal Viewpoint

Hansen, Alvin H., *Economic Issues of the 1960's.* New York: McGraw-Hill Book Company, Inc., 1960. This volume is a statement of the "liberal" economist's view as opposed to a "conservative" (such as Henry Wallich in *The Cost of Freedom*).

Professor Hansen's brief preface points out the need for education to become the "major industry" in view of the accelerating pace of automation and more abundant leisure for all classes and age groups. Underlying reasons are found scattered through the whole book, but particularly so in his section on "Growth, Automation, and the Dual Economy." The other two sections are "The Inflation Debate" and "Developed and Underdeveloped Countries."

The three appendices are on urbanization, trends, and cycles in economic activity and the public debt.

This book is clearly written, well indexed, and an excellent sampling from the over-all Economics Handbook Series.

A Contemporary Problem

Millikan, Max F., and Donald L. M. Blackmer, eds., *The Emerging Nations.* Boston: Little, Brown & Co., 1961. Subtitled *Their Growth and United States Policy,* this book grew out of a pooling of the separate studies in economics, politics, sociology, and psychology of the underdeveloped parts of the world.

Ten different authors submitted their particular studies and viewpoints to the common purpose of giving a broad, cohesive look at the growing problem of newly developing nations. The book covers such topics as the disruption of the traditional societies; their resistance to innovations in politics, economics, and social structure; factors in social change; and so forth. The second part of the book gives the authors' ideas on what the U.S. policy toward these nations *must* be and how this policy can best be effected.

The problem of arising nations is both delicate and immense and one likely to be with us for many years to come. The journalist of today and tomorrow must necessarily have a thorough grounding in basic, over-all information on this subject. *The Emerging Nations* gives this foundation. And it serves as an example of the kind of information available on contemporary problems.

An Interpretation

Galbraith, John Kenneth, *The Affluent Society*. Boston: Houghton Mifflin Company, 1958. This is written from the viewpoint that the "conventional wisdom" of the economists is sadly outdated. The criteria for economic tactics of the "poor" nations no longer apply in this era of affluence, says the author. From this basic stand, he criticizes accepted economic theory and suggests new and possibly radical departures in the whole approach to the business world, profit, production, investment, and government spending. He includes in government spending such things as welfare programs, foreign aid, and the "fallacy" of the balanced-budget theory.

The increased prominence to which the Kennedy administration raised the author makes it even more important that journalists know his philosophies. And the author is not only a widely known economist, he is a witty writer as well. There are many pungent side comments on what he considers some of the more ridiculous aspects of American life.

Agriculture*

Periodical Indexes

Agricultural Index, 1916-   . This is an alphabetical subject index of more than 100 American and English periodicals and a few journals in foreign languages. It indexes many bulletins, circulars, and reports of state agricultural experiment stations, departments, and the U.S. Department of Agriculture. It also includes many books, pamphlets, and reports. It is issued monthly, cumulating during the year and annually, with three year cumulative volumes, and is one of the basic indexes for agricultural literature.

Bibliography of Agriculture, 1942-   . This bibliography is published monthly by the Library of the U.S. Department of Agri-

---

* An example of specialized economic bibliography, prepared by Wayne R. Collings, Librarian, College of Agriculture, University of Nebraska.

culture. It tries to list all current publications, domestic and foreign, in the field of agriculture and is world wide in scope. It now includes almost 100,000 entries annually in broad subject arrangement. There is an author index in each issue and an author and subject index for the year in the December issue.

Experiment Station Record, 1889-1946. This is a monthly digest of agricultural and home economics literature issued through 1946 by the U.S. Office of Experiment Stations, Washington, D.C. It included foreign language materials as well as English and covered a wide range of subject material over a long span of years.

Encyclopedias

Bailey, L. H., *Cyclopedia of American Agriculture,* 4 Vols. New York: The Macmillan Co., 1907-1909. This is a popular survey of agricultural conditions, practices, and ideals in the United States and Canada.

Arranged by broad subjects with an index for each volume, the book consists of signed articles by specialists, with bibliographies. It is now too antiquated for general purposes but is useful historically.

McGraw-Hill Encyclopedia of Science and Technology, 15 Vols., 1960.

Statistics

U.S. Department of Agriculture, *Agricultural Statistics.* 1936-
This is issued annually. Before 1936 the statistical information was contained in the U.S. Department of Agriculture Yearbook.

U.S. Department of Agriculture, *Agriculture Handbook No. 118.* Washington, D.C., 1957-   . This is the major statistical series of the U.S. Department of Agriculture, and it explains how they are constructed and used. Ten volumes have been issued to date.

Yearbooks

U.S. Department of Agriculture, *Yearbook of Agriculture,* 1894-   .
The volumes are issued annually. The volumes published before 1936 contain statistical information and summaries of developments in agriculture during the year. Since 1936 each volume has been devoted to a special subject.

Handbooks

White, J. M., *The Farmer's Handbook.* Norman, Okla.: University of Oklahoma Press, 1948. This is a handbook of ready reference on crops, farm animals, farm engineering, and other major phases of farming.

Ensminger, M. Eugene, *The Stockman's Handbook,* 2nd ed. Danville, Ill.: The Interstate Press, 1959.

Blanck, Frederick C., *Handbook of Food and Agriculture.* New York: Reinhold Publishing Corp., 1955.

17

Man and Mind

If a university were organized in the same way this bibliography has been, probably nothing but chaos would result. However, it seemed logical to place together all of those disciplines which seem, initially at least, to involve an abstract mental approach. In some cases, such as in art, aesthetics and even the subconscious may be involved also. Even a painting is the material result of an idea in the artist's mind.

Thus, you find here mathematics, the fine arts, philosophy, and religion. Actually, religion is included here as a branch of philosophy.

Any number of disciplines might claim each of these subjects. Science might claim mathematics. Science could claim philosophy as the basis for scientific method. And religion could be a part of anthropology or sociology. We chose to put these areas where man's mind, his morals, and his sense of beauty are so important in a separate chapter. Annotating hundreds of books can be a chore. We found annotating these books in particular a delightful mental experience.

Queen or Witch?

To many of us mathematics is a witch. We fear that if we venture too close she will cast a spell, unmasking us to the world as arithmetical idiots.

To the mathematician, mathematics is the queen of the sciences, the arts, philosophy, and almost any of the rest of man's scholarly pursuits.

The difference in viewpoints may lie in something as basic as two plus two must irrevocably equal four. If it were possible for two plus two to equal three, or five, or any other total, we might be less fearful of mathematics. As human beings, many of us accept inconsistency as normal. Anything that is irrefutably consistent may frighten us. It is very difficult to like anyone or anything that is always right. Such an association can lead to a lifelong inferiority complex. Such a complex may have filled newsrooms and journalism schools with mathematical illiterates.

Neither the journalists nor the mathematicians have done very much about it. The nearest the working newsman gets to mathematics are the complications of his expense account. The nearest the journalism student ventures is just as far, and no farther, than the requirements of his college push him. The mathematician too often gives the impression that he couldn't care less about any mathematics course that did not lead eventually to integral calculus. The combination of these viewpoints robs journalists of an acquaintance with one of man's most fascinating and important mental activities.

Newsmen are aware of the gaps suffered by the mathematically illiterate. Many editorials of recent years have called for a return to the "three R's"—one of them being 'rithmetic.

Journalism schools do have mathematicians, if statisticians are mathematicians. The numbers of these statisticians has grown steadily as journalism research also has increased. But, the statisticians are primarily interested in graduate-level research. They are seldom concerned with making mathematics a part of liberal arts education for journalists, or making mathematics a reporting tool that helps dig out statistical facts for a story. There is nothing wrong with research, but there is something very wrong when a student leaves the university atmosphere without learning how to use statistics, not only for a professional critique, but to help produce a good, solid story in depth.

Finally, many mathematicians would like to make mathematics a more useful part of their liberal arts offerings. A few of them have helped to write, or have written, some of the most delightful and enlightening books ever published about an academic discipline.

Some of these books are so excellent that we made a shocking discovery as we read them. We were actually enjoying mathematics.
That experience made us wonder if the mathematicians who had
helped us had not shown us an open door. It is possible that liberal
arts students might shake hands with mathematics through the
popular literature of the field.

For us, the witch's spell had been lifted. We realized almost without knowing it that it wasn't important whether we knew how to
work a problem in calculus. What was important was that we knew
why a mathematician should work a problem in calculus. We realized that mathematicians have to live with the infallibility of their
numbers, but we could simply be good friends.

With the help of basic mathematics courses and a dictionary,
such as the new Van Nostrand volume, we found we could enjoy
several respected books about mathematics and mathematicians. We
also found that at least now and then when a mathematician uses
words instead of numbers he can develop a delightful sense of
humor and a refreshing aptitude for frankness.

One writer confessed in the preface of his four-volume work that
he had started the project with a publication deadline two years
away. He ended up four volumes and fifteen years later. He had
missed his deadline by approximately thirteen years.

Another halted his readers mid-way in the first chapter of his
book to make an admission. Actually, he told the readers, you have
been reading the preface, but it was named Chapter One to confuse
habitual preface-skippers.

Cast aside your normal fears and come half-way to meet the
mathematicians who have written or played major roles in the books
recommended in the following bibliography. They really are not
such a frightening lot after all. Their major problem is that two
plus two simply must equal four.

Meet Mathematics

Bell, E. T., *Mathematics—Queen and Servant of Science*. New York:
McGraw-Hill Book Company, Inc., 1951. The mathematically
illiterate such as we, who inhabit the nation's schools of journalism and newsrooms, should read this book twice.

They should skim it. They should skip gaily through it, oblivi-
ous of formulae and theories beyond their comprehension, or
seemingly so. They should trace a point of interest through the

volume, ignoring for the moment that which is not interesting. An unconventional way to read a book? You read this one that way at the author's invitation. It is not intended to replace a textbook. It is not meant to be a treatise on some phase of mathematics. It is aimed at those with some minimal mathematics matriculation somewhere in the past. It is the author's hope that it will revive a spark of interest, bring a measure of understanding, and encourage the reader to venture further. With these goals Bell has produced something that can be of help to both the student and the professional journalist. And while its distinguished author might wince, we must call to your attention the almost unique cross-referencing within the text. It was designed to eliminate the need for a detailed index. Look for yourself. It had to have been invented by a mathematician—and it was.

Men and Mathematics

Bell, E. T., *Men of Mathematics*. New York: Simon and Schuster, Inc., 1937. This highly readable book is designed to take the reader by the hand and lead him through a side door into the world of mathematicians.

With skill a good depth reporter would envy, the author uses the lives of great mathematicians "to lead up to some of the dominating ideas governing vast tracts of mathematics as it exists today. . . ." In the process, mathematicians become human beings and mathematics less inhuman.

The journalist, and anyone else, will appreciate an author who calls his preface Chapter One to decoy habitual preface-skippers. The journalist will also appreciate the author's acceptance of the ideal that no mathematician thoroughly understands his own work until he can explain it effectively to the first man he meets on the street. Certainly the reporter who deals in complicated stories carries the same problem on his shoulders.

The World of Mathematics

Newman, James R., ed., *The World of Mathematics*. New York: Simon and Schuster, Inc., 1956. This is a four-volume collection of mathematical writings that the general reader can both understand and use for reference.

It took the editor fifteen years to collect the "popular" writings instead of the two years he originally planned to devote to the project. This speaks rather eloquently about the quantity and quality of popular reading in this field. It also speaks refreshingly for an editor, who after missing his deadline by thirteen years, confesses the delay in a preface he calls both a hello and a good-bye.

Of course, when he was finished, Newman had produced four volumes—almost 2,500 pages—instead of one. The popular writing he sought was available, but it had to be dug out. Like a good reporter, he delved through literature in search of his story.

And, like the depth reporter, Newman dislikes "snippets and fragments that tease." As a result, many of the selections are long. However, the number of volumes, the number of pages, the length of selections, the years spent are not the most startling aspect of this collection. More startling to the uninitiated are the names and professions of some of the writers reprinted in this anthology. You would expect to find mathematicians, and you will. But would you anticipate some of the following names? Bertrand Russell, philosopher; Gregor Mendel, the first geneticist; and George Bernard Shaw, a not so obscure playwright.

Some of the subjects are equally startling. You will find mathematics and the social sciences, mathematics and art, mathematics and music, mathematics and philosophy, and so on and on through four volumes into all the areas that make up the world of mathematics.

Mathematics and Culture

Kline, Morris, *Mathematics in Western Culture*. New York: Oxford University Press, Inc., 1953. This book produces a by-product in the historical development of mathematics. A second by-product is the understanding of some of the foundations of mathematics. However, the author's chief goal is to show the part mathematics has played in the development of many phases of what we call Western culture.

That goal carries the reader, via mathematics, of course, into painting, sculpture, religion, and many other places—places with which mathematics is not normally associated. Yet the association becomes normal in this well-written book.

Computers

Chapin, Ned, *An Introduction to Automatic Computers*. Princeton, N.J.: D. Van Nostrand Co., Inc., 1957. In writing about Sir Isaac Newton, the British philosopher Bertrand Russell made this comment: "As a man he was a failure. As a monster he was superb." To many persons, the mathematician's dream, the automatic computer, is an awesome, almost mystical modern electronic monster.

Television has done a better job of dispelling this modern myth than have most of the newspapers. As a matter of fact, television has actually put the computer to work in such special occasions as national elections. The infernal machine has misinterpreted a time or two, which delighted those of us not yet ready for the wheel, but it has served television well at that.

It is conceivable that some highly complicated depth story could be helped along in the research stage by a computer. However, that rather remote possibility is not the main reason the journalist should know something about automatic computers.

Almost inevitably, as science makes break-through after break-through, computers play a key role. For this reason the good newsman needs to know enough about computers to write about them clearly, intelligently, and with no sense of mysticism.

Because this book was designed for businessmen—not engineers and scientists—it can be of obvious help to the journalist. He, like the businessman, will appreciate its clear writing. Terms are carefully defined, and the book has an excellent glossary and a thorough index. We found that you should follow the author's suggestion for reading his book. If you are after a firm foundation, read Chapters 1, 2, 12, 13, 14, 15, 11, 7, and 16 in that order. Then read Chapters 3, 4, 5, 6, 8, 9, 10, and 17.

Are you sure you know the difference between a digital and an analog computer? Then, read.

Over the Embalmer's Shoulder

It is possible that many journalists find philosophy a dead subject because their first glimpse of it is over an embalmer's shoulder. Too often, writers on the subject insist in the preface that philosophy is not dead and then proceed chapter by chapter to bury it. Forsaking the very clarity of thought upon which their art is based, they turn a vital thing into a mummified corpse.

To the many and good men who write well about philosophy, we apologize and have done with it. To the few—and it takes only a few—we complain loudly and bitterly. These may be the men who turn away bright young minds seeking the key to creativity.

Others can share the blame. Who?

Educators who don't insist that young journalists know philosophy. Teachers of philosophy who don't pump life into their subject. College curriculum creators who don't realize that methods of philosophic inquiry should be taught. And the general public, including all parents of journalism students.

To those we call the general public, one image is still conjured up by the word "philosopher." They see a curly-headed Greek lecturing beneath an olive tree to more curly-headed Greeks wrapped in white sheets.

As outlandish as it may sound in the newsroom, from the minds of Plato, Aristotle, Rousseau, Russell, Dewey, and Durant we may take the help for which we have been crying for years. Here may be a tool to help train the creative journalist.

Does it upset you to hear talk about creative journalists and philosophy as a key? Stop and think a moment. What is a creative journalist?

He is a newsman whose news judgment gives him the glimmering of an idea for a story. He sees beyond the bare facts, the surface facts. Because he can organize his facts and his mind, he can get all the facts. He can organize them and write them logically. He can do it clearly and readably. What has he done? He has gone through a mental exercise that started with utter freedom and ended with utter self-discipline.

Now what is philosophy? It is one thing for certain. It is a way of getting an idea, searching out the facts about it, applying the test of logic, and finally coming to an understandable conclusion. This, much as it may shock some philosophers, is our digested version of philosophic inquiry.

If this is one of the contributions of philosophy, what is so wrong about teaching it to reporters?

What do we expect of a truly great reporter? We expect to give his good mind complete freedom as an idea becomes the germ of a news story. Without that freedom, he cannot see the whole story. We then expect him to assemble that story, applying the test of accuracy and logic to his facts. And, finally, we expect him to discipline himself so that that story becomes readable words easily understood and unassailable in so far as the facts and their perspective are concerned.

Within the preceding three paragraphs we have committed the journalistic crime of redundancy. We have said the same thing twice. If necessary, we will say it again. The point is important. Philosophic inquiry, its utter freedom and utter discipline, can be the tool of the creative depth reporter.

It would not upset the philosophers of old, or of new, to have their art of the mind be called a working tool. How can they complain? It was from their mental discipline that came almost every form of government in the world today. It was from this same discipline that came modern science.

Certainly, at least these two—government and science—are the raw materials from which much, if not a majority, of news comes. It may be enough simply to report the raw material. But there's a chance that the reporting might be better if the writer had been based in the philosophies that created government and science.

We also have the philosophers to thank for one other vast area of human endeavor, which is probably more human than all man's endeavors. That area is religion.

To understand how something called philosophy resulted in government, science, and religion, it is necessary to accept the hypothesis that philosophy is alive, rather than dead.

Philosophers have been trying to convince the world of this for centuries. In an atmosphere where nothing is black or white, where there are only half-answers, where few are able to understand because the philosophers themselves have not developed an idea sufficiently to explain it simply, it is difficult for the working philosopher to explain even the life or death of his art.

But he can do it, and rather effectively. He does not accept the theory that philosophy developed the basic scientific methods of research and then died, having given birth. He does not accept the theory that philosophy provided the basis for all kinds of efforts by man to govern himself and then died. He does not accept the theory that philosophy gave the world's major religions a basis and then, having created, died.

He simply says these are history. The philosopher in his efforts to fathom man himself did these things. He asked, "How can I logically figure out the complexities of man's mind?" His answer was a logical method of thought and research—and that resulted in modern scientific method. He asked, "Under what conditions should man live? Is he a totally free being without obligations to society? Should he be controlled?" His answers ran the gamut from no control to total control—and resulted in governments with a like range of power. He asked, "Does man have a soul?" His answer again was varied—and it resulted in the great religions.

Then what happened to philosophy? Having given birth to three major facets of mankind, did it die? The philosopher answers emphatically, "No." No, he says, philosophy was simply the forerunner of these as it must continue to be as long as man is an intelligent being. The philosopher explains that to the uninitiated, philosophy may seem awesome because it is the pioneer of thought. It ranges ahead of man's mental efforts and in doing so acquires the same mysticism that surrounds any pioneer.

Is this too high-flown, too la-de-da, for the newsroom? Not if it is the same newsroom where a depth reporter worries about the rhythm of the words he uses. It is true the reporter may not once in a lifetime write a banner story about the development of a new philosophical school. But he will almost daily report on the results of something which philosophy started.

He can probably cover government, or science, or religion without knowing from whence they sprung. But it gets down to the rather obvious question:

"Would he have covered it better had he known the seed as well as the still-growing tree?"

Modern government provides frequent opportunities for the uninformed reporter to slip. There are politicians who use as a working tool the charge that almost anything is Marxist, Communist, Fascist, and so on. An uninformed public may buy without knowing.

A whole theory of education may suddenly bloom based upon the thoughts of a man named John Dewey. And then, after a decade or two, a reporter may discover that educators are beginning to wonder if they understood John Dewey at all. Would the reporter write more intelligently if he, too, were acquainted with John Dewey?

Thus runs philosophy through the news pages of the modern newspaper. For philosophy deals in mankind, just as does the news. Perhaps in the areas touched by philosophy, as in no other, the problems of hypocrisy, bigotry, and plain stupidity arise every day. In the newsroom, the writers and editors alike may growl and complain at those who use these weapons of the uninformed. But if the newsmen themselves are informed, perhaps the apocalyptic three—hypocrisy, bigotry, and stupidity—would win fewer victories.

It may be because of these three that one area of news coverage is perhaps the whitest washed of all. That area, few newsmen will deny, is religion. Here, where man's soul is at stake, the journalist may feel weak from lack of facts. He may not report bigotry because he is not sure of himself. His editors may not make him report bigotry because they worry about an indefensible position tomorrow.

Yet, here as in almost every case, the reporter need not be afraid to report if he does so upon a sound basis of fact. And while religion deals with the soul, it involves men. And where men are involved, facts are available.

The following bibliography is prepared with all of this in mind. It includes one of several excellent books on philosophic inquiry and a general introduction to philosophy. This is only a start, but it may be an important one.

You will find histories of philosophies. In some cases they are told primarily through the lives of philosophy's great creators. They are readable. They are understandable. They are interesting, and if you read carefully you can learn much about philosophic inquiry and what philosophy started that still lives around you.

You will find a list of some of the important works of some of the world's great philosophers. These are the originals—or translated originals, at least. They are, in some cases, difficult to understand. But when you are ready, they can give depth to your background in philosophy.

Finally, you will find that a special section has been devoted to the much written about, but much neglected field of religion. It, one of the great products of philosophy, is so important that it needs special bibliographical attention.

Histories

Russell, Bertrand, *A History of Western Philosophy*. New York: Simon and Schuster, Inc., 1959. Popularly written, this is the history of philosophy from the rise of Greek civilization to the present day.

It follows chronologically the rise of different philosophers and philosophies, giving the outstanding theories of each. Russell points out the interactions and conflicts of various theories with others and outlines what are, to his way of thinking, the fallacies and contradictions of each. He relates the various philosophies to political and social circumstances and their influence on men and events.

The book is divided into three sections: Ancient Philosophy, Catholic Philosophy, and Modern Philosophy. This history of philosophy gives a good basis for further exploration into more detailed, specialized books on the men and theories presented here with relative briefness.

Durant, Will, *The Story of Philosophy*. New York: Simon and Schuster, Inc., 1926. This is a description of the best-known philosophies told around the lives of the men primarily responsible for their discovery and development.

Philosophy, the forerunner of science and government, gives the journalist insight. This well-written book provides an easy source for the basic ideas from Plato through such moderns as John Dewey. It also is an excellent starting point for journalists who want to go beyond the basics.

An Introduction

Hocking, William Ernest, *Types of Philosophy*, rev. ed. New York: Charles Scribner's Sons, 1939. This is an introduction to philosophy, but still of value to those more versed in the field. As a combination of philosophy and its history, it has a systematic arrangement of kinds of philosophy.

Its value to the journalist is enhanced by the author's effort to produce "a mountain camp from which one makes excursions into the higher trails." Through this book's table of contents, historical index, and subject index, the journalist can find help with relative ease.

Beck, Lewis White, *Philosophic Inquiry, An Introduction to Philosophy*. Englewood Cliffs, N.J.: Prentice-Hall, Inc., 1952. This is an introduction to philosophy organized to: (1) deal with the relation of philosophy to life and to other fields of inquiry; (2) explain philosophic methods of inquiry; and (3) introduce finally philosophies and philosophic schools.

It is valuable to journalists desiring an understandable, readable starting point in acquiring the philosophic basis for such constantly newsworthy topics as government and science.

A Sample Listing of Classics

Aquinas, Thomas, *Summa Theologica.*

Aristotle, *Nichomachean Ethics, Politics, Metaphysics, De Anima.*

Augustine, *City of God, Confessions.*

Aurelius, Marcus, *Meditations.*

Descartes, René, *Discourse on Method.*

Dewey, John, *Democracy and Education.*

Epictetus, *Discourses.*

Hegel, G. W. F., *The Philosophy of History.*

Hobbes, Thomas, *Leviathan.*

Hume, David, *An Enquiry Concerning Human Understanding, An Enquiry Concerning the Principles of Morals, The Dialogues Concerning Natural Religion.*

James, William, *Pragmatism.*

Kant, Immanuel, *The Fundamental Principles of the Metaphysic of Morals.*

Locke, John, *An Essay Concerning Civil Government.*

Lucretius, *On the Nature of Things.*

Machiavelli, *The Prince.*

Marx, Karl, and Engels, Friedrich, *Basic Writings on Politics and Philosophy.* (This particular combination can be found in an Anchor paperback.)

Mill, John Stuart, *Utilitarianism, On Liberty.*

Nietzsche, Friedrich, *Thus Spake Zarathustra, Beyond Good and Evil, The Genealogy of Morals.*

Pascal, Blaise, *Pensées.*

Rousseau, Jean Jacques, *The Social Contract.*

Sartre, Jean-Paul, *Existentialism.*

Spinoza, *Ethics.*

Religion

An Encyclopedia

Ferm, Vergilius, ed., *An Encyclopedia of Religion.* New York: The Philosophical Library, 1945. This is a well-organized, generously cross-referenced encyclopedia. Many authorities contributed, and, helping to lend authenticity to their work, their initials follow their contributions. This approach to subjects that require interpretation is one the journalist with his major ethical tool of attribution can appreciate.

Perhaps the most practical, technical points are very thorough cross-references and the fact that this is in one volume.

This reference, respected by churchmen and college philosophers, can also serve the journalist.

Biblical Interpretation

Harmon, Nolan B., ed., *The Interpreter's Bible.* New York and Nashville: Abingdon-Cokesbury Press, 1952. In 12 volumes, here is the churchman's handbook to the Bible. It can be the journalist's guide.

Its organization is important in its evaluation. As nearly as typographical limitations allow, each page contains: 1) the King James version beside the same quotation from the Revised Standard Version; (2) the Exegesis—the actual interpretation of a concrete passage; and (3) the exposition—an interpretation or lesson that could be the lesson found in the passage.

Obviously, much of the exposition must be opinion based upon education and faith. Yet, when politicians, crusaders, writers, and, indeed newsmen, use Biblical references as examples to make a point, the journalist will find this an authoritative aid.

An Atlas

Kraeling, Emil G., *Bible Atlas*. New York: Rand McNally & Co., 1956. This is a well-written, well-illustrated atlas of the Holy Land.

The geography is integrated with scriptural references. An adequate index and table of contents help guide the reader in search of specific information.

In a history-making period in Palestine and the entire Holy Land, this atlas can be a newsman's handbook. For years the word "Palestine" has meant news, whether it be strife over the Jewish nation or the finding of ancient scrolls.

In this age that has focused attention on the birthplace of Christianity, the journalist may need to know his way around.

A Guide

Rosten, Leo, ed., *A Guide to the Religions of America*. New York: Simon and Schuster, Inc., 1955. This is a collection of the *Look Magazine* series plus statistical and reference materials.

While in some cases the writer of a section may give his personal interpretation, not necessarily a compilation of those of the same beliefs, this book has value to the journalist. The articles and the additional information can provide a question-asking knowledge.

Anthologies

Kaufman, Walter, *Religion from Tolstoy to Camus*. New York: Harper & Row, Publishers, 1961.

Abernethy, George L., and Thomas A. Langford, eds., *Philosophy of Religion—A Book of Readings*. New York: The Macmillian Company, 1962.

Mourant, John A., ed., *Readings in the Philosophy of Religion*. New York: Thomas Y. Crowell Company, 1954.

At first glance anthologies often seem the easy way to publication—via the paste pot. Other times, at first cracking of the cover, they seem the easy way for some professor to fulfill the publication requirements of his profession. Perhaps some anthologies are guilty on both counts. Those deserve a mental snub, and their authors deserve the worst of all censorship—the refusal of a good mind to waste time.

Here, however, are three collections of readings on the philosophy of religion in which the work of the editors is more like picking the rubies from a gravel pile than clipping and pasting someone else's work.

Some so-called religion reporters would be shocked at some of the works included in these readings. But that would only be because these writers are committing a journalistic sin. They are covering only the surface of mankind's all-time quest for truth.

The tables of contents of these books list philosophers, theologians, founders of faiths, leaders of faiths, novelists, poets, and tellers of fairy tales.

It makes little difference how they might have been listed in a *Who's Who*. They had important thoughts on morality and faith.

Any of these could serve as reference books. But for the journalist—and not just for the church writer—they can serve as solid background.

Philosophies

Wells, Donald A., *God, Man, and the Thinker*. New York: Random House, 1962.

> Not only is this an area in which many persons are partially informed, but it is one to which these same persons are seriously committed.

That statement in the preface of this book defines the problem. The same statement could define the newsman's problem when he must—or at least, should—deal with mankind's greatest motivating force.

This book tackles the subject in an interesting way, and though the author may not realize it, organizes the answers as would a master reporter.

Such questions as these are posed: "The Idea of God: to what does the term refer?" "Arguments for the existence of God," "The problem of immortality," "Psychology and religion," "The church and the state," and "Religion and science."

How would the journalist, the courageous one, tackle such earth-and-heaven-shaking stories? He would assemble all the facts, reduce them to the pertinent points, and present them in an understandable way. He would tell all sides—those for, those against, and those in the middle.

That is exactly the approach of this writer.

It seems to us that the thoughtful, professional, aggressive journalist could not read this book without coming up with a dozen ideas for important, readable stories. So, read it.

Trueblood, David Elton, *Philosophy of Religion.* New York: Harper & Row, Publishers, 1957. As a high point in many years of writing about religion, this book was produced "to develop and to expound the essentials of a philosophy which enables men and women of this century to be both intellectually honest and sincerely devout."

The twentieth century journalist finds himself reporting two extremes. On one hand he is told there is tremendously increased religious activity. On the other he is told that Communism rejects religion as an opiate.

This volume was written in part because its author believed "we must have an adequate answer to all those who dismiss all theology as meaningless or irrelevant."

Material Aesthetics

Rich reds become fiery orange and swirl into the deep brown foreground. The brown absorbs the reds to become chocolate and gracefully sweeps into the green background. Light yellows put a wispish crown on the distant horizon. Then, light blues glow and become azure sky.

In the soft early morning light, two children stood before this splash of beauty.

"It's beautiful," said the eight-year-old girl. "But what is it?"

"To the painter it's a landscape," replied her seven-year-old cousin. "To his wife it's a Nebraska landscape. To me, it's a farm. But it doesn't matter what it is to you—if you like it."

Could journalism's few qualified art critics better explain abstract art? Or could the music critics add much of real importance to the supreme praise of the owner of a classical recording who says only, "I like it"?

American newspapers probably would benefit if there were more thoroughly-trained fine arts critics. But even more urgent is the need for broadly educated newsmen who simply understand that fine arts are the translation of man's mind into material aesthetics.

We pretend to produce liberal arts students with educated imaginations, yet they look at or listen to beauty and mouth the excuse of the ignorant:

"It's terrible. I don't understand."

The would-be depth reporter, who wants the reader first, despite the competition's clamor, has a great deal at stake beyond simply knowing something about the fine arts. Oh, he needs that "something," too. He needs background in art and music just as surely as he needs it in the more material products of man's mind.

But, think beyond the surface for a moment. The reporter puts words together. They are the products of his mind. He uses them to convey facts. He can dump the facts, still scrambled, still unorganized, into his reader's lap. So could the artist dump color or the composer musical sounds. But the depth reporter knows that his words, his organization, must turn the facts into an accurate reflection of the ideas that make up a significant news event. Is there a great difference between the problems of the artist and the composer and those of the writer? Would the writer be better or worse equipped if he could add educated sight and sound to his senses?

It would seem, if we claim to be so good with words, that we can't very well have mental blank spots where men's minds use instead color, form, and sound. We are not talking about providing you with phoney intellectualism from which stem shallow comments for the cocktail party after the concert or art exhibit. You can acquire that by listening to other uneducated people. We are talking about the much abused word "appreciation." Many art and music scholars laugh nervously and mutter that word almost furtively.

They needn't. It's a perfectly good word and a perfectly legitimate part of liberal arts education. Artists paint. Composers compose. The rest of mankind either appreciates, or does not. Put that into journalistic perspective:

"Reporters write. And they would be in a miserable fix if readers didn't read."

In fine arts or elsewhere, the fault is not solely that of the artistically uncouth. The artist, the musician, and the scholar of fine arts too often turn to the rest of the world an aesthetic cold shoulder. To a degree it can be forgiven in the artist or composer. Their jobs are to paint and compose, not to serve as their own public relations men. Yet, even they may have to ask for public approval, for economic reasons if for no others. They won't get a fair hearing without a public jury that knows the facts of the case.

The facts, in the case of fine arts, can come from a combination of three sources—the classroom, the literature, and the products themselves. The facts must come from a combination of at least two of these three sources. Lectures and books mean little unless you look at some art or listen to some music. Thus, the following bibliography provides only one source. You have to seek out the second.

Art

Malraux, André, *The Voices of Silence,* trans. by Stuart Gilbert. Garden City, N.Y.: Doubleday & Company, Inc., 1953.

. . . for the artist is by nature secretive and likes to mystify . . .

Malraux makes this statement casually, even enclosing it in parentheses, on page 346. But his whole intent is to fathom the secret of the artist and clarify the mystery. He deplores the fact that "no great painter has ever spoken as we would like him to talk," but words are not the medium of the painter. It is through his paintings that we must judge. And then not the man, but his art.

The author views the world, since the advent of excellent photographic reproductions, as a vast Museum without Walls. And this makes the cumulative visual experiences of the past (and present) the "common heritage of all mankind."

Don't be upset or give up your reading if some of the names or allusions to other art are foreign to you. Just keep reading. One of two things will happen. Either the author will gently and unobtrusively slip in the information you need, or you will not really need a crystallized definition.

The Voices of Silence is both more and less than a standardized "history of art." The history of art is there, but shaped to the author's specialized intent of giving the layman a glimpse into the workings of the artist's mind and how all of us, down to the least artistic, are influenced by the "voices of silence."

Read, Herbert, *The Meaning of Art*. London: Sir Issac Pitman & Sons, Ltd., 1951. In this relatively short book of only 262 pages, the author has tried to give concise meaning to such words as "art" and "beauty" and to trace the great peaks of art from the earliest Greeks to the approximate date of the book's publication.

This is essentially a survey of the plastic arts (painting, sculpture, and so forth) with no great amount of detail. But it does provide a basis for further exploration into the world of art.

There are 70 photographic reproductions, selected by the author to illustrate either a period of art or a point he is trying to make.

Bazin, Germain, *A History of Art from Prehistoric Times to the Present,* trans. Francis Scarfe. Cambridge, Mass.: The Riverside Press, 1959. The author's stated intention is "to give the uninitiated reader as many precise ideas and established facts as possible."

Paintings, sculpture, architecture, jewelry, tapestries, pottery— everything from the major down through the minor arts—all are included in this world-wide, time-spanning history of art.

The 45-page index will help you find the particular artist, school, or work of art on which you need information.

Kepes, Gyorgy, *The Language of Vision*. Chicago: Paul Theobald, 1944. Even if you are an habitual preface-skipper, begin your reading of this book with the two introductory essays by S. Giedion and S. I. Hayakawa. These brief little essays will help you immensely in your understanding and enjoyment of the main text.

The Language of Vision is well illustrated, not only with reproductions of paintings, but also with photographs, compositional designs, posters, and advertising layouts. Each illustration helps the author make his point about how we see and how we should learn to see.

Mr. Kepes was a teacher-artist-designer. His book is therefore written from the viewpoint of one artist to other artists (and art students). It is a "how to do it" book in the sense of explaining some of the artist's technical terms in the manipulation of form.

It might be compared with the reporter's getting new information on an old story—this new information puts a different slant on things. So, too, seeing things in Mr. Kepes's new language of vision will give you new and greater appreciation of the visual arts.

Music

Apel, Willi, and Ralph T. Daniel, *The Harvard Brief Dictionary of Music.* Cambridge, Mass.: Harvard University Press, 1960. This is a compact (341 pages) volume by the author of the much larger and more comprehensive *Harvard Dictionary of Music.*

It was written after adults in evening classes asked for something in line with a lively, but not professional, interest in music. It was designed for both the adult without specialized training and the student just beginning to study. While the authors don't say so, it would seem logical to add a third group—the liberal arts student, including the journalist.

Definitions are concise, clear, and yet complete enough for the audience. Operas and other great works are sufficiently explained to assist the nonprofessional to happier listening.

Blom, Eric, ed., *Grove's Dictionary of Music and Musicians,* 5th ed. London: Macmillan & Co., Ltd., 1954. This is a professionally respected encyclopedia in nine volumes plus a supplement published in 1961 in New York by St. Martin's Press, Inc.

This English-produced encyclopedia is respected throughout the world of music. Its editor with remarkable clarity emphasized that it is written in *correct* English as it is written in England. He complained about the development of a new language that he calls "musicology," and he pointed a half-kidding finger toward the former British colony, now known as the United States.

But having made his jabs, he then added honor to this encyclopedia in his editing of its fifth edition. It is designed for completeness, and, according to scholars of music, very nearly succeeds. The cross-references are plentiful, and the definitions are concise but complete.

Professional musicians respect and use this encyclopedia. Journalists can, too.

Lang, Paul Henry, *Music in Western Civilization.* New York: W. W. Norton & Company, Inc., 1941. This is an almost encyclopedic (1107 pages) history of music in one volume.

However, this book is not encyclopedic in organization. It carries the story of Western music from period to period. A respected work, this is not the kind of book you sit down with in one evening and absorb. You use it for reference and a continuing background over a considerable period of time.

Stringham, Edwin John, *Listening to Music Creatively,* 2nd ed. Englewood Cliffs, N.J.: Prentice-Hall, Inc., 1959. This is a guide to development of personal taste and interested listening.

Its introductory chapter helps put music into perspective with the other art forms. Later chapters introduce the rudiments of music and analysis of great compositions.

Machlis, Joseph, *Introduction to Contemporary Music.* New York: W. W. Norton & Company, Inc., 1961. This is an introduction to twentieth century music.

Like more general "music appreciation" books, this one is designed to help you understand and enjoy. Appropriately, its author has confined detailed discussion to music listed in the record catalogs. He has also given weight to American music. His reasoning—a book written in the environment of America should give extra weight to the product of that environment.

While certain musicians, artists, and critics are perfectly free to ignore the products of their century, the journalist fails if he does. The journalist cannot wait for the test of time to assist his judgments. He is not a historian. He is a newsman, obligated to report the news of his time. If his background fails to help him interpret his contemporaries, it is not a practical background. This book exemplifies that kind of background help.

Bernstein, Martin, *An Introduction to Music,* 2nd ed. Englewood Cliffs, N.J.: Prentice-Hall, Inc., 1951. This volume is designed to encourage intelligent listening to music.

This edition, the second, takes changing listening habits into account. Its author noted the growth in record and radio listening and made several basic revisions. We point this out because he who would acquire background information in music needs to do it within the age in which he lives.

Technocracy has replaced the old crank-wound phonograph in the living room. Technocracy has bred a whole new audience of listeners. No longer is it enough for the journalist to sit in the concert and opera halls. Technocracy has brought them into the living room.

As far as Bernstein is concerned, the preceding paragraph places undue emphasis on the recording industry. But this bibliography is designed to be read, and Mr. Bernstein offered the chance to make a point for journalists. His book can provide the untrained reader with a musical platform. With words, pictures, and musical notes this book uses every method known to the printing business to help you understand and enjoy music.

Ostransky, Leroy, *The Anatomy of Jazz*. Seattle: University of Washington Press, 1960. This is an introduction to jazz music, coupled with an effort to put jazz into its historical perspective.

You will appreciate the position of this author who puts himself in the middle—between classical music and jazz. He, like the sensitive reporter, fears that by trying to explain each to the other he will get into trouble with both.

Mr. Ostransky is, obviously, a member of our club. If he feels lonely up there on his pinnacle of facts between two mountains of opinion, he is only another reporter doing his job in depth. We sympathize, Mr. Ostransky, but we do not pity. To be caught in the middle is high praise.

This book defines well, admits its shortcomings, and ends up giving the uninitiated a foundation in one of America's important music forms.

18

Man and Mouth

Because the English language is the most important background subject for the journalist, it has been separated into a chapter of its own in this bibliography. Much about the use of the language has been spread throughout this book. Here language is dealt with primarily from the viewpoint of usage.

The Last Harangue

As we read in search of an English bibliography for journalists, we became first bothered, then annoyed, and finally thoroughly irritated. We were sick to death of reading repeatedly how reporters are the ruin of the mother tongue. As the irritation became an open sore, we wanted to snarl:

"So, who has a better right?"

A calmer, more logical appraisal does little but bear out that original blunt opinion. Many respected grammarians, experts on usage, teachers, and writers only support the point, whether they mean to or not. Many of them go to great lengths to say that usage is not determined by a few who write about the language but by the some 300 million who speak it. Assuming for the moment that this is the case, then who should have the most influence, those who turn out a few thousand words a week, or those who turn out a few million every day?

262

Of course, among those millions of words that go daily into the newspapers, there are many hastily picked ones that fit like a mother hubbard on Miss America—shrouding the subject rather than revealing it. For those verbal shrouds, obscure phrases, and ill-fitting words there is no excuse.

But there also is no excuse for journalism to continue to suffer a professional inferiority complex about its use of English. After all, who's using the language, them or us?

Stop chortling over that last sentence, fellow journalism teachers. We have not helped the cause very much ourselves. Our tired excuse always is:

"If they would only teach them English in high school or over in the college English department."

Heaven help the working newsman, of course they should teach them English in the high school and the college English department. But it can't end there. In journalism schools and newsrooms the tool is English. We will never be through learning about it or teaching it. It lives; it grows; it changes. No high school or college teacher can be held accountable for what he cannot predict.

He can be held accountable for providing a sound basis, a love of English, and encouragement rather than morphine for the imagination that the language and its literature can ferment. If he does all that, and too often he does not, the English teacher will have performed magnificently. Under any circumstances, he cannot relieve journalists of the responsibility to continue learning for a lifetime, if necessary, how to use an evolving, living language.

This is no carte blanche to treat the language as you please. Three hundred million people won't let you. They use English based, in varying degrees, on rules that have become established by use of the language. The history of English cannot and should not be ignored. It helps us learn why we use the language as we do and it helps dictate future change. The point is that history cannot stop the evolution of our language. And, how newsmen use the language contributes to that constant process of change.

There are, however, newsmen who constantly complain because they must write in English. You have heard them; they inhabit every journalism school and newsroom. Their excuse for poor writing goes like this:

"English is a lousy language in which to express yourself. It lacks the consistency of German, the subtlety of French, and the flow of Spanish."

Come on, now, boys, even if you weren't stuck with English, is it that bad? Of course, English is inconsistent, or, perhaps flexible would be a better word. That flexibility leads to strange things for those just learning the language.

Junior, who is learning to spell, becomes puzzled when he tries to compliment his mother.

"Mommy," he says, "that's good food."

Then, he puzzles, and asks:

"Why do you spell 'good' and 'food' the same way, but say them differently?"

After the flexibility of the language has been introduced to him, Junior has more questions.

"But, why," he persists, "are 'should' and 'would' spelled that way, but you pronounce them the way you do?"

There follows another explanation after which Junior turns back to his meal, grins, and says, "Mommy, this is gud fud."

But these things won't confuse Junior forever. He will learn to live with the language's inconsistency, and it is possible that he may even learn to love it.

It seems almost redundant to point out that most of this bibliography deals with the usage of English. To annotate English literature would take volumes. But to assume that you have some acquaintance with Shakespeare and the King James Version of the Bible seems not illogical.

If English is your tool, usage is your way of life. You should be as up to date about it as a doctor is about new medicine or a lawyer about new legislation.

Before plunging you headlong into a bibliography of English usage, there is one painful observation that must, for the sake of honesty, be made. First, let's use a little novocain. We found many English scholars doing their best in the classroom and in the literature of the language to introduce English as a living, vibrant thing. These scholars are not kicking over the traces of past usage. They treat grammar with respect, but not with awe. They are not convinced that Milton wrote the last decent line of English.

They are teaching and preaching English in the present, not the past. To them the past is valuable background. The present is a living language that can say things as well or better than any other. These men may criticize newspaper writing. They may even sneer "journalese," if they like. For they are the true scholars of living English and have earned the right to monitor its use.

But these men have colleagues whose jabs at journalism hit below the belt. Among these constant critics are some of those who write books about English. It may be naive to expect those who write about English to use the language simply and clearly. Oh, we don't doubt their correctness. How can we? We can't even unravel much of what they say. We get lost in the proliferating complexities of their tangled explanations, groping our way through tortuous, twisted, brambly thickets of phrases, complicated cantos of clauses in complex sentences that should have been written as three instead of one or forgotten entirely.

Perhaps we reacted so violently to obscure writing about English because we were not prepared for it here. We had expected it in such areas as science where we were delighted to find so much that was readable. We approached English with no such foreboding, but we soon found that we had approached with naiveté. Before one of the scholars we have praised earlier in this chapter rescued us, we already had thrown out more poorly written books than in any other area. They had failed to meet the basic requirement of minimal readability.

Our criticism stems from concern, not malice. We firmly believe that a good reporter must have a continuing love affair with the English language.

We thank the scholar who rescued us. More important, we thank him and his kind for rescuing the teaching and writing of and about the English language. With their help, we hope the following bibliography is just another dozen roses in a love affair you have already started.

About Usage

Fowler, H. W., *A Dictionary of Modern English Usage,* 1st ed. Oxford: The Clarendon Press; London: Humphrey Milford (Publisher to the University), 1926. Many of the listings in this specialized dictionary are pointed specifically toward the writer, and in many cases, directly toward the newspaper writer.

Fowler has very definite ideas of what reporters should and should not do to the English language. His point of view differs considerably from that of Bergen Evans (see below), but despite the age of Fowler's MEU it is still regarded by many teachers as the old reliable in correct usage.

This book is "fun" reading, as well as informative. And for the journalist who has an interest in words, apart from their use as his main tool, this is a fascinating, well-written book.

Evans, Bergen, and Cornelia Evans, *A Dictionary of Contemporary American Usage*. New York: Random House, 1957. Although it deals with both the American and British usage, this is written mainly with the American viewpoint in mind. (Fowler's MEU is just the opposite.) The emphasis is on current usage and the examples used are mainly from contemporary speech and writing.

This is recommended both as an accurate authority on present American usage and as fun to dip into at random.

Mencken, H. L., *The American Language*, 2nd ed. New York: Alfred A. Knopf, Inc., 1921. Although published in 1921 and therefore not including many aspects of word usage evolving out of World War II, this inquiry into the development of English in the United States is must reading for anyone with an interest in our mother tongue.

This one volume contains a smattering of history, a dash of word comparisons and origins, bits of peculiarly American usage as opposed to English, and the results of much research into the evolution of the English language on the North American continent in contrast with the English language in England.

Mencken sprays his contempt over all facets of the problem— and most particularly the slavish teaching of "dead English" to youngsters living with and speaking a very lively "American."

Hayakawa, S. I., *Language In Action*. New York: Harcourt, Brace & World, Inc., 1941. This is an explanation and interpretation of the effect of words.

The author says citizens of modern society "need to be scientifically aware of the mechanisms of interpretation if they are to guard themselves against being driven mad by the welter of words with which they are now faced."

This book is primarily about the use and meaning of words as tools of expression and communication. As such it is valuable to the journalist in sharpening his own use and understanding of the language.

About Grammar

Strunk, William, Jr., and E. B. White, *The Elements of Style.* New York: The Macmillan Company, 1959. We frankly admit prejudice in favor of this inexpensive little paperback edition. It is one of our own additions to this bibliography because we could not ignore its success with students who needed brushing up on their grammar.

In a sense, it is a labor of love on the part of Mr. White and a gesture of tribute to his departed friend and professor. White's introduction is itself a masterpiece of characterization.

There are only 71 pages in "the little book" (as Professor Strunk himself proudly entitled it), but those 71 pages contain an amazing amount of information on usage, grammar, and principles of composition. Aside from their sheer practicality, those pages are gems of pungent terseness and prickles for the mind and sense of humor.

You were warned that this is a rave review rather than an austere annotation. We conclude by falling into Professor Strunk's own verbal trap. It is said that he so trimmed the fat from his own classroom lectures that he sometimes found it necessary to repeat himself three times to fill the allotted class hour. So, with a bow to the master teacher, we say, "Read it. Read it. Read it."

Roberts, Paul, *Understanding Grammar.* New York: Harper & Row, Publishers, 1954. This is an English grammar textbook designed to help the student understand the language rather than simply memorize rules.

Respected by many English teachers, it can serve as a reference, a guide, and a basis for grammar.

Curme, George O., *Parts of Speech and Accidence.* Boston: D. C. Heath & Company, 1935.

Jesperson, Otto, *Essentials of English Grammar.* New York: Holt, Rinehart & Winston, Inc., 1933.

These two books are examples of the better grammars from the old-fashioned formalistic approach. The Curme volume has been referred to as "probably the best known of American grammars worthy of the name." The Jespersen book is a one-volume abridgement of his "big grammar" and again presents the old-fashioned formalism view.

Note: The "structural" approach to grammar is exemplified by Charles Carpenter Fries. His *American English Grammar* (study of written English) marked a significant point in the study of English grammar. His later volume, *The Structure of English* (New York: Harcourt, Brace and World, Inc., 1952), is a study of spoken English. *Structure* has a radically new terminology, is very well written, and has had a great influence on subsequent English grammars.

Histories

Robertson, Stuart, *The Development of Modern English.* Englewood Cliffs, N.J.: Prentice-Hall, Inc., 1938. The first several chapters are a brief history of the development of the English language. The remainder of the book takes up such subjects as English inflections, English sounds and their history, spelling and spelling reform, the making of words, vocabulary, and syntax. A particularly interesting chapter is the one on the changing meanings and values of words.

As with most of the books in this section of the bibliography, this one will surely interest the journalist with any love for the language he uses, and in many cases, helps to mold, every day of his working life.

Jespersen, Otto, *Growth and Structure of the English Language.* Garden City, N.Y.: Doubleday & Company, Inc., 1956. (Doubleday Anchor Paperback, 9th ed.) This is only one of several books on the English language by Jespersen, "the great Dane," generally conceded to be one of the world's great philologists.

He states that English has always seemed to him to be a masculine language, and cites reasons and examples. Although he does give a historical sketch of our language, he does so only as it is connected with contemporary English, or by way of contrast.

There is a chapter each devoted to the influence of the Scandinavians, the French, the Latins, and the Greeks upon our language. Another chapter each is devoted to "various sources," to "native sources," and to "Shakespeare and the language of poetry."

This relatively small book nevertheless contains an abundance of information. For those journalists who give no further thought to words than how best to string them together more or less intelligibly, this book will be an eye-opener.

Baugh, Albert C., *A History of the English Language.* New York: Appleton-Century-Crofts, Inc., 1957. This is the second edition of Mr. Baugh's history. Although usually regarded as the standard book on the subject, the Robertson volume annotated above is a good complement to it.

Wyld, Henry Cecil, *A History of Modern Colloquial English,* 3rd ed. New York: Barnes & Noble, Inc., 1953. This is an examination of English as it has been spoken for the past four or five centuries. The origin of the English of literature and its relation to spoken English is also considered.

This is a highly detailed examination of spelling, pronunciation, usage, and semantics. It may be too much for many journalists. Yet some, for whom the study of English is an avocation, will find its intricate trails fascinating.

It is offered in this bibliography as an example of the detail available for those who never cease to study the major tool of their profession.

Literary Histories

Spiller, Robert E., Willard Thorp, Thomas H. Johnson, and Henry Seidel Canby, eds., *Literary History of the United States,* rev. ed. New York: The Macmillan Company, 1953. A survey of the body of American literature from colonial days to the mid-point of the twentieth century, this volume of some 1,400 pages attempts to "draw a new and truer picture of our literary tradition." Background material on American writers and their writings and interpretations of the men, their works, the particular locale of the United States and its effect upon their lives and writings are all here. Some of the major American writers are given complete biographical treatment.

Baugh, Albert C., ed., *A Literary History of England.* New York and London: Appleton-Century-Crofts, Inc., 1948. This is a comprehensive one-volume history with which the journalist should make at least an index-acquaintance.

While literature is best appreciated by reading that literature, a thorough (1,673 pages) history such as this can serve as both a base for questions and a reference. This work of five scholars puts examples, interpretation, and historical perspective at the reporter's mental fingertips.

Benet, William Rose, *The Reader's Encyclopedia*. New York: Thomas Y. Crowell Company, 1948. Subtitled *An Encyclopedia of World Literature and the Arts,* this gives in alphabetical order authors, titles of works, when written, and in many instances a brief résumé of the piece of literature being defined. There are explanations of literary phrases and expressions, and also various brief references to painters, sculptors, musicians, and so forth. As a starting point for further research and reading, or simply to find who wrote what and when, this could be *the* reference book.

Dictionaries

New English Dictionary. Oxford, 1933. Twelve volumes and supplement.

Century Dictionary and Cyclopedia. New York: Century. Six to ten volumes, depending upon edition.

Dictionary of American English. Chicago: Chicago University Press, 1944. Four volumes.

Webster's New International Dictionary, 3rd ed. Springfield, Mass.: G. & C. Merriam Co., 1961. You will be better off if you also have the second edition of this famous dictionary. The third edition has considerably fewer words than its predecessors. A combination of the two is ideal. While there has been some criticism of the third edition, many linguists agree that the some 200,000 words eliminated from the second edition are generally considered archaic. However, many believe the third edition to lack the style of the second.

Dessert

Evans, Bergen, *Comfortable Words*. New York: Random House, 1962. Here are 370 pages of popularly used words, clichéd expressions, and commonly used terms—all used daily by millions of English-speaking people. They use them, but have no idea of their real meanings or the twists and turns by which they have arrived (and survived) in our everyday speech.

We have saved *Comfortable Words* for the last in our English bibliography for two reasons: (1) It can help the writer under-stand why words and phrases mean what they do, and (2) we thought we'd like to leave you laughing. Mr. Evans has a light touch on a sometimes too pedantic subject. If you can read his little explanations of word and phrase etymology without at least a responsive smile, then you are surely in the wrong lan-guage. You might like to try a really dead one, for example, reading the hieroglyphics on Egyptian mummy cases.

19

Man and Miscellany

What started as a search for a bibliography for journalists also became a liberal education on liberal education. You cannot look for the literature to help plug holes in what is called a liberal arts education without some kind of definition. But as this bibliography grew, definition became less important as it was overshadowed by a disturbing question:

In this age of specialization, who needs a liberal arts education?

That led to other equally disturbing questions:

To what practical use can a liberal arts education be put?

Is there a place in the world for the liberally educated?

Is anyone really teaching the liberal arts student?

Does anyone really want to teach the liberal arts student?

Is anyone writing textbooks for the liberal arts student?

And, finally, the most disturbing of all—

Can anyone really afford to teach or write textbooks for the liberal arts student?

Though those questions might be loaded with obvious prejudice, don't try to dismiss them with the usual defenses. Of course, there are strictly liberal arts colleges. Of course, every great university includes a major college of liberal arts. Of course, everyone pays lip service to the philosophy that liberal arts must show us how to live with the atomic bomb and other products of the age of technocracy. Of course, there are many other answers. But they simply do not refute the facts.

Even many of the nation's editors and journalism educators have neglected the facts in developing their favorite theory on education for the newsman: Journalism needs men who know the techniques and have a broad liberal education.

Unfortunately, that theory does not become fact simply because it is said or believed. The harsh fact may be that if this is what we want for journalism, our student may very well represent the last stronghold for the well-rounded man. It may very well be that it will take a special curriculum, special courses, and special text-books to provide the journalist with the kind of education we have been talking about for at least half a century.

Of course, journalism cannot be the last stronghold for the well-rounded man. The world needs this kind of education in many places. Journalism only puts a finger on the need. If it is difficult for the journalist to acquire such an education, then it is also difficult for others.

Truthfully, we are probably talking about a man educated in miscellany—a Bachelor of Miscellany, if you please. There should be nothing disparaging about such a degree, but say what you will, the acquisition of a Bachelor of Miscellany in the age of technocracy is looked down upon. There is plenty of lip service, but it may be difficult as a practical matter to acquire such a degree. Somehow, the journalist needs during his college tour to combine a Bachelor of Science in the techniques of his business and a Bachelor of Arts in miscellany.

In some fields really good literature for the liberal arts student is practically nonexistent. That does not mean that there is not one book. There may be two or even a half a dozen. That is not enough. It is a violation of the concept of thoughtful education to confine any student to as few as a half a dozen books about a whole academic area. Yet, that is what happens. The books, and possibly the course work, are directed at two opposite audiences.

The first is for the shopper, who may also be the liberal arts student. This student must fulfill certain beginning requirements, and he often does it with as little work and as little thought as possible. These courses and usually the books for them shoot beneath the feet of the student. Usually their intelligence is insulted, whether the students realize it or not.

The second audience for course work and books is the student majoring in the subject. For such a student there are plenty of

books and plenty of courses, for this is the curriculum of technocracy. And technocracy is the father of specialization.

While the nation's scholars and writers are swept up in the drive
for specialization, the student who really needs a liberal arts education is going to have to work for it on his own. He will find many
sympathetic professors—probably far more than he would imagine.
As we talked to representatives of the academic disciplines, invariably we found not only sympathy, but concern. But these men serve
two masters. One is the specialization upon which technocracy
feeds. The other is the ethical responsibility of the educator to
produce a well-rounded man. These sympathetic professors seemed
almost delighted to be told that journalism has a very great need
for what some of them fear is an outmoded product—the liberally
educated student.

But be forewarned. If a liberal education is what you need, you
are going to have to work for it. In fact, you are going to have to
work for it harder and longer than all the technicians who sit
around you in classrooms.

You will not get everything you need by sampling beginning
courses in various departments. You will not get everything you
need by reading the textbooks for those courses. Too often the men
who teach and write for those beginning courses are dissatisfied
and frustrated because they must shoot their scattergun at such a
broad audience. It is not easy to teach a course that really introduces a liberal arts student to an area in which many men spend a
lifetime learning about only one tiny phase. Don't misunderstand.
You must take the beginning courses. But then you must nourish
the seed that you get there with your curious mind and an insati-
able appetite for reading.

Do not be distressed because much of what you read may also
resemble the shot pattern of a scattergun. If you want to conduct
an interesting experiment into the split personality of book writers,
start reading prefaces. Here you may be surprised to find the clear-
est, the frankest, the most direct writing in the whole book. Here
the author lets down his hair and directs his comments at you. His
style is often informal, even chatty, but then, following those fatal
words, "Chapter One," he starts shooting with a scattergun in an
effort to satisfy some kind of a vague cross-section of readership. As
a newsman, you know the problem. You shoot at a cross-section of

humanity every day. But you know by now that the best way to reach the largest share of that cross-section is to direct your writing at one reader who lacks information.

Whether the writer of a book shoots with a scattergun or not, if you are to be liberally educated, you are going to have to read. The foregoing bibliography can serve only as a starting point. Do not use it as you might the bibliography produced by the theory that a well-educated man can become so by reading all of a certain "one hundred books." Pick and choose from this bibliography for journalists as your needs dictate. In some areas you will need far more than the origins of the ideas that form the base of an academic discipline. Your course work should have shown you that. Because you have found that you needed a great deal of history, political science, or economics, you have sacrificed many academic hours to acquire advanced knowledge in these fields. Having done this, you have been unable to spread yourself thin enough to acquire depth or possibly even introduction in many other valuable areas.

You have been told repeatedly that certain general bibliographical material would wind up in this section. But, if you think for a moment, you will realize that you have already been exposed to a great deal of what might be considered general background reference. The academic disciplines that have served for the division of this bibliography actually use much common reference material. For example, how many of these areas use census statistics? Economics, sociology, political science, and history just start the list. As a matter of fact, many of the references you need on census statistics have already been discussed. All that remains are the raw materials themselves. These do deserve a moment of attention.

As you must be aware, census reports are a great deal more than the counting of heads and the reporting of numbers every ten years so that legislators can battle over reapportionment. In the years between, the Census Bureau pours out a flow of statistical material on almost literally every subject under the sun. You need to get acquainted with the census publications. To help you the Census Bureau also produces a pamphlet as an index to the publications.

There are, of course, other governmental sources for statistics. One of the most valuable is the Statistical Abstract of the United States. You already have met it in the political science bibliography. You would also find it on the bookshelves of economists, sociologists,

anthropologists, historians, and many others. Such reports help
form part of the base of raw material for research used by many
scholars.

We could not possibly acquaint you by name with all statistical
sources—not even all that come from the federal government. But
we can guide you to some guides. The federal government publishes
a paperback directory to its own publications. There are a number
of other publications designed as directories and aids in the use of
governmental literature. Let us quickly list a few of those:

Schmeckebier, Laurence F., and Roy B. Easton, *Government Publications and Their Use,* rev. ed. Washington, D.C.: The Brook-
ings Institute, 1961.

Boyd, Anne Morris, revised by Rae Elizabeth Rits, *United States
Government Publications,* 3rd ed. New York: The H. W. Wilson
Company, 1949.

Liedy, Philip W., *A Popular Guide to Government Publications.*
New York: Columbia University Press, 1953.

Of course, the source for most federal government documents is:
The Superintendent of Documents
Government Printing Office
Washington 25, D.C.

We are not trying to escape a list of all the usual newsroom
factual sources. After making our way through several hundred
books and annotating at some length more than one hundred, a
few more would make little or no difference. However, it would not
be in keeping with the philosophy of our approach to you. We
have no intention of shooting beneath your feet. By now you are
acquainted with the usual sources. You must know about the
yearbooks, *Facts on File,* the *World Almanac, Bartlett's Familiar
Quotations,* city directories, and postal guides. As for atlases, gazetteers, maps, and dictionaries, you have already met these as the
products or major tools of academic disciplines discussed earlier.

You were warned that this was not an ordinary bibliography.
Had it been, it could have been just as well set in small type in the
back of the book and allowed to die there, as do most bibliographies. This bibliography provided the vehicle for some facts and
messages to the liberally educated journalist. That vehicle may

276

have run over some professional feelings in just about any area you could name, including journalism. This was not hit-and-run by intent. The intention was solely to convince you that journalistic techniques alone will not make of you a journalist. Techniques must be coupled with the kind of education we call liberal arts if you are to be equipped to produce worthwhile stories.

Introduction

This section deals with the newspaper problems which have created a need for depth and the newspaper problems depth reporting itself has created. In other words, the time has come to talk about the problems of the publisher, the editor, the city editor, and the copy editor. This does not mean that suddenly this book designed for advanced journalism writing students and young reporters is shifting audiences. The audience remains the same.

Books have been written on lesser subjects than those to which this section is devoted. Books need to be written about the editor's problems in the coming age of depth. All this section is intended to do is to acquaint the depth reporter with what he should know about the other parts of his business. These are the other members of the team, without whom his depth story would never reach the reader and might just as well never have been written.

Once again, you, the depth reporter, must look over my shoulder as we talk to the people who put your stories into the newspaper.

20

Cobwebs on the Cash Register

The journalist who does not think his business has problems, perhaps more than ever before in history, needs to start his depth studies in his own backyard.

The problems are multiple and obvious. Production costs have risen astronomically. Competition has shifted the proportion of the national advertising dollar in favor of television. Television has taken something else, too—hours of the reader's time. Radio has changed formats and advertisers. Today radio ad salesmen are in hot competition with newspaper ad salesmen at the local marketplace.

One of the problems, then, is the health of the cash register. Need the newsman worry about the health of the company cash register? While the money-spending news department and the money-making advertising and circulation departments are traditionally separated, every newsman soon learns one simple fact of life. He normally can spend money for better coverage only if there is money in the cash register to be spent.

Happily, of course, the quality of the work done in the newsroom usually is reflected in the cash register. Studies of mail order advertising response gives substance to this favorite newsroom theory. Identical mail order advertisements have been run in newspapers known for their quality and in newspapers known for their lack of it. The ad response to the quality paper has normally been much higher than that to the identical ad run in the less reputable competitor. This is fairly obvious proof of the pudding. Quality in the newsroom pays off in the business office.

Then, are America's newspapers in good economic health?

At first glance, the answer seems "Yes." Most newspapers are making money. They are running more lines of advertising than ever in history. They are circulating to more people than ever in history.

But that is a surface answer to a depth question. Closer examination tells a different story.

First, this business of making money is relative. An investor wants to do more than simply end up in the black. He wants a return that compares favorably with the return on a similar investment in other stable and safe businesses.

How good is the return on an investment in a newspaper?

It seems to vary proportionately to the size of the newspaper, with the larger newspaper coming out on the smaller end of the profit margin. For example, each year *Editor & Publisher* faithfully reports the profit-and-loss statement of some of the country's major newspapers. That annual report on some of the best never fails to create a stir. Often those reports show margins of profit of somewhat less than one percent of the investment. From the investor's viewpoint the money put into those newspapers could be drawing a very safe four to five percent.

Other statistics and comments by publishers indicate that the weekly newspaper is the best investment for margin of profit. Next comes the small- and medium-sized daily. And finally at the top of the heap in size and at the bottom of the heap in profits sits the metropolitan daily.

Strangely enough, though most of the depth work is now being done at the metropolitan level, the profit story might indicate that smaller newspapers could afford a proportionately larger share of depth.

The news department spends money, and two other departments, advertising and circulation, bring it in. To get a depth picture of the health of the cash register, let's take a look at each of these money makers.

What Slice of the Pie?

How about that steadily increasing advertising linage? Newsmen are as human as anyone else when they discuss their own business in generalizations. When they talk about advertising linage they make two generalizations, but usually fail to apply their own zest for the complete story to their own statements. They say:

1. Advertising linage in newspapers is at an all-time high.

2. The newspapers' percentage of the national advertising dollar has dropped steadily in the face of competition.

On the surface, both statements are correct. However, both need much closer examination. For instance, do declining percentage figures in the national advertising column of the ledger indicate declining dollars? The answer is that they do not. As a matter of fact, they represent rather fantastic increases in the dollar income of newspapers. To make this point ultraclear, examine briefly the national advertising picture starting at the end of World War II.

During the war, national advertising fell off drastically, except for the rather small space devoted to institutional ads. When the war ended, wartime manufacturers were anxious to get their share of the postwar consumers market. They jumped into the national advertising arena with gusto.

However, along with the end of World War II came the encroachment of television in the living room. At first, there was a mad scramble for the unbelievable national audiences offered by television. And while this scramble has not necessarily decreased, the national advertisers made a discovery.

They discovered that all advertising is essentially local advertising. They realized that it is very well to boost a product in general advertising through television, magazines, and radio. But they discovered that moving that product at the local level requires something else.

That something else developed into the local tie-in or cooperative advertisement. The manufacturer paid half the cost, or some percentage, for the local ad and the local dealer paid the rest. This, by the way, has tended to throw off the linage figures when com-

piled on a national basis. Now, let's examine the statistical picture
for a few years after World War II.

Total advertising expenditures in the leading media in:

	1946
Magazines	$168,700,000
Newspapers	150,200,000
Radio	124,000,000

In 1950 newspapers moved into first place:

	1950
Newspapers	$533,400,000
Magazines	514,900,000
Radio	326,000,000

Then came TV which became the toughest competitor. By 1955
the picture looked like this:

	1955
TV	$795,000,000
Newspapers	750,000,000
Magazines	685,000,000
Radio	225,000,000

By 1955, television took over first place. However, close behind
television, newspapers showed a $200,000,000 gain over their na-
tional advertising figure in 1950. By 1960 television was well ahead,
with newspapers and magazines bringing up a close second.

Obviously, simple percentage figures do not tell the whole story.
It is easy to say that not too many years ago newspapers depended
upon national advertising for from a fourth to a third of total
income. Then, if you want a truly black picture, you simply have
to point to the nonmetropolitan dailies and show what a very small
percentage they count on today.

Smaller newspapers can now plan on only about eight to ten
percent of their total advertising to come from the national advertising pie. Newspapers with circulation from 50 to 100 thousand
anticipate about 18 percent from the national advertisers. Obviously,
the national advertising percentage figures have dropped at a
frightening rate. However, the dollar figures tell a more accurate
story. Those smaller percentage figures represent a great deal more
money. Newspaper income from national advertising was more than
500 percent greater in 1960 than it was in 1950.

What the percentage figures really describe is a change in advertising patterns. As the national ad ratio dropped, newspaper ad salesmen put more emphasis on local display and want ads. Not too many years ago newspapers counted on from five to six percent of the total to come from classified or want ads. Today, nonmetropolitan dailies expect to get from 24 to 26 percent of their income from want-ad sections.

And while this was happening in the want-ad department, the local retail or display department was building up a phenomenal head of steam. In fact, increases of ten percent or more each year were not uncommon in the decade between 1950 and 1960.

Now let's take one more look at the national advertising pie. Obviously, the slices have been cut quite differently since World War II. Who is getting the large slices?

Television, of course, has become the big knife in redividing the pie. Between 1948 and 1958 TV increased its slice of national advertising by $660 million annually. And while it was about it, TV made other inroads which indirectly affected the newspaper.

For one thing, television and other competition for the ad dollars shrunk the newspapers' total share. In 1935, the newspapers carried about 45 percent of all advertising. By 1960, the figure was closer to 30 percent.

And when the Big Eye replaced the Big Ear of radio in the American living room, radio made violent changes to survive. Stations shifted to a new format of news, music, and sports. The days of fat network contracts were over. Radio had to turn more than ever to new advertising markets—the local ones. The radio ad salesman began to tread the paths to those local markets with increased vigor, right on the heels of and sometimes ahead of the newspaper ad man.

However, you need one more statistical picture to complete this review of the cash register. Taking all kinds of advertising, who gets the biggest share? In the 1960's, the newspapers were far out in front. In one year, for example, they exceeded the nearest competition—direct mail—by two billion dollars. Newspapers are still the king of the hill on Madison Avenue and hundreds of Main Streets all over America.

Our Share of the Crop

Now, how about circulation with its new all-time highs? Statistics indicate that America's daily newspapers seem to be getting their share of the new readers. A study by Wilburn Peterson at the State University of Iowa indicated that the newspapers were attracting young readers as they reached their twenties in the 1940's and 1950's. In the 1940's, when the population of twenty-year-olds represented 15.3 percent of the total, newspaper circulation went up 33.2 percent. In the 1950's, the twenty-year-olds increased 8.1 percent and the newspapers picked up 9.4 percent more readers. Only time will tell whether these figures will continue their trend. But, remember, they are statistics. They do not tell us whether we are getting our share of the young readers' time. To find this out, we can only take a look at their reading habits.

How well, for instance, do university students read the newspaper? The answer can be found on the front steps of fraternity and sorority houses and dormitories on every campus in the country. Too often, a lone copy of the newspaper lies there awaiting the occupants of a fraternity house with some 50 residents. A dormitory with from 300 to 400 students may take five copies of the paper. While from these front-stoop statistics it would be foolhardy to draw hard conclusions, they acquire a good deal of statistical backbone from a survey of student circulation in the Big Eight college conference of the Midwest.

Circulation managers of the 18 major off-campus newspapers which serve the Big Eight schools were asked to estimate their student circulation. Their figures indicated that about one daily newspaper was delivered for each 15 students living on the campus.

However, all students do not live on the campus. While the circulation managers had understandable difficulty arriving at an estimate for these off-campus students, they did their best. It helped the ratio considerably, indicating that about one daily newspaper was delivered for each seven or eight students including both those who live on and off the campus.

Off-campus and married students considerably improve the stu-

dent body's average. One circulation manager estimated the following readership among students:

Married Students	50%
Graduate Students	90
Students Living Off-Campus	40
Students Living On-Campus	10

Another circulation manager put it less statistically when he said:

"I have included the married students in the figures given you, because if I didn't there wouldn't be any figures to report!"

Circulation manager after circulation manager pointed out that
his major difficulty was reaching the single student living on-cam-
pus and composing the large bulk of the student population. Some
of the circulation men sought consolation from the theory that a
single newspaper gets a great deal of passing around in places
where students live. However, they admitted that there is a limit
even to passing around. In all the Big Eight region no newspaper
estimated a circulation of more than four to any fraternity or sorority house and some fell as low as one. The average was 2.5 per
house, and those to be passed around among 40 to 60 students.
Dormitories fared no better with an average of 7.5 newspapers for
from 100 to 500 students.

There is little use in belaboring the point or arguing about how
many times a newspaper can be passed from student to student. It
may be best simply to admit that students are somewhat less than
avid newspaper readers and go on to other aspects of circulation.

For the circulation manager it may be enough to know how
many newspapers are delivered. It is not enough for the newsman.
He needs to find out how his newspaper is treated when it comes
to the number of people who read it and the time they spend on it.
These factors, as has been pointed out before, are vital to the
depth reporter whose story may require 20 minutes of a reader's
time. This is important enough to look at it once more.

Television, according to several surveys, gets more than four hours
daily in viewing time in the average home. Newspapers, other
surveys indicate, get an average of some 20 minutes. Comparison of
the surveys turns up sharp discrepancies. But the discrepancies
cannot be sharp enough to change the picture. Television is still
way ahead in the time-consuming department.

Yet, all this does not change too greatly the accepted measurements of newspaper prosperity:

1. Advertising linage is at an all-time high.
2. Circulation is at an all-time high.

It becomes very logical to ask:

If newspapers are so well off in advertising and circulation, what's all this talk about short profits?

The answer to that one can be found in production cost figures. Each year in recent history they have climbed. In the 1960's we find ourselves paying 400 percent more to produce newspapers than we did just before World War II. Payrolls alone have increased from 350 to 400 percent. And the harassed production managers of hundreds of newspapers can tell you that everything else has gone up, too—paper, ink, machinery, maintenance, and every other item that makes every newspaper a complicated manufacturing process. *Editor & Publisher* estimates that, in ten of eleven recent years, production costs have increased more rapidly than revenues.

At last, in this depth examination of the newspaper's cash register, the real reason for shrinking profits emerges. While advertising has shown not only a normal, but a healthy increase, and while newspapers have maintained their advertising linage in the face of the stiffest competition in history, production costs have outstripped the increase in income. It only follows that the margin of profit has shrunk year by year. Newspapers are not a dying investment, but it seems safe to assume they are, as the boys at the Chamber of Commerce say, no barnburners.

Is this a problem for the editorial staff?

Quality Makes the Difference

Directly and traditionally the answer is "no." But indirectly every newsman must ask himself:

What does the business office have to sell that makes this newspaper better than the competition?

The answer is another question:

What does a newspaper have to sell its advertisers and its subscribers?

The answer to that is, the newspaper has to sell exactly what the quality of the newsroom has made it.

It is true that some newspaper readers subscribe for the advertisements. That's fine, except a throw-away shopping guide would serve the same function without the added cost of the newsroom.

However, if the newspaper is not going to be an advertising throw-away, the problem is tossed back once more into the lap of the newsroom. What, then, can the newspaper do that makes the product different from and better than other media?

First, the newspaper is responsible only so far as the newsroom has made it responsible. This kind of responsibility is what Turner Catledge means when he says that the staff of *The New York Times* is "devoted to the idea that the press is an instrument of integrity."

Or, it is what the *St. Louis Post-Dispatch*'s Crowley meant when he said, "*The Post-Dispatch* regards it as its journalistic duty never to be satisfied with merely printing the news, always to remain devoted to the public welfare, and always to fight for progress and reform."

Add to these viewpoints an opinion upon which Crowley, Catledge, and every other responsible editor can agree. That opinion, which amounts to a beacon for the American press, is just this old-fashioned:

The newspaper's first duty is to inform its readers.

That does not mean to entertain. That does not mean to tease with abbreviated news stories. That does not mean to editorially crusade in the news columns. It means only one thing—to inform the reader.

Those who find these are high-flown viewpoints should recollect briefly the history of American journalism. The newspapers of the nation assumed a special responsibility the day the Bill of Rights was ratified. In return for the privilege of freedom of press, the newspapers were expected to pay in responsibility. True, there has been much irresponsibility, but there has been much responsibility, too.

The penny press, which rose in the early nineteenth century, thrived on irresponsibility, gossip, and schemes to build circulation. So successful were several of these newspapers that it was worth a woman's reputation to have her name appear in their columns.

Civil War times found an increase in responsibility and almost a zenith in editorial influence. Without a blush, such giants as Horace Greeley told the nation what to do—and sometimes the nation even did it.

In subsequent years some of the giants of today started building a reputation based on integrity and responsibility in informing the reader. At the same time, there were several champions of irresponsibility involved in an all-out circulation war. Indeed, these newspapers are credited with helping to start the Spanish-American war as part of their unbelievable fight for readers.

The twentieth century found certain newspapers adding another precept to the tradition of the American press. The crusaders, *The Portland Oregonian, The St. Louis Post-Dispatch, The Kansas City Star-Times,* were among those who punctuated with courage the obligation to "progress, reform, and public welfare."

The 1930's brought one of the first broad hints that the newspaper, the giant among public opinion molders, might be losing some of its punch. Inklings could be found in the study of newspaper backing of presidential candidates. From 1932 through 1948, the winning presidential candidate did not have the majority support of the American press.

Did the lack of influence in national elections mean that the newspaper had lost its power to influence? No such thing. The power was still there, particularly at the local level. It made no difference how many readers read or believed an editorial directed, for instance, at city council action, as long as the city council members read and believed. And at the local level, the newspaper was still the only place for the confused voter to get advice on the relatively unknown candidates running for local office. And in recent years we have begun to understand better than ever the importance of knowing candidates at the lowest level of government.

Actually, whether they objected violently in their editorial columns or not, no one doubts that the newspapers influenced re-election after re-election of Franklin D. Roosevelt. Day after day the voters saw stories in the news columns about FDR and his administration. No one who really believes in advertising could deny that this was promotion in favor of the Democratic president. The loss of influence at the national level seemed to be on the editorial pages, not the news pages.

Why this loss of influence?

Some blamed the newspaper giants of the nineteenth and early twentieth century. In some instances their dogmatic arrogance finally brought a typical American reaction:

"We are tired of that editor trying to tell us what to do."

Also, the American people were becoming steadily better educated. With education came the ability and the desire to make up our own minds. Any number of editors have conducted private experiments with their editorial power in an effort to find out what opinion means when there is a shortage of information. They were trying to determine if the voters would follow their advice in a political race where the candidates were unknown. One Midwestern editor, who had become a powerful voice in national, state, and local affairs, realized that he could not accurately test the influence of his well-read editorial opinion in races involving widely known candidates. There were too many imponderables.

He picked instead relatively small races between relatively unknown candidates. These races were not those upon which he normally gave editorial opinion. In each of his experiments he backed an unknown and the voters followed his advice.

Technocracy also has had its part in reducing the editorial power to influence the masses. With wires, airwaves, jet planes, and rockets, the size of the world has been shrunk. It has become possible for anyone to be a world traveler without leaving his living room.

And World War II did its part in shrinking the world. In this war as in no other in the nation's history, Americans were sent to all corners of the world. While few GI's became foreign-affairs experts, millions saw first-hand what they had been reading about.

When those GI's returned home they were the source of embarrassment not only for newspapers but for professors. It became a rather common campus joke when some ex-GI raised his hand in class to say politely, but emphatically, "I'm sorry, sir, but that's not the way it is. I was there and. . . ."

Even in the business of informing people, which was not involved with the opinion of the editorial page, the newspaper's position was being changed. The Big Eye in the living room pushed radio into a new format of music, news, and sports. In this new climate, radio was not only willing, but anxious, to break into any program for a hot news break—even some that were not so hot.

On television, where scheduled minutes actually devoted to news were relatively few, there also was a willingness to break in for hot news flashes. Furthermore, television could disrupt its schedule for a visual examination of world-shaking news in the form of half-hour and hour-long documentaries. And it was so easy to absorb news via television. All the viewer had to do was sit and look.

It took no pundit at the midpoint of the twentieth century to determine that the newspapers' editorial power to influence the masses on national and international problems had been reduced. To top it off the newspapers had been chased right out of the business of reaching the reader first with hot, breaking news.

In the face of the competition by radio and TV, a number of newspaper trends appeared. One defense was to completely ignore the Big Eye and the Big Ear. This seemed a head-in-the-sand viewpoint when both the "eye" and "ear" could often provide only enough to whet the reader's appetite for what the newspaper could do in depth with its columns of space.

Another trend was toward the abbreviated story. It became popular on a number of the nation's best city desks to order that "no story is worth more than 300 words unless the reporter has special permission." Far-sighted newsmen pointed out, however, that while there is a place for the bulletin approach in the newspaper, when it is applied to every story the reader gets no more than he can from a 60-second television spot.

A summary of the newspaper in siege past the middle of the twentieth century could paint a black picture:

For investors there were easier ways to make money than to put it into a newspaper.

For readers there was competition for time that some claimed left the newspapers with only 20 to 30 minutes a day.

For the editorial writers there was doubt that their opinions were being felt on such issues as national elections.

For the newsroom there was a certainty that the competition would be there first with the hot, breaking news.

In the face of all this, the newspapers could do either of two things. They could concede the battle and relegate themselves to a second-rate position in the communications world. Or, they could give a depth answer to their problems. They could use the competition.

When radio and TV rode the airwaves to be there first with the news flash, the newspaper could train its readers to look to it for the complete story.

When magazines dealt in depth on a weekly or monthly basis, the newspapers could beat them by days. And the newspapers could deal in local depth, something none of the competition could afford.

There may be a few cobwebs on the newspaper cash register, but there are not as many as the critics would have us believe. Technocracy must help publishers find the answer to rising publication costs. But the newsroom already has its share of the answer. It can give the business department something to sell—something the competition cannot touch. It can give the business department the integrity of depth in the news columns.

21

Action to Replace Lip Service

"We preach depth," said a weary news editor, "but we practice antiquity."

In its own terse way that statement summarizes the problems of the other half of the depth reporting team. It is true that there can be no depth without the raw material—the story written by a highly professional reporter. However, that story could be lost, wasted, or ruined without editors at all levels who could edit in depth. In fact, without a good editor, the reporter probably would never have been given the time to do a depth story. Earlier in this book you have heard reporters say that the depth approach in the newspaper would be impossible without a good editor.

It goes much further than that. Editors will point out that this is not possible without a good publisher. It is a simple fact of modern newspaper life that the responsibility for depth starts at the top in the Old Man's office. Then it goes down through the ranks of thinking, intelligent editors.

True, some editors are already practicing what they preach for the newspaper of the future. T. C. Harris of *The St. Petersburg Times* talks about the "newspaper of tomorrow" and adds appropriately, "that's very soon." If Mr. Harris won't mind, that probably should have been yesterday. Mr. Harris and others were doing it yesterday and there is evidence to prove it: a relative newcomer to *The Washington Post* says, "I have done more depth coverage on this newspaper in three months than I did in three years back in. . . ."

Ben W. Gilbert, city editor of the same paper, describes his staff organization for depth and says, "to us, this is the answer to television and the news magazines."

Frank Eyerly, managing editor of *The Des Moines Register and Tribune* finds this approach "the best guarantee against deterioration. . . ."

Erwin W. Canham, editor of *The Christian Science Monitor,* calls depth "a way of life for us."

The Wall Street Journal, already convinced of the daily approach to depth, started *The National Observer,* a Sunday newspaper devoted almost entirely to depth.

These men and newspapers talk about the newspaper of tomorrow as if they were editing it today. They are. But unfortunately, their action is not shared by enough of their colleagues. And this is not necessarily the fault of the colleagues.

Newspapers are an American institution based in tradition and coupled to the democratic growth of the country. They change slowly over the years. Their readers take an extrapersonal interest in what "my" newspaper prints.

The story goes that one of the nation's leading editors had his own research technique for keeping a finger on the reader's pulse. He periodically turned up in the circulation department and sat down at the complaint desk. He then kept tab as the readers who were missing their paper called in. If the angry reader on the phone demanded, "Where is *my* newspaper?" the editor scored one for *My.* If the reader asked, "Where is *the* newspaper?" the editor reluctantly marked one up for *The.* When he was finished, if he found the *My*'s well outnumbered the *The*'s, the wise editor felt good about the kind of newspaper he was producing.

This editor and others like him have no way of knowing how these close friends—the *my* type of reader—might react to apparently violent changes in their newspaper. Thus, change in any newspaper must consider the reader. It also must consider the problems that tradition has passed down to the modern editor.

He lives and works in a "rat race" that has accumulated during the history of his nation. There is no separating the American newspaper from America. Unlike many institutions which evolved, like children, from the American Revolution, the newspaper emerged more like a parent. Just as the pre-Revolutionary journalists spread the word and bound the colonies together in their dissatisfaction, the post-Revolutionary newsmen had to assume a great deal of responsibility along with their freedom.

Bound in the tradition of freedom they started, and bound in the tradition they remain today. Nobody is going to knock that. But there are some traditions which have utterly nothing to do with freedom that could bear an examination. Somehow, the newspaper business has become steeped in traditions that may extend to the tiniest detail. Many times the things our modern newsman does may have been dictated by his predecessors once, twice, and thrice removed. Perhaps it goes with backshop techniques that have hardly changed since the invention of the linotype machine. But the journalists of the twentieth century know that to change the newsroom and its product requires a good deal more than simply deciding to do it. In some cases, it may take dynamite.

Let's look for a moment at the confusion the modern editor faces daily. Many times his day and that of his staff starts early because they are still shackled to an edition structure that came in with the iron horse. This is literally so, because circulation in the early days of the steam locomotive was dictated by the departure schedule of the railroad. Edition after edition was cranked out to meet a schedule set not in the newspaper office but in the home offices of railroad companies.

Even the circulation patterns of newspapers were defined by the rail lines, often from east to west. Many of those general patterns remain today, particularly in the Midwest. But the patterns are not all that remain. There are those back-breaking edition schedules. There are still too many newspapers turning their newsrooms into pandemonium to make five or six editions a day.

This same outmoded edition schedule dates back to the days when in every town from two to a half-dozen newspapers fought it out on the street corners for circulation. Today, the proud publishers boast that 90 percent of their newspapers are delivered to the front doorstep. The publishers like it. The advertisers like it. Yet, in many cases, it has not occurred to anyone that this should mean a change in edition structure. If we are delivering most of our papers to the doorstep, if we are sending our newspapers out by truck instead of by a long-forgotten railroad schedule, we no longer need that edition schedule. Furthermore, we are only kidding ourselves if we think the difference of an hour or two is going to make any difference to our reader out in the trade area. Radio and television still will have brought the first word of major news breaks to him. We would do better to exchange that six-edition schedule for quality in two editions.

Why exchange? Because today's newspaper takes more time to write, to edit, and to organize. There is no such thing as depth reporting all by itself. As *The Des Moines Register*'s Eyerly puts it, "there is depth editing, too." Depth editing, like depth writing, takes more time because it produces a better job—a neat package, well laid out, well organized, and fully equipped to leave the competition out in the cold.

What does it take to produce that neat package?

The solution of the outdated edition schedule is just one of the problems that must be solved before the American editor can find time first to think, then plan, and finally produce. The edition schedule only contributes to the hubbub in which he works. Look at some of the other factors that add up to a hectic day in the newsroom:

The editor must inform. He cannot forget that his readers depend upon him to keep them acquainted at all levels of news, despite radio and television. Somehow, he must separate the trivia spawned by tradition from the truly informative news. And every day he is surrounded by mountains of trivia.

He must find space for the news. He knows at the start of any given day that enough news will pour into his newsroom to fill his newspaper ten times over. The idea of finding even a couple of columns for a good depth piece may seem overwhelming as the wire service teletypes pound out their wide ribbons of news and reporters' typewriters tap out additional mounds of copy.

He must have personnel. Interwoven in the problems created by those twin mounds of trivia and too much so-called news is the major problem of personnel. Good writers must have time to produce good depth stories. Good copyreaders must have time to edit them. Good layout men must have time to display them, lest they be lost. Somehow, the editor hoping to turn out a neat package complete with depth must arrange manpower to do the job.

To do the job he must have depth editing. It will not be enough to find the manpower; that manpower must be equipped with a depth philosophy and be given time to apply it. It is possible that before the editor can find his way out of the squirrel cage he will have to take a close look around the rim of his copy desk.

He must make sure that the readers are going to read his depth stories. It makes little economic sense to take expensive time, talent, and space to produce a depth story that is lost in a poor layout philosophy. Handled as a run-of-the-mill story in a system that may have developed more through tradition than thought, the battle may be lost for want of a nail.

Let's be redundant for the sake of emphasis. The best depth story will never reach the reader if certain problems are not solved at the editor's desk. He must make sure that he does keep up with the breaking news. He must find space. He must find personnel. And he must provide a new philosophy of copy editing and of layout. Every one of these points becomes such a stumbling block on most newspapers that they will be discussed individually and in detail in later pages of this book.

The point is that none of this can succeed without planning. Planning, the time for which most editors have lost in the daily turmoil, is the key. The key cannot be turned until American newspapers solve the basic problems of informing, space, personnel, copy editing, and layout.

The solutions suggested on following pages are, just as were those for depth reporting, no magic potion. They are solutions suggested by a combination of research and the experience of some of the nation's best editors. Many of them are not new. However, like many of the words applied to reporting, they have been lost in a weary semantic maze. In the hubbub that is part of the production of a daily newspaper, there are more good ideas than tried ideas. The need now is to try to equalize the two.

No Escape from Information

There are critics of the press who admit—with a note of apology and delight—that "if I were running a newspaper, it would go bankrupt in 30 days." What they mean to imply is that they have such grandiose ideas for the American newspaper that it would be impossible to continue publishing and making a profit. This, for them, is a combined rationalization and apology for their criticisms. While the American press probably can benefit from such criticism, it sounds more like a death knell than progress. The intelligent newsman knows that he can neither make a living nor do the things he would like to do as a journalist if he is not working for a healthy, profit-making organization. Hence, the practical approach to the newspaper for today—sometimes erroneously called the newspaper of the future—is a combination of things that are expensive without abandoning the traditional role of keeping the reader informed of the news.

Certainly, news in depth is the answer to the critics, and more important, the answer to reader wants. However, any newspaper which tried to do everything in depth would indeed wind up bankrupt in 30 days, give or take a few days. No newspaperman with his head in the clouds and his fingers pounding out a rhythm of depth on his typewriter can forget that the newspaper of yesterday, today, and tomorrow still has one basic job—to inform. Nobody not anticipating bankruptcy in 30 days is going to tell the newspapers to stop covering the news. Depth or not, the newspaper loses its basic excuse for existence if it does not do a better job than its competition in simply covering the day's news.

An examination of the competition's routine coverage of news indicates that neither radio nor television can usually expect to do much more than provide a bulletin approach. While there are critics who claim educational TV channels could replace the newspaper, no commercial station can afford to cover all the news and expect to avoid bankruptcy itself.

Now, once more, what does the competition do? As far as radio and television are concerned, they digest the news until it can be read to the listener or viewer in something less than a half-hour. In the magazine business, the news approach must be at least on a week-to-week basis. This places the newspaper squarely in the middle. Newspapers publish daily and have space enough to do a great deal more than give the barest facts.

In its advantageous position the newspaper can give its readers daily, local depth in competition with the magazines and it can offer a greater quantity of current news coverage than either radio or television. But, within the budget of any given newspaper, there is only so much money. With that money there must be a combination of depth and breaking news. How, then, can the newspaper do both?

One way, perhaps, would be to give some attention to the so-called bulletin approach. It is practiced hourly on the airwaves and daily by some newspapers. For example, *The Wall Street Journal* publishes a newspaper for "everyone interested in making a living." However, as this newspaper continues to grow in national standing, its readers have not been forgotten when it comes to being informed on other than business news. The editors of *The Journal* try to give their readers at least as much national and international news as could be had during the half-hour 10:00 P.M. telecast.

To do the job *The Wall Street Journal* employs top editors to work almost solely on the news bulletin column for page one. The same technique is applied to other areas of more specialized coverage, such as taxes, business trends, commodity reports, and special news from the nation's capital.

Some newspapers have carried the bulletin approach a bit further—in fact, a great deal further than just a bit. There are city editors and news editors whose job it is to force reporters and copyreaders to tell all the news in sardine-can space. It has become popular on certain newspapers to dictate that "no story is worth more than 300 words." Or, "if you can't tell it in one typewritten page, it's poorly written."

While such a philosophy crams literally hundreds of stories— bulletins, if you please—into a newspaper, it can very well defeat itself. Is the answer to the competition on the 10:00 P.M. telecast to beat them at their own game? If it is, then it would seem logical that we relegate all of the writing in depth to the competition breathing over our other shoulder—the magazines. Once again, it probably comes down to what many might call a compromise. The newspaper cannot afford to stop covering the breaking news, but it must make time and space for depth.

Some newspapers have for years given their readers a page-one column of bulletins for which there are detailed stories inside. This, however, has not necessarily meant that the detailed stories were in depth. Frequently they were only longer.

A different approach to the bulletin column is now being con-

298

sidered by such editors as T. C. Harris of *The St. Petersburg Times.*
He says:

> As I see the newspaper of tomorrow (and that's soon), it will contain
> most of today's news, but the relatively unimportant and yet interesting
> will be logged more and more and the depth stories will have greater
> play. *The Wall Street Journal* may be setting a pace on this with its
> two front-page enterprise or depth stories and its tersely written para-
> graphs of the run-of-the-mill news.

Harris said what many newsmen have been thinking. And several
good newspapers have been practicing it. Really good bulletin columns and tight writing of a semibulletin approach to routine news
can help fulfill the newspaper's obligation to inform. As a matter
of fact, those who insist any story can be written in 300 words are
at least partly right. There are a lot of less important stories that
must go into the newspaper that can be written in a good deal less
than 300 words.

The bulletin column and the other tightly written stories can
then allow depth to make the best use of the newspaper's advantageous daily publication and space. If a bulletin or an apparently
routine item needs depth treatment, it may have to wait a day or
two. Meanwhile, the readers will have been informed by their newspapers at least as well as they have been by TV and radio.

Obviously, the answer is planning and organization. Someone
must decide what will be covered in depth, what will go into the
bulletin column, and what less-important news must be wrapped up
as tightly as possible. While it might seem so, there is no real conflict in writing style between these three courses in a daily news
meal. Only the bulletin column may require a different approach,
but it, too, will specialize in good, tight writing. Never forget that
depth does not simply mean length. If a depth story is long, it can
only be because it has more to tell.

Editors who discard depth as simply verbose writing have themselves abdicated their right to edit. These editors must decide which
stories have more to tell. They must decide which stories are left
out entirely, and which will get brief treatment. This is simply editing by thought rather than by routine.

The same thought must be applied to bulletins and bulletin editing. Here again a misconception arises in the minds of newsmen
who imagined the paper being turned into a series of little bold-

face paragraphs stuck under a standing head. That, of course, is
what a bulletin column is. But that does not mean that it has to
be done routinely without imagination or editing. There is no rule
that says a bulletin column need have a boring appearance, the
greatest effort toward good typography being to automatically alter-
nate boldface and lightface paragraphs.

Bulletins can have headlines, and probably should. They needn't
be set regular column width, and probably shouldn't. There is nothing that says art work cannot be tastefully inserted into the bulletin
column.

New Dress for Bulletins

Even this, the well-dressed, prominently displayed bulletin column, is far from new. A few newspapers have been using it successfully for years. A great many others have tried it and either let it
die or continue in a dried-up state that makes it almost worthless.
Often the very philosophy which established the "news in brief"
column is lost.

Why, when the newspaper lacked the competition of the airwaves, did it start using bulletin columns?

The very earliest reasons were mechanical. It was an expedient
way to shove last-minute items into the paper when there was no
extra time for changing the makeup of page one. This was a perfectly legitimate reason for a bulletin column and remains so, even
today. However, since radio or TV can give its listeners a bulletin
in seconds, this approach has lost some of its punch. Even so, it still
protects the newspaper's readers on last-minute breaking news.
There are some readers who will not get it from the airwaves and
others who will not be able to say, "I saw it on TV, but why isn't
it in my paper?"

Another reason that newspapers started several decades ago to
use bulletin columns was part of a philosophy of reader service. It
involved making it easier for the reader to quickly scan the major
news. It gave him that digest on page one where he could find it
easily and first. This news-at-a-glance philosophy was a good one.
Unfortunately, over the years it, too, has been too often lost in the
routine. Often the job of producing this column falls to a less-

experienced copyreader. Sometimes it is just an additional, last-minute burden for a competent, but harassed, wire editor. In either case, the result is usually neglect, and it is not unheard of for the bulletin column to become a dumping place for short items that would not have even been in the paper otherwise.

There is nothing wrong with the reasons that originally led to bulletin columns. In fact, in the age of depth the bulletin idea gains new strength. See how you feel about bulletins if you add the following reasons to the list:

1. They could save primary space on page one and other good readership pages. A bulletin column solidly anchored in a given spot on page one, taking an allotted amount of space every day, often makes it easier to plan the rest of the page and give good display to a depth story. *The New York Herald-Tribune, The Wall Street Journal, The Des Moines Register* and the *Des Moines Tribune,* and many other good newspapers already use this technique. The theory is—and it works—that by including a hot item in the bulletin column you have protected your reader and need not devote other prime space to that particular story.

2. They can enhance inside space where the reader may have to go for more detail. Often, the bulletin approach can be coupled with a reference which guides the reader to more details on an inside page. Later, we will take a closer look at references and promotions. However, at this point you need to note that reference can be part of the bulletin approach.

3. They can give the reader the latest facts about a breaking news story and, at the same time, save space. This approach requires the very best of news judgment, plus a good deal of courage on the part of a news editor. The idea is simply to provide the reader of the bulletin column with enough beautifully condensed information so that the competition can offer nothing new. However, because of time or space there may be nothing more than the bulletin synopsis in that particular day's paper. It may very well be that the same story will require depth tomorrow or the next day, but meanwhile the reader will have been informed by his newspaper.

This approach to the bulletin column for page one makes another important point. You have heard much preaching in this book about the quality needed to write and edit depth. It takes equal quality to produce even a good bulletin column.

It also takes skill in layout. But, the bulletin column need not drastically change the appearance of page one. It can be edited to fit any kind of a makeup philosophy. I am convinced that in the serious consideration of bulletins we can help solve some of the problems created by the depth approach to the news. However, there are other problems to be considered, and one of those is space.

22

Nightmare of the Newsroom

In the business office, space is the commodity that pays the bills. In the newsroom, space is a precious thing to be guarded against the pressures that would eat it up.

Yet, in the hectic rush to get out the paper every day, the pressures may win and space may be wasted.

It isn't that the city editor, the state editor, the wire editor, and every other editor does not fight to protect that precious space. They say "No" a hundred times a day, but the battle may have been lost long before they even became editors.

Some of what we might call tradition in the American newsroom might better be called habit. One of these habits is a bondage to a kind of blanket coverage that started when city hall was the size of a chicken coop.

This philosophy of total surface coverage developed when there wasn't much news from city hall, and every scrap of it had to be covered. Every zoning petition, every minor personnel change, every utterance of the part-time mayor became news. As we replaced the shanty-sized city hall with, in many instances, one of the largest buildings in town, we went right on covering city hall on the surface and with unbelievable triviality.

City hall just happens to make a good example. It happened at the police station, the courthouse, at the state capital, over at the Chamber of Commerce, and, heaven help us, at every spot up and down Main Street where the ancestor of the modern newsman trod his beat.

302

The trivia mounted from a molehill into a mountain, and, yes, the newspaper grew, too. The newspaper added pages. It added more columns of news. It became the country's leading advertising medium. But the size and prestige of that newspaper could not possibly have kept up with the growing mountain of trivia that came from the beats.

In fact, did the size of the newspaper really keep up with the volume of news, let alone the trivia?

A study of the newshole of a Midwestern metropolitan newspaper tells a provocative story. The study covered the years from 1900 to 1960—a period during which better communications systems and growing population multiplied many times the significant news of the world.

During those 60 years, this is the way the city involved in the study grew:

Year	Population
1900	102,555
1910	124,196
1920	191,601
1930	214,006
1940	223,844
1950	251,117
1960	301,598

The following are the 10-year averages of the newshole for each Tuesday:

Years	Pages	Newshole
1900-1909	9.6	950.8″
1910-1919	12.6	1025.4
1920-1929	19.4	1598.7
1930-1939	21.6	2218.7
1940-1949	21.1	2083.9
1950-1959	32.8	2431.1
1960 (one year only)	32.0	2485.0

This study appears to speak well for news-hungry readers. The number of pages had increased more than 300 percent. The newshole had increased about 250 percent. There was just one catch—or maybe two—the type size and the column width.

Let's take the column width first. During that 60 years the width of the column shrank from $2\frac{1}{4}$ inches to $1\frac{7}{8}$ inches.

The type size took the opposite tack. It grew from about 7 points to 9 points.

No one is going to criticize either the column shrinkage or the type expansion. Production costs dictated the first and readability the second. Nevertheless, the combination of the two did drastic things to that beautifully expanded newshole.

In 1900, there was an average of 80 words in each column inch. By 1960 the average was 35 words.

Take from the newshole almost two full pages of comic strips, of which there were none in 1900. Also note that many modern non-metropolitan newspapers devote 17 percent to 26 percent of their space to syndicated features. Now, look at that newshole. While it had more than doubled in 60 years, the number of words in each column inch had been cut to less than one half. If this example is borne out on other newspapers, then there is actually considerably less news space on the average than at the turn of the century. Small wonder that thinking editors shudder at the waste of a single line.

There are a few editors in the country who occasionally have to worry about filling the newshole, but these are as rare as that anti-quated news peg, the dog-biting man. In the early days, there was some concern over filling the newshole, but by World War II every inch of space became a precious newsroom commodity.

However, in most cases it is not treated with the loving care it deserves. The newshole is quickly gobbled up early in the day and it takes momentous happenings to shake loose the trivia stored away in those sacred columns.

True, some newspapers have tried to do something about that precious space. Some have developed the cult of tight writing. Others make and remake pages as new editions send papers out into different parts of the circulation area. Here, news is not judged on its value, but by geography. For an edition going to Clay Center, we put in items from Clay Center whether they are news or not.

Once more we have run into the antiquated edition schedule that bred an antiquated regionalizing of the news.

There was no time, it seemed, to halt the treadmill and take a long, earnest look at the mountain of trivia and the edition schedule. And what happens if you do stop and look? This is what John H. Colburn, former president of the Associated Press Managing Editors found:

Take a pencil and go through any edition of your newspaper 24 hours after it hit the street. See how much you can delete. Make the rounds with your beat men asking "What's new today?" or handling some routine that should be the job of a clerk.

How much of that time could be spent on penetrative reporting . . . developing news stories in depth? Stories that would make the reader proud of his community . . . stories that had the guts to make the reader demand action to correct faulty administration.

Where would you put such stories? Why not fill up those newsholes where you had copy that is perishable within 24 hours? That's the kind of news you get every hour on the air. Let it perish on the air-waves, not in your news columns.

I followed up Colburn's suggestion. The news editor of a news-paper was paid to take the time to take a red pencil and second-guess himself. Here are some of the things he discovered 24 hours after he had published a paper that he considered fairly well done. He found that he agreed with what had been done with 58 percent of the copy in that particular edition. He found that he could trim without hurting about 10 percent of the strictly news copy. He felt by careful editing he could pick up yet another 10 percent. Exclud-ing everything except strictly news—no society, sports, or editorial space—this news editor discovered that he could have picked up 196 inches from a total of 989 inches of space.

The newsroom can frequently do little but cry about the out-moded edition schedule. But cry the newsman must, and it wouldn't hurt the publisher to listen. However, what the newsman can really do is go to work on that mountain of trivia. Until he whittles that down there will be no time, no space, and no money for depth. It is all very well for the editor to pound on the publisher's door and demand more space and more money to do a better job in depth. It makes more sense, if, along with the pounding, he finds out where the space and time are being used right now.

At this point there is not even any need to start a hassle over what alleged news we should be putting into or leaving out of our newspapers. Without ruffling a single feather of a single news edi-tor, it is fairly easy to find out what we are now running that is of minimal interest to the reader.

Just to get a glimmering about the amount of this minimal brand of news, five newspapers were sampled. They ranged from 7,500 to

225,000 circulation. With the help of several news executives and a week's copy of each paper we examined the following categories:

1. News of interest to less than 25 readers.
2. News of interest to less than 50 readers.
3. News of interest to less than 100 readers.
4. News of interest to less than one percent of the readers.
5. Duplication where tight editing would have saved space.
6. News of absolutely no local interest or national significance.
7. Obvious filler.
8. Regular features—columns, and so forth—which run on a schedule without any judgment as to the worth of any individual feature. In other words, in this category, we were asking if any news judgment was applied to the use of syndicated material.

From the outset no one even suggested that all the news in all these categories should be left out of the paper. We knew, for instance, that anyone who would try to make a newspaper fit without fillers is fooling himself. All we sought to find were the readership soft spots, and once finding them, determine just how soft they were.

The following are the daily average totals of minimal news in all categories. (Details on individual categories are listed later in this chapter.)

Paper	Circulation	Page Average	Newshole Average	News of Minimal Interest Average
A	7,500	12	1022"	223"
B	18,500	19	1476	246
C	25,000	26	1793	187
D	45,000	23	1830	181
E	225,000	20	2178	77

While it would serve no purpose to identify the first four papers, there is no harm in naming the fifth, with its almost rock bottom 77 inches of minimal news a day. That paper is *The Des Moines Register,* generally conceded to be one of the most tightly edited and depth-conscious newspapers in mid-America.

The individual areas of minimal readership, which were examined, deserve some attention. We need to look at the "why" as in "why do we still use them?"

Back in the days when city hall was a shanty and we developed the tradition of coverage like a blanket, it made some sense for news-papers to cover every meeting—every collection of more than three people—that took place in town. But homo sapiens has a way of joining up, and the opportunities are unending. Luncheon clubs meet every day of the week. Discussion clubs meet every night. Women's clubs meet day and night. You take your choice and if you don't want to spend any time at home, you don't have to.

There grew up with the clubs a job called "publicity chairman." His or her job was to remind the newspaper whenever more than three members got together. And most of the newspapers went right along with it. When the city hall had become a skyscraper, many newspapers were still covering every meeting of every organization in town—and they called it complete coverage.

Now and then, after World War II, a city editor would shove back his chair for a minute or two and ponder his assignment list. He would scratch his head and ask, "Why am I sending even an inexperienced man to all of those luncheon meetings? The only ones who care about the meetings are the members, and they know what happened, anyhow. They don't even depend upon me to tell them when they meet, although they always want it in the paper. Every member gets a postcard before every meeting, and, further-more, the speakers are on a circuit. They will talk to fourteen clubs on the same subject in fourteen weeks."

It isn't that newspapers have to ignore completely the much-abused luncheon-club speaker. But the speakers themselves will admit wearily that they have been trapped. In a weak moment fourteen weeks ago they agreed to make a talk to luncheon club No. 1. The program chairman of luncheon club No. 2 was also a mem-ber of luncheon club No. 1. When the speaker had finished his talk, the program chairman of luncheon club No. 2 dashed up to pump his hand and say, "That was great. Will you please make the same talk for luncheon club No. 2?"

A week later at luncheon club No. 2 sat the program chairman of luncheon club No. 3. And when the speaker had finished his talk, the program chairman of luncheon club No. 3 dashed up and. . . .

Now, the first time the speaker spoke for luncheon club No. 1 it may conceivably have been news. But from that point on there was no question about it. It wasn't news; it was wasted space if it got into the newspaper. Not only was it a waste of space, but it was a waste of time for the reporter and the copyreader who handled it.

Thinking city editors have had to decide if items of interest to small groups are going to take up space that might serve a good many more readers. Ben Gilbert of *The Washington Post* is such a city editor. He says, "We are also eliminating minor one-point items of interest only to a minority of readers. For instance, we no longer publish the names of high school graduates nor do we record every zoning action. We try to be selective and to highlight those that are significant."

Gilbert has started to lick his problem. Most others are still fighting it. Here is what the space survey of five papers showed about use of limited readership items: (All figures are daily averages).

Categories from 25 Readers to 1 Percent of Circulation

	(Readers)				
	25	50	100	1%	Total
			(column	inches)	
Paper A	68	7	10	6	91
7,500 (Circulation)					
Paper B	111	11	5	4	131
18,500					
Paper C	51	10	5	17	83
25,000					
Paper D	59	5	2	21	87
45,000					
Paper E	9	2	2	10	23
225,000					

Selectivity, like trivia, extends beyond the luncheon clubs. It extends, as Gilbert hinted, to those beloved beats where a reporter has it made if he can spend day after day covering his beat in all the detail—or more—as did his predecessors down through the years. Some newspapers have dared to take a look at those beats and have found that both they and the reporters were being robbed. It is no insult to the hard-working beat reporter to be told that he is wasting his time if all he is doing is going as hard and as fast as he can to cover every detail. He may need some rescuing, too, from the traditions established by his predecessors.

His publisher and his editor may find it comfortable to brag that "we cover every zoning move down to the last detail." But is that really coverage? Newsmen are beginning to wonder if attention to trivia has not taken away from them the right to judge and edit the news. What can we expect of the beat reporter who is expected to come into the office with his daily columns of agate? We certainly cannot expect very much depth.

For the large newspaper the answer is relatively simple and very expensive. The metropolitan newsroom budget may be able to afford two staffs—one for routine and one for depth. For example, *The Washington Post* has reorganized its local staff so that the regular beat men can still cover the old geographical beats and give spot news protection. The other staff, comprised of depth writers, goes beyond the surface news.

That is fine for the large paper, but what about the editor of the paper with 25,000 circulation? Does he have time or money or space to use two staffs? Of course not. He is already filling his paper three times a day as it is.

Is that an exaggeration? Does that much so-called news pour into the newsroom each day? Think about it for a moment. Assume that you are editing a newspaper with both United Press International and Associated Press wire service. Perhaps you also have the Chicago Daily News foreign wire or the New York Times service. From those sources you can expect approximately a half-million words a day off the wire. A reporting staff of 15 to 20 members provides column after column. Those reporters probably are capable of almost filling your newshole by themselves. A throw-away spike at the city editor's elbow holds 50 or 60 releases that arrived in the mail during the day. Perhaps 75 correspondents pour in their offerings by mail, by wire, and by telephone. In some cases a bureau established out in your trade area provides regional news. On the society and sports desk the same thing is happening. And how much space is there for the news in that day's edition? Perhaps on a good day you have 40,000 words worth of space. Now look again at the half-million words alone pouring off of those teletype machines. It is no myth that more so-called news pours in than the paper can run. It is piling up there in the wire editor's waste basket.

The surplus of what seems to be news further complicates the problem of deciding what we mean when we say we must inform the reader. What, of all this mound of raw copy, informs the reader and what does not? Obviously, there is no direct answer to that question. The answerable question is, "Which of that news informs the most readers the best?" The answer to that is thoughtful editing. Somebody has to decide.

Somebody has to decide how much coverage the newspaper is going to give to clubs and other small minorities of readers who actually know what happened at their meetings and apply pressure on the newspapers to build up their scrapbooks. Somebody is going to have to decide if we want clerks or reporters on the beats. It may be that there are jobs for both of them there. The clerk can collect the detail we feel we must run and the beat reporter can start covering his beat. A couple of malicious city editors have experimented with their beats by giving the beat men free rein to decide what should be covered, but insisting that they cover the beat in half the normal time. Both reporters and editors have been shocked to discover how little the coverage suffered. They were pleased to discover how they had created both new space in the newspaper and more time for the beat reporters to work in depth.

Of course, not all the space can be found by readjusting the work of reporters. A good deal of space can be found by a copy pencil in the hand of an adept copy editor. The amount, of course, will vary with the quality of the copy editing. Remember the news editor who second-guessed himself and found the copy could have been tightened about ten percent?

Duplication, poor news judgment on the value of a national story to local readers, and filler also account for a good deal of space. Our five-paper survey showed:

Paper	Duplication	No Local Reason	Filler	Total
A	13"	26"	14"	53"
B	8	14	8	30
C	4	14	13	31
D	8	18	18	44
E	1	8	3	12

The above table doesn't prove anything startling except that here is some more space that is not exactly directed at informing the reader.

Having plunged this deeply into desecration of newsroom tradition, turn now to the hallowed editorial page. Is there any space to be had there? A good many editorial writers have put aside their personal egos to answer that question affirmatively. They point out that most editorial pages carry some syndicated columnists. They add that there is nothing so hallowed about a columnist's work that it dictates he do a good job each day. In fact there are a few snide souls who say the good job is a rarity. Someone else can argue that, but no one can cite any news rule that says you can't throw out a syndicated columnist on the day he misses the boat. There are, in fact, some newspapers which have thrown out all columnists—permanently. This may be a bit extreme, but it certainly is not extreme to suggest that the columnists face up to daily news judgment just like everything else in the paper. So a columnist cost you ten dollars; would you sell ten inches of your newshole for that price? This is not an attack on the editorial page, it is simply a suggestion that here, too, there may be tradition that started when the city hall was a shanty.

In the five-paper survey an effort was made to estimate which regular features, excluding such items as comics, of course, were run on schedule no matter whether the writer had a bad day or other demands for space outranked him. This included syndicated features both on and off of the editorial page.

Syndicated Material Run on Schedule

Paper A	79″
Paper B	84
Paper C	75
Paper D	51
Paper E	42

Again, let me remind you that I am not suggesting we throw out these syndicated columnists. I am only saying that if we need space, we might be able to pick up a little when the columnist has a bad day. There are, as a matter of fact, editorial pages where the good depth story has found a home alongside locally written editorials. And readership surveys have indicated that the well-dressed depth story was not only read, but it drew some attention to a page that sometimes suffers from lack of readers.

But let's not stray too far from the point. We are concerned only with finding some space. Along with the space we have to find time to write the depth, which is also saving money to pay for it. The first step may be examining our newspapers, as any reasonably run business should do periodically anyhow. Call off the rat race for a moment. Take a look at the edition structure. Stand back from the mountain of trivia.

No one says you should throw out all the filler, all the columns, and all the minority readership items. But it seems perfectly reasonable that within the ten or twelve columns you are giving this stuff every day, you ought to be able to find two or three columns as a starter for some depth.

Happily, the question of time, space, and money need not be divided up into three questions. When you create more space by eliminating trivia, you also create more time by eliminating the work that went into the trivia. And that time, which really is money, can help solve the budget problem. It all gets back again to this— on a very practical basis, we must ask ourselves:

"Have we abdicated from editorship in favor of our predecessors who made their decisions on the basis of a shanty-sized city hall?"

23

"Feet-Up" Editing

"Oh, I can finish this all right," said an editor reading copy on a reporting job that had taken months. His statement wasn't so bad; it was commendable, in fact, since it was at the end of one of those long, frustrating days that can develop in the newsroom. But then the tired editor added:

"I can't write when I am tired, but I can sure edit."

The copy editors, and the reporters, too, for that matter, should have risen indignantly from their desks and marched in protest to the nearest tavern. But, as happens far too often in American newsrooms, it was late and the few reporters and copy editors left around had already capitulated to the need simply to get the job done and out to the composing room.

This is a far too common example of what often happens to the single most important man in the newsroom—the really good copy editor. Reporters and copyreaders traditionally disagree right up to a point just short of fists. And perhaps, since most good news personnel men recognize that they are two dissimilar species of feline, that's just as well. But deep down in his egotistical heart a good reporter knows that a good copy editor is his most trusted ally.

However, newsroom conditions may often tend to widen the gap between the two, rather than narrow it. A tradition born in the need for speed has turned too many copy editors into copyreaders. And a copyreader is as bad as a hack reporter. A copyreader is a low-grade copy editor who is an expert with paragraph marks and trims stories with his scissors. Spikes piled high with copy to be

314

processed for the next edition have reduced too many copy editors to copyreaders. And those same spikes have robbed the copy editor of his chance to think.

As much as we need depth reporters in this business, we need copy editors. In the machine that too many copy desks have become, a good depth piece can be cut up and rolled out the same thin gage as all the rest of the surface coverage in the paper.

The reverse, of course, is true when copyreaders become copy editors. And the good reporter knows that the other half of his team is just as good or better than he. We do not need reporters to tell copy editors how to do their job. The job of reporting in depth is plenty for any one man. We need copy editors with a combination of ability and decisiveness that can perhaps best be matched by the big league umpire.

In fact, one of the best copy editors I have ever known used to parody one of the best baseball jokes I have ever heard. The joke goes that one of the major league's umpires was asked in a newspaper interview how it felt to make decisions under such tremendous pressure as a World Series game. "Does it bother you?" he was asked.

He replied, "They may be strikes. They may be balls. But they ain't nothing until I call 'em."

My copy editor friend, a genius with a black pencil, made a parody of the punch line:

"They may be sentences. They may be paragraphs. But they ain't nothin' until I mark 'em."

That Godlike attitude of the master copy editor may seem both irritating and arbitrary to the reporter, but it is exactly the kind of dedication necessary to handle a depth story. Every news editor, every slot man, and every city editor in the country has been dismayed by copyreaders who write paragraph marks, cut a story in half with the scissors, slap a headline on it, and then have no idea of what it says. The depth story must be placed in the decisive hands of a copy editor who feels that he is the last word for every word in that story.

The copy editor must serve two major functions. Jaded as he may become with the thousands of words that may pass daily beneath his pencil, he must react as the reader might to his first reading of a depth story. Then, he must edit. He must make sure the point of the story is made. He must spot the unanswered questions. He must cut the excess verbiage, but not the life, from the story. He must love and respect the language in which he works, and insist that the reporter do likewise. He must demand a rewrite if necessary. And most of all, he must think.

Just as there is no formula to replace thought when the reporter writes, there is no formula to replace it around the rim of the copy desk. In fact, many good newsmen are disturbed because the highly systematized approach on most copy desks can produce speed but reduce thought.

Some newswriters would like to have the copy editor in on the story from the start. However, such togetherness would destroy the copy editor's ability to react freshly to the final result. At the risk of sounding as if I proposed a team with two quarterbacks, I do not believe that the copy editor should have any more confinement than the depth reporter. Each man has a job, and each man should do it separately for the best results. There are times for team work when a depth story is under way, but the times are neither when the reporter writes nor when the copy editor edits. We either want this kind of quality personnel or we probably do not want depth.

This section obviously is not a complete or near-complete dissertation on copy editing. Copy editing is an art unto itself and deserves to be treated that way. You, the student writer or the young professional writer, need to understand the vital part good copy editors play in the depth approach. That, and for no other reason, is why you are sitting behind the men at the rim of the copy desk as we discuss their problems.

Some newspapers, such as *The Wall Street Journal,* have even established separate desks for the depth pieces. Here men with the combined talents for rewriting and editing deal as master copy editors should. Such specialization is not absolutely necessary, even if desirable. It is possible to maintain copy editors on a universal copy desk whose talents are available to bring a depth story to its culmination. Either of these techniques requires one major ingredient beyond talented copy editing. That ingredient is time to think. A depth story spiked with the run-of-the-mill news at the copy editor's elbow stands a good chance of receiving run-of-the-mill treatment.

But assume the talented copy editor, of whom there are too few, is given time when he works on a depth story, of which there are too few. With time as his ally, what then is his role in the approach to depth?

First, he becomes the toughest critic in the newsroom. He takes the time to read the story completely through. With his pencil behind his ear, he enjoys the luxury of reading the whole piece without a thought for style, punctuation, paragraph marks, or any of the technical tools of his art. Nothing can destroy both the depth story and its author more quickly than a surface copyreader who starts marking up the story before he has read the first sentence. If he insists on using his pencil before reading, he gives up his function as the critic.

Let's call this the "feet-up" philosophy as opposed to the "heads-up" philosophy so popular in the athletic locker room between halves. As the coach says, "Let's play heads-up ball," the editor should say to his copy editor, "Let's do feet-up editing."

No editor should care if grooves are worn in the edge of the copy desk if it means that thoughtful copy editors have leaned back, planted their heels on the edge of the desk, and read thoughtfully and critically a major story. If this seems a poor economy of time and copy desks, think for a moment about a really uneconomical practice too often found in our newsrooms.

At least hours, usually days, and sometimes weeks before the copyreader starts his job, an editor and a reporter have started spending the newspaper's money on a depth idea. First, in consultation and planning they eat up time, which is always the equivalent of dollars. Then, through those hours, days, and weeks, a reporter researches, interviews, and organizes his story as his schedule allows. More hours—more dollars—have been committed to the project.

Finally, the story is produced and space is allotted. If the story is good and the editor recognizes it, prime space may be set aside on page one or some other choice spot. If you want to know what that space is worth, consult the advertising department. You should take the figure given you and double or triple it at least to determine the worth of news space.

Now, for the question. Does the story go to a copyreader or a copy editor? If a copyreader gets the nod, look out. With a busy pencil, flashing scissors, and speed, but no time for thought, he can, in minutes, waste hundreds of dollars. If he is a copy editor he can use the same tools plus talent and time to enhance your investment.

Just as the rest of the newsroom needs to examine the traditions, more aptly called habits, developed in an atmosphere of haste, so does the copy desk. A thoughtful copy desk can help reduce minimal stories into minimal lengths, and even suggest quick death for fourth-rate stories. Remember, if minimal stories are left out of the paper, the time it would have taken to edit and head them is saved on the copy desk. It works a little like an algebraic equation— fourth-rate copy thrown away equals space and time.

As far as depth is concerned, the same rules apply for the copy editor as for the reporter. The rules are mostly lack of rules in favor of more opportunity for thought. However, just as in the case of the reporter, there is no formula the copy editor can learn that will help him do a thoughtful job. In this atmosphere where thought and quality become the only real rules, the copyreader becomes a copy editor who is the most valuable partner a depth reporter can find.

What can that copy editor do? First, of course, is a vitally simple point. Did the reporter come on out and make the point of his story? Don't laugh when a good copy editor looks for the answer to that question. He may save the depth reporter from his research and himself.

As you write in depth you will understand why this is the first commandment for a copy editor. All newspaperdom chuckles every time a beginning reporter misses a routine story because a major catastrophe has eliminated his chief source. You know the kind, the kind involving the wedding story that couldn't be written because the bridegroom ran off with the company funds. Depth writers of considerably more experience run the same risk. They can become so bound up in the research of their subject that they miss the point entirely. Oh, they know what the point is, and in a vague way it is in the story. There are hints, statistics, innuendoes, quotations, and all kinds of circumstantial evidence. But unfortunately, the reporter may have done his research so well that he assumes everyone understands quite obviously what the story is all about.

The copy editor who thinks and reads before he pencils is the best-equipped person in the newsroom to catch this natural but serious omission. If he uses his pencil first, the chances are good that he will join the reporter in his own fact-filled, research-glutted never-never land.

Beyond that first great omission, not making the point, there are many holes into which the depth reporter can fall and out of which a good copy editor can pull him. Throughout the story there may be unanswered questions. There may be points that seem obvious to the writer but are totally lost for the reader. When a good copy editor finds someone referred to as "the second woman in history to reach this rank in state government," he asks the reader's question, "Who was the first?" When the same copy editor reads, "Legislative Bill 119," he asks, "Does that number also stand for the statute that raised my taxes?"

While filling in the holes, the good copy editor may also have to level mountains of words that have little to do with telling the story. This war on excess verbiage frequently puts reporters and copy editors on opposite sides of the barbed wire. Good reporters love all their words, but good copy editors have to decide between love and information. A combination of the two is possible, but there can be no love without information.

There is also a difference between excess verbiage and words and phrases that make a story live. The real copy editor feels his way along this fine line between baloney and beauty. An example helps make the point. Read the following lead:

> To the outsider, the Cornhusker football fan may seem to be some kind of a superloyal nut.

That sentence started a story examining the fantastic support of a losing football team. The lead itself trod the razor's edge between an unintended insult to the Cornhusker fan and a dull approach to a good story. The words "to the outsider" eliminated the danger of insult. The description, "superloyal nut," promised good reading. Now, see what happened to that lead in several newspapers who used a digested and nervous wire service version:

> Cornhusker football fans are some kind of superloyal nuts, according to Hal Brown.

Those few changes, intended for attribution, established the unintended insult and created antagonism in place of reader interest. And the attribution, in this case, instead of being laid to one of the sources was to, of all people, the reporter who wrote the original story.

For the word-counters, this change was a four-word victory. For the story it was a distortion and sure death.

For another example, let's go back to the beginning of this book where among the definitions the death of Joe Jones, a cigar-smoking mechanic, was discussed. Take the cigar out of Joe's mouth. Eliminate the fact that he helped youngsters build safer soap-box racers on the weekends. And the story is just as dead as its subject.

The copy editor who can tread the razor's edge is also a copy editor as much in love with the English language as the good reporter. He knows not only how to spell, but he knows what words mean. He knows, for instance, that the difference between emigrant and immigrant is probably several million people in the U.S. alone. He may have his peculiar quirks. He may insist that people do not drop dead, but fall dead. He may insist that no one dies instantly. He may insist that there is no such thing as an advisor, but only advisers. But all this simply means that he is a professional at the copy desk. He wants the reporter's words and his own headlines to tell the story in the best way possible.

He glows with pride of authorship when he does his job well and is respectfully envious when the competition does it better. I wonder how many good editors said, "I wish I'd written that," when they saw how a West Coast newspaper handled America's initial effort to put a satellite into space. After weeks of build-up, the attempt fizzled. Many headline writers told millions of readers that the effort had flopped, but how many banners said this?

"10-9-8-7-6-5-4-3-2-1-Phfftt!"

For the real copy editor rewriting is another part of his job. It often amounts to using a typewriter when there is too much correction needed for a pencil. Most newspapers give the depth story back to its author when rewriting is necessary. And when circumstances allow, this is probably best. However, after the reporter has done his best at the rewrite someone else may still have to give the depth story the last touch.

For example, the Page-One Desk of *The Wall Street Journal* is greatly involved in rewrite. From all parts of the world come depth story candidates that usually already have been rewritten a time or two. In the New York office topnotch rewriters give the stories the final polish. In such cases some measure of rewriting is almost assumed. It is only the degree that varies.

But on smaller newspapers rewrite is also the job of the copy editor. When that is the case the simple choice of tools usually makes the difference between enough rewriting and not enough. If the copy editor sticks to his pencil, he probably will not rewrite enough. If he is willing to turn to the typewriter and then do a little clipping and pasting, his rewriting runs a good chance of enhancing the story, even if it enrages the reporter.

Actually, where rewriting takes place doesn't make too much difference. But unless a newspaper can afford a specialized rewrite desk for depth, it may be best that the copy editor also rewrite. As a matter of fact, the rewrite man on such a desk as that set up by *The Wall Street Journal* is also a copy editor, so we are talking about the same thing. If the copy editor is the man responsible for getting the story from the reporter to the reader, then the copy editor probably should have the total responsibility for the story's final form.

But he cannot be responsible unless he is given time for thought. And I don't much care what his eccentricities are, if he will think. Let him lean back and plant his heels on the edge of the copy desk. Copy desks are cheap compared to the newspaper's most valuable man, the honest-to-goodness copy editor.

24

Depth Deserves the Best

No one will deny that new twists in layout, makeup, and other devices sometimes called readability have done great things for the twentieth-century newspaper. But newsmen must be cautious. Those who feared depth reporting was only a gimmick now know that it is hard work and a thoughtful way of newspaper life. Nothing will substitute for either the work or the thinking. The same applies to the typographical devices that have immensely improved our modern newspapers. Hard work and thought are behind these, too. However, those of us in the newsrooms and classrooms must avoid our natural tendency to try to turn them into hardbound rules—formulas of mechanization. We must use them, but to make sure they do not use us, we must take care to preserve that old-fashioned ingredient called news judgment, which is just another way of saying, "Think!"

It is very well to develop a more readable newspaper. Scholars of typography have jarred us out of nineteenth-century traditions of layout. They have given us better body type and more readable headline faces. The old folks, for instance, discovered their glasses were not so bad the day their newspaper shifted from $7\frac{1}{2}$-point to 9-point type. An attractive headline has been known even to draw the reader's attention away from that Big Eye in the living room. But, 9-point body type and attractive headlines will not replace thought either in the story or in the layout.

Time after time as I have approached cautious editors for assistance on this book they said "depth editing" in the same breath that they said "depth reporting." They mean the kind of planning, editing, layout, and makeup that brings maximum returns for all the dollars spent on a depth story.

Of course, throughout the production of depth, planning is the key. It does not mean that we call in an eager junior executive and say, "You are responsible for giving this newspaper depth." It means that the men at the top must say to themselves, "I am responsible for giving this newspaper depth." Togetherness and delegation of responsibility are fine, but where the most important ingredient of the future newspaper is concerned, the someone with responsibility has to take the responsibility.

A number of excellent newspapers are already doing this kind of planning. They are already pulling out the stops when a good depth story deserves it. Remember that *Des Moines Tribune* team that did nothing else for several days but prepare for the announcement of a freeway that would change the face of the city? Or, perhaps it is such a team as *The New York Times* public-affairs team. Editor Turner Catledge says its function is primarily planning. Weekly meetings are held with public-affairs reporters with the city editor running the show. An assistant city editor is assigned the liaison job with the reporters. Assistant managing editors provide the links with the managing editor, the national desk, and the Washington bureau. How does it work?

Take for example a story that every newspaper in the country knew was coming up at least ten years in advance. It was the announcement of the preliminary 1960 census figures. *The Times* reporter assigned to the census story joined the public-affairs group. Discussion centered on the meaning of the expected drop in city population. This started the planning. And this was the result:

On the day after the preliminary figure was announced *The New York Times* provided complete coverage with sidebars explaining the political and economic effects of the reduced population in the city and the potential gains in representation of expanding suburban counties.

The same kind of planning can be found on several of the country's better newspapers, but unfortunately they are for the most part metropolitan. It may seem that they have the time, money, and staff to do this, when the smaller paper is beaten before it starts. That is not true. While the pace in the editor's office of the smaller newspaper may be more hectic, he, too, can find time if he is willing to examine critically some of the traditions and formulae passed down to him by his predecessors. Let's look at the more technical aspects of getting a depth story well dressed and into the paper.

Now, we are talking about makeup and layout philosophies, which very often operate by formula. For instance, there is a newspaper tradition that says the right-hand column of page one is a proper spot for the top breaking news story of the day. The left-hand column operates in much the same light, according to this formula. Newspapers with horizontal makeup, though it be newer in the business, have their traditions, too. The over-the-roof spot usually goes to a story of "featurish" nature. A spread display across the bottom is usually used the same way. In other words, no matter what the makeup philosophy of your newspaper there are probably certain rules of thumb that dictate the play of certain kinds of stories in certain places. Depth, as a newcomer in the planning of many newspapers, may upset these rules.

What honest news editor or makeup editor can really say that the breaking news day after day provides a story really worth the right- and left-hand columns of page one? Before the arguments start, let's remember the history of newspaper makeup. That big, bold, black headline leading to the left- or right-hand story was the weapon of the street corner fight for circulation. Many newspapers still have that big bold headline as part of their philosophy though the circulation and advertising departments are boasting more than 90 percent home delivery. That does not mean they should throw out the big headline. If it is part of the face that greets your reader each morning or evening, then removing it could very well be like removing the nose from the face of a family friend. The point is that when newspapers were there first with the breaking news that headline and the right- or left-hand columns belonged to the hottest story available, even if it was surface news. Today neither the headline nor the columns serve the same function. Would it be so out of order to give that spot to a far-reaching depth story? Some newspapers, such as *The New York Herald Tribune, The Wall Street Journal,* and others, are already doing it. These two newspapers make excellent examples because they represent almost opposite kinds of layout philosophy. *The Journal* uses a conservative approach of vertical layout. *The Herald Tribune* exercises the flexibility of a horizontal makeup. Yet, without changing their faces these newspapers can guide readers to depth in good spots on page one. The conclusion seems to be that page one may be the answer to that question: "If we get this depth, where in blazes do we put it?"

The next most obvious place for depth on some newspapers has been provided by the development of a "second page one." Sometimes it is page two. Sometimes it is the first page of the second section. And, with apologies to Little Orphan Annie, it has even chased the comics off the back page of one of the sections. It makes little difference where it is; it is designed to provide better readability on an inside page. If it is well done, it increases the readership on that inside page.

Some newspapers use their second page one for top play for depth. Usually when they do it they promote both the page and the story from page one. It seems to me that the excellent philosophy of the second page one—sometimes called a local page—is destroyed when it becomes a dropping place for last-minute items or those that might not get into the paper otherwise. Here is the perfect opportunity to reserve space for depth. Here is the perfect opportunity to make that space so attractive that it hauls the reader into the story.

If it is possible to chase Little Orphan Annie off the back page of a section, it is also possible to take a covetous look at the editorial page. Some newspapers have also done this, and in doing so have found both space for the depth story and readership for the editorial page. What space on the editorial page? The answer was given a couple of chapters ago. Does every columnist ring the bell every day? Does any writer ring the bell every day? Are the letters to the editor, as widely read as they are, always sufficient to fill the space? Are there always three or four or five good subjects upon which to produce locally written editorials every day? If the chief editorial writer and his editorial writers apply this kind of news judgment to the contents of their page, they might just possibly find space for a well-written depth piece.

It might interest you to know that in our experiments with depth at the University of Nebraska we discovered editors voluntarily taking a look at their editorial space when a good depth story was available. A number of them took a well-written student series on taxation and ran it once a week in place of their editorials.

Some newspapers have taken over editorial space for depth on a more regular schedule. For years *The Milwaukee Journal* has run a well-played, well-edited, well-illustrated background story on the editorial page every day. The subject may be anything from background on baseball to foreign monetary exchange, but it is treated like a gem that needs a good setting.

The Milwaukee Journal and such other newspapers as *The St. Louis Post-Dispatch* and *The Kansas City Star* also produce special editorial sections on Sunday. This does not mean more editorials; it means more depth. These sections carry beautifully laid out stories that challenge the best the magazine layout men have to offer.

But we must not forget in this enthusiasm for depth the problems of the smaller papers. Someone has to write it. With a look at ways to cut his trivia, the editor of the small paper may find reporter time for depth. However, that is not his only answer.

The answer was in the making as early as 1951 when *The Washington Post*'s Alfred Friendly wrote a summary for the domestic news section of the APME's continuing study reports:

> The essence of the findings of these special topic studies was that AP must move steadily toward reporting of increasing depth and seriousness for an audience of growing education and sophistication. To AP's credit, it has long since graduated from the notion that a budget of fires, rapes, and train wrecks suffice for the daily domestic report. It must maintain its awareness that the dimensions of news growth steadily, year by year, become deeper as well as broader—and that the challenge of covering the news more expertly and more seriously grows greater each day.

That was 1951. Today both the AP and the UPI include many good depth pieces in their budget. Unhappily, many of their clients, bound up in tradition and tight newsholes, have trouble finding space for depth. Perhaps the editor of the small newspaper where local depth must be a limited luxury should look into the wire editor's waste basket. It is no more difficult to put a good depth story from the wire services on the editorial page than it is to lay in a column from the syndicates.

Now, let's turn to the rest of the inside pages. Here, on most newspapers, the advertising department determines the amount of space and, to a large degree, the makeup. Day after day, the dummies come in from advertising with the inside pages almost planned in advance for the news editor. True, he decides what he puts on those pages. However, every news editor knows the frustration of a page with a few inches of news space spread out over the top of eight columns of ads. He also knows the problems of writing a decent head and using decent art with a long story that traipses, wraps, and winds its way over the top of pyramided ads.

No newsman who gives a hoot for payday is going to suggest that the ads be thrown out. But it might not hurt both the news and ad departments to see if they, too, are not trapped by tradition. Most newspapers pyramid ads on the right-hand side of inside pages. This leaves news space in the upper left-hand corner. Is that the best arrangement of space for a news story?

Some newspapers do not believe so, and as a result, have dared experiment with ad layout on inside pages. They have tried, for example, *well* makeup. This involves building ads both to the left and right sides of the page. It leaves the top and the middle for news display. For advertisers who like to see their ads run close to news copy, *well* makeup actually gets more ads next to news columns. More important, it gives the makeup editor a chance to lay in an attractive story that might just possibly draw more readers to the page. And who ever heard of an advertiser who didn't like more readers in the vicinity of his ad?

There is in the newspaper business an excellent tradition that separates the news and advertising departments. However, this separation should not exclude close cooperation where space for a good depth piece is involved. Whose virtue is going to be tarnished if the news editor, planning a good depth story for tomorrow's paper, asks that special attention be given to providing good space on one inside page?

It should be apparent that there is space to be found for depth stories. But that does not answer all the questions. Two major questions remain:

1. How do we use that space so it drags the reader into a story that may be longer than usual?

2. How do we make sure that the reader knows that story is in the newspaper?

Let's look for answers to the first question over the shoulder of the skilled layout man. Actually, the opportunity to take a good chunk of space and make it as attractive as possible is a challenging one for the layout man and his art. For lack of something better to call it, let's call this *unit* makeup. The idea of a unit involves taking a tip from our competitors in the magazine business. In their smaller format the magazines can pull the stops on one or two pages just to get the story off to a good start. The reader's attention is focused by every trick of the trade on that particular offering. Normally, this would be impractical on a newspaper, where a full page is a great deal of space.

Then, why not plan for units of space within those eight-column pages? Perhaps we could commit one-fourth, one-third, one-fifth, or one-eighth of a page. It might be a horizontal one or a vertical one, depending upon the newspaper's philosophy. It might be on the editorial page, page one, an inside page, or it might start on page one and jump to an inside page. But suppose that the layout man can be told, "Here is a hole five columns wide and eight inches deep. Have at it. Make this story grab the readers by the eyeballs."

Without changing the face of the newspaper, without creating too much of an upheaval in the backshop, that layout man can use art, attractive heads, decks, subheads, odd measure type, and all the other tools of his craft. You can bet that given a little time to think and a little space with which to work, he can turn out a unit fully competitive with his magazine counterparts.

There is one more point involving the layout man. If he is to use units of space to best display depth, he needs a crack at tomorrow's dummies in advance. It may very well be that before anything else is laid into the paper, the unit of space for depth must be picked. Then there is no unbreakable tradition that says the rest of the paper cannot be built around it.

There is another much larger unit of space that not only gives the layout man an opportunity to practice his art, but gives the newspaper an opportunity to improve its educational position. This unit is the special section. I am not talking about the special sections that are primarily advertising vehicles. These are the new homes sections, the new cars sections, and countless others which carry related copy with the ads. Frankly, I have never been able to get too upset about the suggestion that this type of section compromises the newsman's ethics. Such sections are obviously promotion sections. Even the least perceptive of readers knows that. Furthermore, labeled as promotion sections, they make money for the newspaper. And if you have read anywhere in this book that I have any objection to newspapers making money, then it will be removed on the first revision.

However, I am talking about special educational sections. This is the kind of section that is produced primarily to give information and only secondarily to make money, if indeed there is any immediate dollar profit at all. But the indirect profits are almost as incalculable as those for the newspaper's transition from surface to depth. To find out how these special sections are involved in both depth and education, let's look at a couple of them.

In 1961 *The Cleveland Plain Dealer* produced a special section about Ohio—"From Wilderness To Wealth." The section carried not one line of advertising. For those who wished additional copies the price was 35 cents.

While *The Plain Dealer* most certainly did not get rich on the edition, its profits could not be counted in immediate dollars and cents. What *The Plain Dealer* did was produce a popular, well-written, well-illustrated history of Ohio. And that history helped to buck the newspaper tradition that makes it quite acceptable to wrap the garbage in the newspaper before it is a day old.

Other newspapers have done the same thing. *The Kansas City Star* regularly produces beautifully illustrated special sections in its regular eight-column format. However, the type is not usually set one column wide, and subheads, pictures, maps, and boxes give the reader the impression that he is looking at a large-size magazine.

The University of Nebraska School of Journalism has also experimented with this kind of educational special section. An examination of the results can more clearly indicate the indirect profits the newspaper can expect from this kind of public service.

The Nebraska special section, written entirely by advanced students, dealt solely with the state's unique political creature, the unicameral legislature. The primary objective of the experiment was, of course, education. As they tried to explain as well as to examine the successes and failures of the unicameral legislature the students were making an important step in their education as journalists. They were combining their journalistic techniques with their liberal arts educations. Hardly a subject in the special section could have been written without reference to one or more of the academic disciplines in which these students had taken course work. Furthermore, as they interviewed senators, governors, lieutenant governors, party leaders, and any number of other official and semi-official sources, they discovered practical application of such background courses as political science and history. Were they successful?

The resulting 36-page section in Sunday magazine format dealt with every aspect of the state's one-house legislature. Its history was reviewed. Its founding fathers were described in word profiles. Its gears were examined to the smallest bolts and nuts. And for the first time since its founding 25 years before, most of its legislative leaders were given a chance to say thoughtfully how they thought the experiment had worked.

That was the educational experience. That was what the School of Journalism gave first priority. But the by-product resulting from the section can give you some notion of the indirect profits a newspaper can expect.

Its initial circulation was 5,000—less than the daily circulation of almost any paper in the state, and even less than many of the weeklies. It went primarily to newspapermen and educators. Hence, Nebraska readers and those in other states had to hear about it indirectly. Yet, the word did reach readers, not only in Nebraska, but in most of the other states. Soon, orders poured in from libraries, legislative councils, schools, and from people who were simply interested. The classroom orders were the most significant. Hundreds of copies went out in bundles of from 25 to 80 so that every student in a class could use it as a textbook supplement.

Now, this is important. These youngsters were paying 25 cents a copy. The 25 cents is not important. It did not pay for the publication. But, it meant that young people—our future readers—were paying their money for a newspaper product to be used where they best understand information. To them the classroom is the place where they get reliable information. When they used this product of journalism, they were accepting its reliability and appreciating its readability as part of their educational experience.

Now, we are getting to the point. When newspapermen realize, when they are educated, when they are convinced that depth is the answer for the newspaper, the battle is only starting. For decades many of our newspapers have trained their readers to expect flashing glimpses of the breaking news. Now, in the age of depth, those readers must be trained to expect thought-provoking depth. In other words, it will take a while to educate our readers to expect the complete story in their newspaper.

But every time a special educational section—be it from Cleveland, Ohio, or Kansas City, Missouri, or Lincoln, Nebraska—reaches into the classroom a big step in that education has become a fact. We have not only escaped wrapping the garbage, but we have been placed on top of that pile of magazines set aside for future reading.

About that time we begin to get this reaction:

"This is the stuff I expect in my magazine, or in books, or maybe in a TV documentary program. But here it is in my newspaper."

That is the important reaction. The newspaper, still the giant of the communications industry, has struck back at the competition in a positive way. The minute the newspaper, or a section of it, escapes the first garbage wrapping, it has acquired more reader time. And when it does this, it also may very well make a new bid for new advertising dollars. No one denies that the merchants who sell perishable goods as well as common, everyday staples know they must turn to the newspaper for help. No one but the newspaper has continued to sell successfully hams, avocados, and even soups, skirts, and used automobiles. But when the newspaper begins to hang around the house, there may be advertisers who will wonder if they can't sell in the newspaper the way they do in magazines and on television. And don't forget that the advertiser doesn't forget that the newspaper arrives once a day.

That very problem, the inability of the newspaperman to understand the value of his own product, brings us to the second major question involving use of depth in our newspapers. The first was how to lay it out so it would haul the reader into the story. The next is how to be sure the reader knows the depth story is in the paper.

For as long as any of us care to remember a newspaper has been a multicolumn, multipage, larger-than-average publication. As the years have gone by, we have put the best news on page one, and relegated the less important news to inside pages. Logically, we assume high readership on page one and lower readership inside. As a matter of practicality, a change in the format is out of the question in the reasonable future. We have no choice but to work with our multicolumn, multipage, larger-than-average publication.

But for the moment let's assume that we could change to a smaller magazine format. If we did, not one of us doubts that we would use page one and the index to promote like the very dickens what could be found on the inside pages. We know we aren't going to change to a magazine format, even if we wanted to. But is there any reason that we cannot thoroughly promote what we have on our inside pages?

Promotion to inside pages from page one is hardly an innovation. But the newspaper business needs to ask itself if it is promoting half as well as it should. Many newspapers run an index on page one. Often it is little more than an almost telegraphic phrase to hint at something of significance that takes two columns to tell on page 17. Too often the typographical dress of the index is the dullest on page one. In some cases, it is even set in agate. Other papers may relegate the index to page two or three.

Obviously, when we treat an index like that, we do not practice what our ad salesmen preach. They tell a customer that he will sell more in 48-point type than in 8-point type. Yet, sometimes, we try to sell all our inside pages on the basis of a dull little list tucked away somewhere at the bottom of page one.

Newspapers that know how to promote inside pages make their promotions as attractive as anything on page one. A depth story promoted under a two-column head in two-column type with an inset picture runs a good chance of being read even if it is tucked between the grocery ads on page 31.

Newspapers also use *reference lines*. These are indications within or near a page-one story that there is more information inside. Often that information may be depth already available for a breaking story on page one. The idea is fine. Its execution may be doubtful. How many readers are going to be aware of the inside information if they read about it in a boldface, centered, 9-point line at the bottom of the page-one story? How many more are going to turn to the inside if they are told to in 24-point type ruled into the top inches of the page one story.

Let's not fill up page one with promotions for inside pages. But let's remember that page one simply isn't big enough to carry all of the major breaking news, a good bulletin column, and all the

332

depth. And we waste the depth if we tuck it away inside but fail to tell the reader about it.

That depth is the future of the American newspaper. With depth, the profession attracts and holds the kind of intelligent men it must have. With depth, it uses the competition and then beats it with thoughtful, quality reporting. And with depth, the American newspaper continues to build and enhance its only really important tradition—that of informing its readers.

Bibliographical Index

Author's Note: To make this index work most easily and quickly, look for your subject under the name of a specific academic discipline. For example, you would find governmental statistical references under the main title of Political science. Subtitles under Political science would guide you to municipal, state, national, or international statistics. Where there is some question about the placing of your subject, cross references have been provided to help guide you to the proper discipline.

334

General Index